WRITE EVERYTHING RIGHT!

Let the world's highest-paid
writers show you
the secrets of making
readers love your:
e-mails, letters, memos,
blog, reports, speeches, ads,
press releases, articles,
books, PowerPoint, website
and yes, especially your résumé!

Denny Hatch

WRITE EVERYTHING RIGHT!
Let the world's highest-paid writers show you the secrets of making readers love your: e-mails, letters, memos, blog, reports, speeches, ads, press releases, articles, books, PowerPoint, website and yes, especially your résumé!

ISBN: 1-931068-73-9

Direct Marketing IQ
1500 Spring Garden Street, 12th Floor
Philadelphia, PA 19130
215-238-5300

Denny Hatch Associates, Inc.
310 Gaskill Street
Philadelphia, PA 19147
215-627-9103
DennyHatch.com
dennyhatch@yahoo.com

To arrange bulk purchases of this book for educational purposes, please contact the publisher.

Also by Denny (Denison) Hatch

Nonfiction

• *Million Dollar Mailings* (1993), (2001)

• *2,239 Tested Secrets for Direct Marketing Success* with Don Jackson (1998)

• *Method Marketing: How to Make a Fortune by Getting Inside the Heads of Your Customers* (1999)

• *Jack Corbett, Mariner* by A.S. Hatch, (2002),
Edited by — and Afterword by — Denny Hatch

• *PRICELINE.COM: A Layman's Guide to Manipulating the Media* (2003)

• *The Secrets of Emotional, Hot-Button COPYWRITING* (2010)

• *Career-Changing Takeaways: Quotations, Rules, Aphorisms, Pithy Tips, Quips, Sage Advice, Secrets, Dictums and Truisms in 99 Categories of Marketing, Business and Life* (2011)

Fiction

• *Cedarhurst Alley* (1969), (2005)

• *The Fingered City* (1973)

• *The Stork* (1976)

• *Coldcocked* (2010, Kindle edition)

Newsletter

• *WHO'S MAILING WHAT!* (1984-1994)

Online

• *Business Common Sense* on the *Target Marketing* website

Thanks, Bob ...

This book is dedicated to Bob Scott for a lifetime of sound advice and editorial excellence including the painstaking work on this manuscript.

Contents

Two Quickies

A world renowned author once asked the Welsh master of best-selling thrillers, Ken Follett, if he thinks about the reader when writes. Follett said he thought about the reader all the time.

"I never think of the reader," the author said. "I always write for myself."

"That's why you are a very great author," Follett said. "And why I am a very rich author." *—From a Charles Osgood PBS Interview with Ken Follett*

....

"What do you do?" a guy at a cocktail party was asked.

"I'm a brain surgeon," was the reply. "What do you do?"

"I'm a writer."

"Ah," said the brain surgeon. "I've often thought when I retire I'd like to try some writing."

"And when I retire," said the writer, "I plan try a little brain surgery." *—Old anecdote*

PROLOGUE

Below is an e-mail I received from former Pennsylvania Governor Ed Rendell. Presumably it went to a list of Democratic voters — average folks.

Statistically, half the people who received it could not understand it. Here is the governor's e-mail in full:

> **A really big deal**
> Friday, Mar. 22, 2013 9:21 AM
> **From:** "Ed Rendell" democraticparty@democrats.org
> **To:** "Denny Hatch" dennyhatch@yahoo.com
>
> Denny—
>
> Right now, Republicans in our state are trying to diminish Pennsylvania's importance in future presidential elections — meaning that the issues that are important to you and me will get less attention at the national level. They know they can't win our state on the issues, so they're resorting to underhanded tactics and undermining the influence of our voters.
>
> Their plan would change the way Pennsylvania allocates its Electoral College votes — splitting our votes between the winner and the loser, rather than the traditional winner-take-all approach we've used for centuries. It would end our historical role as a critical electoral state, and create a detour around Pennsylvania on the road to the White House.
>
> In short, it's a bad idea that will hurt every Pennsylvanian, Democrat and Republican alike. And it's up to us to do everything we can to stop it.
>
> **Call Governor Tom Corbett's office right now at (717) 787-2500 and politely let him know you oppose this plan because it's neither fair nor the right thing for Pennsylvania. Here's a sample script you can use:**
>
> *My name is (YOUR NAME) and I live in (CITY). I am calling today because I am opposed to changing the way Pennsylvania allocates its Electoral College votes. This plan will diminish Pennsylvania's importance in future elections and its historical role as a key swing state where candidates spend time and money focusing on issues that are important to Pennsylvanians. I urge you to publicly oppose Senate Bill 538.*
>
> **After your call, let us know how it went.**
>
> Look, it doesn't take a genius to figure out why Republicans are trying to pull this trick in Pennsylvania: They haven't carried our state in a presidential election since 1988. They haven't been able to beat us, so now they're trying to rig the game.

This isn't the first time we've seen Pennsylvania Republicans try to rig the election in their favor. In 2012, they tried to change the rules by passing burdensome voter ID laws that would have had the effect of disenfranchising thousands of Pennsylvanians. We fought those laws in the courts, and won.

Now let's join together again and make sure this latest scheme doesn't fly.

Call Governor Corbett at (717) 787-2500, and tell him to stop this bill. Then, click below to report your call:

http://my.democrats.org/PA-Call-Report-Back

Let's do this,
Ed

Governor Ed Rendell

P.S. — I can tell you from my experience as Governor: these calls make a difference.

Call right now and tell him you oppose this bill.

....

Before writing to average folks, know this:
• "Nearly half of all Americans read so poorly that they cannot find a single piece of information when reading a short publication." *—UNESCO: Institute for Statistics*

• A sentence of 29 or more words is very difficult for readers to comprehend.

What's going on here?
Ed Rendell had three goals:

- Infuriate voters.
- Scare hell out of us.
- Get action.

This should be a short, red-hot communication, immediately understood and acted upon. Instead, voters received a 422-word lesson explaining the arcane workings of the Electoral College. Only a policy wonk could make sense of this gibberish.

Misleading subject line
"A really big deal" sounds like an investment opportunity. It has no relation to the actual message.

The incomprehensible, blah lead sentence

Right now, Republicans in our state are trying to diminish Pennsylvania's importance in future presidential elections — meaning that the issues that are important to you and me will get less attention at the national level.

Of this monstrous 35-word sentence, nine words (more than 25 percent) have three syllables or more:

- Republicans
- Diminish
- Pennsylvania's
- Importance
- Presidential
- Elections
- Important
- Attention
- National

Using the words "importance" and "important" in the same sentence is sloppy prose. The average American voter — able to read at the level of an eighth grader or below — would have a one-word question: "Huh?"

The entire e-mail is blather. A position paper. No research. No specifics.

The response mechanism
This is direct marketing. Governor Rendell wants a response. He gives the reader one option: use the phone.

Personally, I avoid the phone. I am a "write guy," not a "talk guy." I would respond by e-mail or not at all.

Others might like to use snail mail — a letter or postcard. Or possibly a fax. The point is, when you ask for an order, it is imperative to make it easy to respond in the method most convenient to the prospect.

I took the liberty of rewriting Gov. Rendell's e-mail.
Remember, this is coming from the most famous politician in the state of Pennsylvania. Ed Rendell would not lie or do anything to hurt his reputation.

When he says this is serious business, voters will take notice.

Urging the average voter to read a 56-word script over the phone to the governor's answering machine is preposterous. Voters will stammer through it. The governor's people will not listen to it.

The only message: "Oppose Senate Bill 538."

What works is an avalanche of messages. 100,000 messages from upset voters will get attention in Harrisburg.

Here's my version of the governor's e-mail:

> **Urgent. Act At Once!**
> Friday, Mar. 22, 2013 9:21 AM
> **From:** "Ed Rendell" democraticparty@democrats.org
> **To:** "Denny Hatch" dennyhatch@yahoo.com

Denny,
You're about to lose your vote.

Right now in Harrisburg, state Senator Dominic Pileggi has written a bill to steal all future presidential elections in Pennsylvania in favor of the Republicans.

For example, under this scheme, President Obama would have won only 7 of Pennsylvania's 20 electoral votes in 2012. Yet he won the popular vote by 309,840 votes.

This is a major scam in the making.

With this vote-rigging scheme, no Democratic candidate for president will ever again win Pennsylvania.

You must act now. Otherwise Republican Governor Tom Corbett will sign the bill into law.

If it becomes law, every vote you cast in presidential elections will be wasted.

It's easy to contact Governor Corbett.
Four choices:

1. Phone Governor Corbett's office:
(717) 787-2500
Sample script:
This is [YOUR NAME] from [YOUR CITY]. I urge you to publicly oppose Senate Bill 538.

2. Letter or Postcard
Governor Tom Corbett
225 Main Capitol Bldg.
Harrisburg, PA 17120

Dear Governor Corbett,
I urge you to publicly oppose Senate Bill 538.
Sincerely,

[YOUR NAME] [YOUR ADDRESS]

3. Fax:
(717) 783-4429
Use the letter above.

4. E-mail: governor@state.pa.us
Subject Line: *Oppose Senate Bill 538.*

Use the letter above.

Do not let the Republicans steal your vote.

Contact Gov. Corbett today.

Ed
Governor Ed Rendell

P.S. I would appreciate your telling me how you contacted Governor Corbett.
http://my.democrats.org/PA-Call-Report-Back

....

Takeaways to Consider

• "Nearly half of all Americans read so poorly that they cannot find a single piece of information when reading a short publication." *—UNESCO: Institute for Statistics*

• "Short words. Short sentences. Short paragraphs." *—Andrew J. Byrne*

• If you create sentences longer than 29 words, split 'em up.

• "Your first ten words are more important than the next ten thousand." *—Elmer "Sizzle" Wheeler*

• The first 10 words by Ed Rendell: "A really big deal ... Right now Republicans in our state ..."

• The first 10 words by Denny Hatch: "Urgent. Act at Once! You're about to lose your vote."

• Ed Rendell (or his writer) delivered a 422-word civics lecture. My down-'n'-dirty version is 243 words with four ways to respond.

• Why offer four response options? Because everywhere Gov. Corbett turns — phone, fax, e-mail or pile of snail mail — he'll find pissed-off voters. He can't get away from us.

• The operative copy drivers — emotional hot buttons — to make people act in this case are fear and anger.

• "Make it easy to order." *—Elsworth Howell*

• "What surprises me most about people's skills is how poor their writing and grammar are, even for college graduates." *—Eleonora Sharef, Founder of HireArt*

• Few top executives achieved their positions by being good writers. Yet writing is something they must do every day and, frankly, should do well.

• Put another way, if you're a sloppy writer, your message will be lost.

CHAPTER 1

We Are All Writers — And We Are All Selling

"In the modern world of business, it is useless to be a creative original thinker unless you can also sell what you create. Management cannot be expected to recognize a good idea unless it is presented to them by a good salesman." —*David Ogilvy 20th century advertising legend*

"Whether you like it or not, life is one long sales pitch — and most of that selling is done in writing." —*Drayton Bird, partner and friend of David Ogilvy*

....

Whether creating a letter, memo, e-mail, article for publication, blog, special report, proposal, press release, advertisement, or a full-blown book, we are all writers.

And the greatest challenge to a writer is capturing the reader's attention and holding it.

Meet the elite
WRITE EVERYTHING RIGHT! will introduce you to the tested and proven attention-getting (and attention-holding) secrets of an elite, anonymous cadre of writers. They earn six and seven figures a year.

These are advertising copywriters who have been mobilizing the English language and sending it out to sell for the past 800 years. Their unique skill is coming up with copy so powerful and smooth it's easier to read than to skip.

"I have always believed that writing advertisements is the second most profitable form of writing. The first, of course, is ransom notes." —*Phillip Dusenberry, chairman of BBDO Worldwide.*

Any time you put words on paper (or a screen) for somebody else to read, you too are selling.

You are selling the reader on *continuing on to the next word, next sentence, next paragraph and next page, all the way to the end.*

To put it another way: Write one or two boring paragraphs and your reader is gone. This is especially true in the digital world where we are all one mouse-click away from oblivion.

Stay on message … or else!
I am personally terrified of boring or confusing my readers.

When writers go off-message, self-indulgently show off with words requiring a lookup and employ horrendously long sentences; they have no respect for the reader's time. This is typically found in academia, the courts, government, blogs, social media and all over the business community.

Some writers' prose negates what they preach. Check out the disgust of the U.K.'s greatest living direct marketer, the late David Ogilvy's associate, Drayton Bird:

> So I read about a seminar in "power talking" and "communication skills" with great interest — especially when it said that 80 percent of people fail at work because they don't "relate well" to other people ... "a clear case of failed communication"...
>
> Well, the seminar was cheap, the course leader is practically a genius — "multi skilled as an Occupational Psychologist, Executive Mentor, Presenter and Counsellor" — and the subject is highly relevant.
>
> But the copy put me off. As far as I or anyone else who cares for the English language might be concerned it was indeed a case of failed communication. It had more clichés and jargon in it than a politician's speech.
>
> I was promised "user-friendly, high-level skills" and "solution-focused communication techniques". There was obsessive use of expressions based on the word "impact" — "impacts on," "impactful," "high-impact" and "positive impact." And naturally that shop-soiled word "engage" popped up (why not "intrigue" or "interest"?)
>
> If that's how people who teach communication write, it explains a lot of the mindless tripe we all have to plough though — in documents, on the Internet, in meetings: everywhere.
>
> Every day you are trying to get colleagues, bosses, customers — maybe family — to do what you want. Whether you like it or not, life is one long sales pitch — and most of that selling is done in writing.

Appalling linguistic assaults

Over the years I kept seeing serious lapses in communication skills by people who should know better. Some examples:

- As a business trade journalist, I routinely get pitches from PR firms to interview this person or write a story on some subject. The majority of them are unemotional, filled with "we," "us" and our" (as opposed to "I," "me" and "you"). The prose is so overflowing with techie corporate-speak as to be unintelligible. I find myself screaming at the computer screen, "For heaven's sake *make it fascinating!*"

- Newspaper and magazine journalists — who should know better — often start with cute anecdotes and bury the "who," "what," "where," "when" and "how" throughout the story.

- I regularly receive special e-mails, reports and articles made up of depressing "gray walls of type" containing prose badly written, boring and splayed out from one side of the computer screen to the other.

- On my Kindle, I find authors routinely wander off-message and journey into the world of self-indulgence. This has nothing to do with the business at hand and is as boring as a distant relative's home movies.

• Important e-mails are not received because a word in the subject line triggers a spam filter and the message is consigned to e-Limbo.

• E-mails from young people are rife with texting gibberish such as a "?4u AAA TX" (question for you, any advice appreciated, thanks).

• When e-mails, memos and letters are written entirely in lower case, form overpowers content and the message is diluted. (The only person getting away with this affectation was the Bollingen Prize American poet e. e. cummings.)

• At business conferences I find myself in sessions where nitwit presenters read their speeches off PowerPoint screens. The type is so small, even people in the front row cannot read it.

• Why are e-mail inboxes glutted with spam? A spammer can make money on as little as three replies per million and doesn't care a rap if 999,997 others are inconvenienced.

• Put another way, dealing with a piece of spam takes time to decide whether or not to open or delete it. If each spam requires a penny's worth of a person's time, then 1 million spam messages costs the economy $10,000 in lost productivity.

• You have to wince at the avalanche of misspellings, wrong words, mucked up structure and typos.

• Publicists and PR types blitz the media with ill-written, cliché- and jargon-riddled press releases. The people, events and products they describe could be made riveting in the hands of a good writer.

• In Chapter 18 you'll find the 50 words most likely to cause *The New York Times* readers to scurry to the dictionary. If you want people to read what you write without interruption, never use any of these words. Never!

All of the above — *all of it!* — could be avoided if the writers were tipped off to the techniques advertising copywriters have known for centuries.

The day the egg hit the fan

A story in *The New York Times* jerked this book out of my dark subconscious and put it squarely on the front burner.

In 1980, John R. (Rick) MacArthur — son of the late Bankers Life and Casualty Company gazillionaires John D. and Catherine T. MacArthur — bought the 160-year-old *Harper's Magazine*.

On Jan. 30, 2010, as owner, savior, president, publisher and major financial contributor, he addressed the editorial staff. According to *The Times*' Stephanie Clifford, Mac-

Arthur announced to the somber assemblage, "We are going through a crisis."

> In a rambling 40-minute monologue that left many attendees perplexed, Mr. MacArthur, 53, talked about the problems facing *Harper*'s: readership was down 35,000, newsstand sales were plummeting, the only direct-mail piece that seemed to work was 20 years old. Worse, Harper's seemed irrelevant — "the mainstream media is ignoring it to death," he said — according to people who were at the meeting.

Normally I would scan the headline and lede of a story such as this and move on. However, four years earlier in late May 2006 at Philadelphia's 30th Street Station newsstand, I picked up a copy of Harper's. On the train to New York, I opened the magazine and was hit with the worst lead paragraph I ever encountered in my 77 years on this planet. It was so gawd-awful I saved it in my private archive:

On simple human decency
by Ben Metcalf
I.

> Before I attempt to fill these pages with my disgust, which the odd reader who knows me will surely expect, I am obliged to address a preliminary concern, which that same odd reader may safely ignore. Some time has passed since I last raised my voice to the multitude, and whereas literary taste does not seem to have advanced much in the interim, and I assume is still arrayed so as to engage only the weak-minded and dull, I find that I am no longer able to discern with any accuracy where the bounds of simple human decency lie. This would bother me even less than does the taste issue were it not for the fact that ground gained or lost in the theater of decency tends now and then to affect the law, and it has long been a personal goal of mine to avoid capture and imprisonment.

Here are three sentences averaging 50 words each. By all standards, these sentences — in terms of word count and complexity — are incomprehensible. (For ease of reading, no sentence [of mine] in this book is longer than 29 words.)

I dipped in and out of the rest of Ben Metcalf's 2,850-word essay to see if it were equally dreadful throughout. It was. And I vowed never to buy a copy of *Harper's* again.

How in the world, I wanted to know, could a professional magazine editor allow this tangled twaddle to see print? Here's how: Ben Metcalf, the author, was also literary editor of *Harper's*. If *Harper's* was in deep doo-doo, Ben Metcalf was most certainly a large part of the problem.

An advertising copywriter submitting anything this tortuous and unreadable for an ad or a direct mail letter would immediately be cashiered into account management. The copy chief who OK'd it would be fired.

P.S. Mercifully for *Harper's* Ben Metcalf was axed in January 2011.

We frequently write to people who are not expecting us

In his masterpiece, *How to Write a Good Advertisement: A Short Course in Copywrit-*

ing, the great Vic Schwab (1898-1960) threw down the gauntlet to all advertising copywriters. In his chapter, "You, the Uninvited Guest," Schwab addresses every author who commits words to paper (or computer screen) meant for others to read:

> Do not underestimate the fierce competition you face in getting attention. Nobody in the world (except you) is waiting for your advertisement to appear. Everybody in the world (except you) would much rather read the news, comics, stories, articles, editorials or even the obituaries.
>
> You, the advertiser, are the Uninvited Guest — actually, let's face it, an intruder. No reader asked you, or paid you, to join the party, which he is having with the publication he has bought. You paid to get in.
>
> The reader has bought the publication for news, entertainment or instruction, which is of helpful personal value. So that is what your advertisement also has to provide — if you are to stand any chance of competing with the publication's editorial matter for the interest of the reader. And then, to make him pay you for your product, you must make it pay for him to read about it.
>
> Successful advertisers purposely start from this premise: People don't want to read advertising — not even mine. Then they work their way around this 8-ball by shooting that much harder for advertisements that, as Arthur Brisbane defined good writing, are "easier to read than to skip."

A letter, e-mail or résumé can be totally unexpected. The whole point of *WRITE EVERYTHING RIGHT!* is to help make your writing "easier to read than to skip."

Successful advertising copywriters have spent years learning the tricks and secrets evealed between these covers. Go forth and dazzle!

Denny Hatch
310 Gaskill Street
Philadelphia, PA 19147
dennyhatch@yahoo.com
www.dennyhatch.com
215-627-9103 (rings on my desk)

Takeaways to Consider

• "Advertising is the greatest art form of the twentieth century." —*Marshall McLuhan (1911-1980), pioneering media guru*

• "The force of the advertising word and image dwarfs the power of other literature in the 20th century." —*Daniel J. Boorstin (1914-2004), historian, essayist, Librarian of Congress*

• "If I were starting life over again, I am inclined to think that I would go into the advertising business in preference to almost any other. The general raising of the standards of modern civilization among all groups of people during the past half century would have been impossible without the spreading of the knowledge of higher standards by means of advertising." *—Franklin D. Roosevelt*

• "Advertising nourishes the consuming power of men. It sets up before a man the goal of a better home, better clothing, better food for himself and his family. It spurs individual exertion and greater production." *—Winston Churchill*

• "In the modern world of business, it is useless to be a creative original thinker unless you can also sell what you create. Management cannot be expected to recognize a good idea unless it is presented to them by a good salesman."*—David Ogilvy*

• When words are committed to paper or to a computer screen and are meant for others — like it or not — we are all selling.

• We are selling the reader on continuing on to the next word, next sentence, next paragraph and next page, all the way to the end.

• "Every day you are trying to get colleagues, bosses, customers — maybe family — to do what you want. Whether you like it or not, life is one long sales pitch — and most of that selling is done in writing." *—Drayton Bird*

• "Good writing is easier to read than to skip." *—Arthur Brisbane*

CHAPTER 2

Four Horrifying Roadblocks

Why Americans can't, don't, won't and don't want to read
Here is what every writer is hit with:

Roadblock No. 1: time crunch
One of the greatest practitioners of advertising was Claude Hopkins (1866-1932), author of My Life in Advertising. Among his clients: Schlitz beer, Quaker Oats, Pepsodent toothpaste, Studebaker Automobiles and Goodyear tires.

In his Scientific Advertising, Hopkins' analysis of people and their reading habits is relevant today. We live in a dizzying multi-media world where the folks we want to reach are constantly connected to iPhones, iPads, TVs, radios and laptops. Some of us even read old-fashioned print via magazines and newspapers. Hopkins wrote back in 1923:

> Always bear these facts in mind. People are hurried. The average person worth cultivating has too much to read. They skip three-fourths of the reading matter, which they pay to get. They are not going to read your business talk unless you make it worth their while and let the headline show it.

Disheartening numbers all authors face

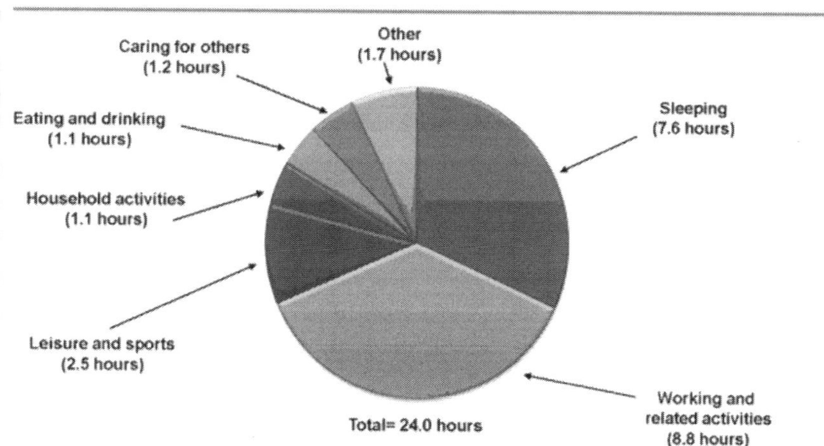

NOTE: Data include employed persons on days they worked, ages 25 to 54, who lived in households with children under 18. Data include non-holiday weekdays and are annual averages for 2011. Data include related travel for each activity.
SOURCE: Bureau of Labor Statistics, American Time Use Survey

The American Time Use Survey collects information about the activities people do during the day and how much time they spend doing them. For example, on an average day in 2011, Americans age 15 and over slept about 8.7 hours, spent 5.2 hours doing leisure and sports activities, worked for 3.6 hours, and spent 1.8 hours doing household activities. The remaining 4.7 hours were spent in a variety of other activities, including eating and drinking, attending school, and shopping. —*Bureau of Labor Statistics*

The 31-hour day
People now surf the Internet while watching television. Their children instant-message friends while listening to music. They all talk on the phone and check their e-mail while they cook. "Our research showed that people somehow managed to shoehorn 31 hours of activity into a 24-hour day," said Colleen Fahey Rush, executive vice president for research at MTV Networks, which worked with an online research company, OTX, last year. "That's from being able to do two things at once." *—Sharon Waxman, The New York Times*

The e-mail overload
According to Fortune/CNN, the average person receives 147 e-mails a day and deletes 71, or nearly 50 percent. Each delete operation requires 3.5 seconds.

The average worker spends 28 percent of the workday dealing with e-mail — or roughly 14 hours out of a 50-hour week.

This may seem dreadful. However, imagine if it were snail mail rather than e-mail and 147 envelopes landed on your desk every day!

Teen texting time
Pew Research has discovered half of all teenagers send 50+ text messages a day or more than 1,500 texts every month. One-third of teens send 100 texts a day and 15 percent send more than 200 texts a day. Matt Richtel of *The New York Times* described one avid texter:

> Allison Miller, 14, sends and receives 27,000 texts in a month, her fingers clicking at a blistering pace as she carries on as many as seven text conversations at a time. She texts between classes, at the moment soccer practice ends, while being driven to and from school and, often, while studying.

Do you want to reach Allison Miller with a sales pitch or a message?

Fuggedaboutit.

The bizarre world of Web gamers and Twitter
In August 2007, *The Wall Street Journal* reported on secondlife.com, a multi-player Web game with 10 million registered users. The guts of the story:

> A typical Internet "gamer" spends 20 to 40 hours a week in a virtual world.

In 2009, I was persuaded to "tweet" on Twitter to increase my online presence. Within two years, I had 690 followers, some of whom report they are following hundreds — and in some cases, thousands — of tweeters. Example: a reader in Utah is following 1,744 tweeters. Another follows 10,263 Tweeters and has 9,430 followers. How in the world do these folks have time to do much else?

Incidentally, I follow no one on Twitter.

Roadblock No. 2: the literacy problem
• 50 percent of adults cannot read a book written at an eighth-grade level.

• 45 million are functionally illiterate and read below a fifth-grade level.

• 44 percent of the American adults do not read a book in a year.

• 6 out of 10 households do not buy a single book in a year.

• Between 46 and 51 percent of American adults have an income well below the individual threshold poverty level because of their inability to read.

• Approximately 50 percent of Americans read so poorly that they are unable to perform simple tasks such as balancing a checkbook and reading prescription drug labels.

Roadblock No. 3: poor attention span
These self-conversations are frequently interrupted: a baby crying, a kitchen timer going off, a dog barking, someone at the front door, a fire engine going by, a piece of direct mail or catalog, a TV infomercial or a telemarketing call.

If your headline or writing is dull … if they do not interrupt and keep on interrupting … the interruption you are trying to achieve is interrupted.
Whereupon we resume the conversation with ourselves.

Once you have captured the attention of your readers, it is imperative to hold it. Otherwise, they're gone. And you, the writer, have failed.

> • "Every man is constantly holding a mental conversation with himself, and the burden of that conversation is himself — his interests, his loved ones, his business, his advancement." *—Robert Collier (1885-1950), copywriter, author of The Robert Collier Letter Book*
>
> • "The average attention span of an adult is 20 minutes." *—Brad Vander Zanden, University of Tennessee*
>
> • "On the Internet, the average attention span is three to five minutes. We have to cater to that." *—Steven Hirsch, co-chairman, Vivid Entertainment*
>
> • "The addictive nature of Web browsing can leave you with an attention span of nine seconds — the same as a goldfish." *—Dr. Ted Selker, MIT Media Lab*
>
> • "The technology is rewiring our brains," said Nora Volkow, director of the National Institute of Drug Abuse and one of the world's leading brain scientists. She and other researchers compare the lure of digital stimulation less to that of drugs and alcohol than to food and sex, which are essential but counterproductive in excess … Scientists say juggling e-mail, phone calls and other incoming information can change how people think and behave. They say our ability to focus is being undermined by bursts of information. These play to a primitive impulse to respond to immediate opportunities and threats. The stimulation provokes excitement — a dopamine squirt — that researchers say can be addictive. In its absence, people feel bored. The resulting distractions can have deadly consequences, as when cell phone-wielding drivers and train engineers cause wrecks." *—Matt Richtel, The New York Times*

Roadblock No. 4: the glut of prose
We are drowning in a tsunami of humanity screaming for our attention.

Ads are everywhere you look — on cars, jet plane fuselages, garbage trucks, golf carts, kids' report cards, over urinals, on billboards and gas pumps. Ads are also found on cell phones, sports uniforms, skywriting, plus, of course, on radio and TV as well as in newspapers, magazines and the Internet.

"Somewhere between 254 and 5,000 is a number that represents just how many commercial messages an average consumer gets each day," wrote Matthew Creamer in adage.com.

Internet by the numbers

- Number of e-mail users worldwide: 2.2 billion.

- Total e-mail traffic per day worldwide: 144 billion.

- Share of e-mails that were considered non-essential: 61 percent.

- Number of e-mail clients worldwide in 2012: 4.3 billion.

- Percentage of all e-mail traffic that was spam: 68.8 percent. *—pingdom.com*

- "When one of the most important e-mail messages of his life landed in his in-box a few years ago, Kord Campbell overlooked it. Not just for a day or two, but 12 days. He finally saw it while sifting through old messages: a big company wanted to buy his Internet start-up. 'I stood up from my desk and said, "Oh my God, oh my God, oh my God," Mr. Campbell said. 'It's kind of hard to miss an e-mail like that, but I did.' The message had slipped by him amid an electronic flood: two computer screens alive with e-mail, instant messages, online chats, a Web browser and the computer code he was writing." *—Matt Richtel*

Takeaways to Consider

- "People are hurried. The average person worth cultivating has too much to read. They skip three-fourths of the reading matter, which they pay to get. They are not going to read your business talk unless you make it worth their while and let the headline show it." *—Claude Hopkins*

- "Research showed that people somehow managed to shoehorn 31 hours of activity into a 24-hour day. That's from being able to do two things at once." *—Sharon Waxman*

- According to Fortune/CNN, the average person receives 147 e-mails a day and deletes 71, or nearly 50 percent. Each delete operation requires 3.5 seconds.

- Pew Research has discovered half of all teenagers send 50+ text messages a day or more than 1,500 texts every month.

• A typical Internet "gamer" spends 20 to 40 hours a week in a virtual world.

• 50 percent of adults cannot read a book written at an eighth-grade level. *—Literacy Project Foundation*

• 45 million are functionally illiterate and read below a fifth-grade level. *—Literacy Project Foundation*

• 44 percent of the American adults do not read a book in a year. *—Literacy Project Foundation*

• "The addictive nature of Web browsing can leave you with an attention span of nine seconds — the same as a goldfish." *—Dr. Ted Selker, MIT Media Lab*

• Think of the endless distractions on an iPad, iPod, smartphone, DVDs, TV and texting. Compared to these dazzling high-tech media, being forced turn boring little black letters of the alphabet into words, thoughts and paragraphs is tough. Quite simply, reading is work.

CHAPTER 3

Your Private Archive Can Make You Rich

A personal digression — Harry Kursh
My first job after the Army in 1960 was in the publicity department of Prentice Hall's trade book division in Englewood Cliffs, N.J. One of the authors assigned to me was thoroughgoing, professional, no-nonsense nonfiction writer Harry Kursh, who lived in a small town in Westchester County, N.Y.

Kursh wrote books on all kinds of subjects. A sampling of his titles:

- *The Franchise Boom*
- *This Is Alaska*
- *Inside the U.S. Patent Office*
- *How to Get Land from Uncle Sam*
- *The United States Office of Education*

I asked Kursh how he knew so much about so many things.

"My files," he said, as a beatific expression crossed his face. He described how he subscribed to a slew of newspapers and magazines, spent many hours eyeballing them and cutting out articles he thought would be useful. I was given to understand his home contained a mass of filing cabinets. This was a tedious, labor-intensive, time-consuming task. And after paying for all those subscriptions, it was also very expensive.

I really admired the guy. He was a kind of Renaissance man, who knew something about everything and could become an expert on anything in very little time. When a publisher called Kursh needing a book or article, he could agree to it before knowing the subject.

Harry Kursh was my role model
Forty-five years later, in order to create the e-zine *Business Common Sense*, I started doing what Harry Kursh did — only using the Internet. I spend 20 to 30 minutes a day, seven days a week scanning three print newspapers, surfing the Internet and downloading news stories and feature articles for my private archive. It currently contains more than 80,000 entries in 383 major categories — indexed and cross-indexed.

I can do in 20 minutes what Kursh spent hours doing. Instead of a basement full of file cabinets, the entire archive fits easily in my laptop and travels with me everywhere. With the exception of a paid subscription to *The Wall Street Journal* online and two morning print newspapers, it's all free!

In the nine years I've been publishing, a number of readers have asked what software I use to create the archive. I tell them I don't use software. I've created my own system.

Why a private archive?
An archive — indexed and cross-indexed — is a private information source, idea trove and swipe file.

No matter what your profession, an extensive file of retrievable, cutting-edge information directly relating to your business and industry is a huge asset.

If you are a journalist, a private self-created encyclopedia dedicated to your beat can be invaluable.

You can lace your memos, e-mails, letters, reports, stories, speeches, PowerPoint presentations and whitepapers with tidbits, factoids and statistics. Readers will immediately see 1) you know a lot, 2) are on top of your job and 3) are a force in your industry.

You are unique

Your archive makes you one of a kind. Assemble a private archive — and nobody else in the world has anything exactly like what you will be working from.

With a private archive, you'll be far less likely than your colleagues and competitors to suffer writer's block. Put another way, without all this private material, I would have to start every new assignment from scratch.

Instead, I have an invaluable series of dossiers on industries, people, businesses, business practices and events — indexed and cross-indexed, with everything easily retrievable.

Many correspondents and presenters want to dazzle their audiences with personal cleverness and brilliance.

I like being known as a journeyman aggregator of information, a connector of dots and a fair researcher. Whenever possible, I credit the source of a fact, factoid or quotation. This lends credence to my argument and makes me appear smart for knowing something about a lot of stuff and knowing how to do research.

How to create an archive

Surf the Internet, read newspapers, trade magazines, journals and books. Attend conferences and take notes.

When you come across something you might be able to use someday, get it into your private, computerized archive immediately.

Downloading from the Internet

Many stories on websites are presented on more than one page. You must click on "Next" or "2" to get to the next part. Don't waste your time.

Click on the "print" or "single page" link, and the entire story appears on one page. Copy and paste it into a word-processing document — Word, AppleWorks or whatever you use.

I suggest you put all stories in one or two formats — say Word and PDF. They will all look alike and are always accessible on whatever computer you end up using.

Often the name of the publication and date are omitted from the "Print" version of a Web story. Be sure these are in the story you save. If not, type them in.

If the story has helpful illustrations, charts, graphs or timelines, you can paste them into most word processing documents.

Paste in the URL
Also it is imperative to copy the URL of each story and paste it at the top in small type. If you need to see the original someday, you have the link. This is also handy if someone challenges your accuracy or source. Send off the URL and you're done.

How to download from print
If you come across an item in a magazine, newspaper or other print source, go to Google and type in the first sentence surrounded by quotation marks. Google will probably find it.

Outsmarting a 'pay wall'
If a "pay wall" exists — whereby the online publisher requires payment — you may well find the same story on other sites for free. This is the result of a deal between the original copyright holder and licensees.

If not available online because of exclusivity, use the print version to scan the text and illustrations into your computer.

The file name
Once in your computer, the document must be labeled. Do not rely on the actual headline, because writers and editors frequently use cute or clever headlines to attract attention. These sappy headlines will make no sense six months or a year later. Instead, let your file name to tell you immediately what it's about.

Private shorthand
This is your private archive, so you can use shorthand (e.g., "2" for "to," "4" as "for," "FU" for "follow-up," etc.). These may not make sense to an outsider, but I recognize the stories. Examples of file labels from my archive:

- Home, 2nd = 40% of Mkt
- Blogs 4 Lo-Cost Mktg
- Search Engines R Thieves
- Wyeth 2 Cut Detail Force 30%

Whatever works for you.

Your private cookbook
Think of your filing system like a cookbook. You would not file recipes under "Scrambled Eggs" and "Fried Eggs." Instead use "Eggs, Scrambled" and "Eggs, Fried," so all of them appear under "Eggs."

With people, use last name first (e.g., Obama, Barack rather than Barack Obama).

Where and how to file
The first thing I see when I go into my private archive is a series of file folders. The first 10 major subject headings are shown here:

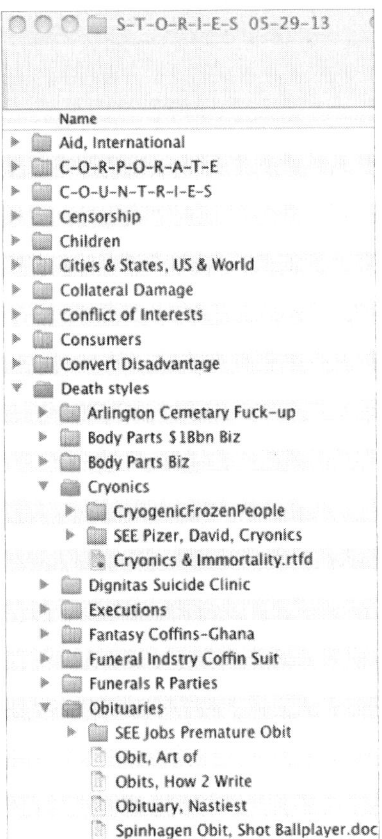

The 11th file reflects my morbid fascination with all facets of death. One of the sub-heads is "Obituaries," with several articles on how to write one. In all, my Death Styles file has a total of 75 sub-files and stories.

Note the first sub-file under *Obituaries: SEE Jobs Premature Obit*
This is an example of my primitive cross-index system. When Apple's Steve Jobs was close to death, Bloomberg News screwed up big time. Someone posted on the Internet an obituary-in-progress before the young mogul actually assumed room temperature. Bloomberg instantly retracted it, but gawker.com picked up the story and ran it. Included was a long list of notables throughout the world to be contacted for comments and recollections. This insider's peek at what goes into creating a major obit runs a whopping 27 pages.

In a private archive, no need exists to maintain two individual copies of a 27-page story in two files (in this case, under "Jobs, Steve" and "Obituaries"). So for cross-indexing purposes, I filed the original of the full story in the "Jobs, Steve" master file and referenced it here with an empty folder, "SEE Jobs Premature Obit."

Throughout the archive are empty file folders with the cross-reference information.

Takeaways to Consider

- Note: You do not own what's in your archive. Most of it is under copyright and owned by others. *(See Chapter 7 for a discussion of copyright and "fair use.")*

• An archive — indexed and cross-indexed — is a private information source, idea trove and swipe file.

• No matter what your profession, an extensive file of retrievable, cutting-edge information directly relating to your business and industry is a huge asset. You can lace your memos, e-mails, letters, reports, speeches, PowerPoint presentations and whitepapers with tidbits, factoids and statistics. Readers will immediately see 1) you know a lot, 2) are on top of your job and 3) are a force in your industry.

• Your archive makes you unique. Assemble a private archive — and nobody else in the world has anything exactly like what you will be working from.

• With a private archive, you'll be far less likely than your colleagues and competitors to suffer writer's block. Put another way, without all this private material, I would have to start every new assignment from scratch.

CHAPTER 4

Don't Get Hung Up on QWERTY. Learn It!

Many years ago my mother gave me two pieces of advice:

- Always leave the john seat down.
- Learn to touch-type.

She was wise on both counts.

In 1954 during a break in my schooling, I commuted to Brown's Business School in Rockville Centre, Long Island for six weeks. I learned to touch-type on a massive, clunky Remington office typewriter.

In this one area, my mother was far seeing.

My Aunt Gertie was a crackerjack typist. She could take dictation directly onto a typewriter keyboard with no mistakes. Her typing sounded like a machine gun. Gertie was dazzling!

The good news
Sixty years later, thanks to my mother and Brown's Business School, I can operate a computer keyboard at about 65 words a minute.

The bad news
I cannot operate a pen or a pencil anymore. I can begin to take pretty good notes with a writing implement, but within minutes I start creating unreadable scrawl.

It is astonishing in the world of computers — where information can be processed in nanoseconds — the major source of input is the ancient QWERTY keyboard. It was first developed and used in 1878 to keep the keys from jamming. It remains relatively unchanged since then.

More astonishing is to see people of all ages clumsily two- and three-fingering a computer keyboard to enter data into these magic machines. They could achieve the same results twice as fast — or faster — if they were touch-typing.

Takeaways to Consider

- If you plan to do any serious writing, I urge you to learn touch-typing.
- With touch-typing, your fingers become an extension of your thought processes.

CHAPTER 5

Never Start With an Outline or a Title!

For the first 25 years of my career I was a writer — publicity releases, sales letters, memos, business plans, budgets and advertising copy.

In 1976, I was fired yet again and decided to try my hand at freelance copywriting.

In the early `80s I heard *US News & World Report* circulation director Dorothy Kerr speak at a Direct Mail Creative Guild luncheon.

How Dorothy Kerr changed our lives

"The way to be successful in this business," Dottie said, "is to see who's mailing what. Track the mailings that keep coming in over and over again, because they are successful and making pots of money. And then steal smart."

I immediately started collecting and cataloging junk mail. By 1984, I had six filing cabinets full of the stuff.

Becoming entrepreneurs

My wife Peggy and I gambled $10,000 to create a dry test mailing — an offer to the direct mail community for a non-existent monthly newsletter. The title: *WHO'S MAILING WHAT!*

The test was successful and the rollout brought in enough money to get up and running.

Within a couple of years, I was the country's foremost authority on junk mail. I wasn't a wizard or particularly smart. I happened to be the only guy collecting, analyzing, archiving and writing about the stuff.

My new audience of readers was made up of direct marketers, copywriters and designers. Another segment was suppliers to the direct marketing industry. Those were the folks seeking information on what was in the mail, so they could get leads and sell their services to people who used mail. Included were advertising agencies, consultants, printers, list owners and brokers, envelope manufacturers and lettershops doing the inserting and mailing.

For the first time in my life I was a regular writer of articles.

Contrary to what many English teachers, copy chiefs and writing coaches suggest, *I never, ever start with an outline.*

In fact, any time I tried to make an outline of what I was going to write, I was hit with a serious case of writer's gastric block — an intellectual and emotional backup from my brain to my innards.

Becoming a magazine editor

In 1992, Peggy and I sold our little business to North American Publishing Company.

Suddenly I was not only writing articles, but also I was running *Target Marketing* magazine with editors and writers reporting to me. I had just three pieces of advice for them:

1. Don't fake anything. *Target Marketing* magazine and *WHO'S MAILING WHAT!* are trade publications, I told them. You are experts writing for experts. It doesn't matter how complicated the story may be — the business model, the execution or the marketing techniques. You must grasp it so well you can explain it to your grandmother. If you run into something you don't understand, keep asking questions until everything falls into place. Never fake it.

"The only stupid question is the one you don't ask," former *DM News* editor Ray Schultz once said to me.

2. Never start with a preconceived point of view. I once had lunch with a couple of producers for *60 Minutes*. They had come to Philly to research a story about political direct mail fundraising. It became obvious early on they were under orders from above to slant the story a particular way.

This meant the mailings they picked out fit the preconceived story line. All the people who would be interviewed would be in lockstep with how the story was expected to turn out. In order to give a "fair and balanced" segment, one or two experts who disagreed with the thrust would be interviewed. But frequently these were wild-eyed nut cases who simply reinforced the original premise.

Let's just say I operate under a perpetual distrust of what Gov. Sarah Palin labeled the "lame-stream media."

3. Never start with a title. Start with a "working title." Consider this an interim label. Feel free to change the working title as the project takes shape.

In the end, your first title may indeed be the final version. But don't be surprised from of the torrent of words you have generated, a few of them will pop out of the text and 1) say precisely what the work is about and 2) grab the reader's attention.

"There's a story here. . ."

I would tell editors this:

"Say to yourself, there's a story here. You have to do research, get inside people's heads, take a lot of notes and see where it leads. You want the finished piece to be completely understandable, accurate and fascinating. And if it takes off in a direction you never expected, all the better!"

"I read books and articles and any kind of authoritative materials about my subject I can find," wrote freelancer Malcolm Decker, "until I feel comfortable — or, as Frost said, 'easy in my harness.'"

I can't speak for other writers, but only after I've done the research can I begin to discern an outline. This means taming an unruly mass of information, notes, interview quotes, reading material, samples of the products or services, illustrations and maybe videos. Eventually I can begin to get my head around the various facets of the story. Pieces fall into place and take shape — the lede, the direction, the middle and the end.

A writer too facile

We once hired an editor/reporter who could generate torrents of very readable prose. She never had writer's block and always met deadlines.

Generally, when a writer I knew and trusted submitted a story, I skimmed it and sent it into production. With new writers, I spent time on their work.

"The most essential gift for a good writer is a built-in, shock-proof, shit detector," Ernest Hemingway said. "This is the writer's radar and all great writers have had it."

Every two or three stories by this new editor would contain something to cause the red flag of my shit detector to start waving in my brain.

I was never an expert in all facets of direct marketing. If I were a physician, I would be a GP — general practitioner. I knew the business and the industry. I knew what I did not know. I knew the experts to ask.

"I'm sorry," I would say to her, "I'm not sure I understand this."

Her answer more than once: "I don't understand it either, but that's exactly what the guy said."

This kept happening and, alas, we finally had to let her go.

Another editor — usually very reliable — pulled this same stunt. "What the hell is this?" I asked him. "I don't get it."

"I don't either," he said blithely. "I left it in and figured you'd catch it."

I was ticked.

Takeaways to Consider

• I never, ever start with an outline.

• I can't speak for other writers, but only after I've done the research can I begin to discern an outline.

• This means taming an unruly mass of information, notes, interview quotes, reading material, samples of the products or services, illustrations and maybe videos. Eventually I can begin to get my head around the various facets of the story. Pieces fall into place and take shape — the lead, the direction, the middle and the end.

• You are experts writing for experts. It doesn't matter how complicated the story may be — the business model, the execution or the marketing techniques. You must grasp it so well you can explain to your grandmother. If you run into something you don't understand, keep asking questions until everything falls into place. Never fake it.

• "The only stupid question is the one you don't ask." *—Ray Schultz*

• Never start with a preconceived point of view.

• I would tell editors, "Say to yourself, there's a story here. You have to do research, get inside people's heads, take a lot of notes and see where it leads. You want the finished piece to be completely understandable, accurate and fascinating. And if it takes off in a direction you never expected, all the better!"

• "I read books and articles and any kind of authoritative materials about my subject I can find, until I feel comfortable — or, as Frost said, 'easy in my harness.'" *—Malcolm Decker*

• "The most essential gift for a good writer is a built-in, shock-proof, shit detector. This is the writer's radar and all great writers have had it." *—Ernest Hemingway*

CHAPTER 6

Research Has Never Been Easier or Quicker

Writing a column is easy. I just sit down at the typewriter, open a vein and bleed it out, drop by drop. *—Red Smith (1905-1982), Sportswriter*

....

Don't open a vein. Do research.
When I got out of the Army in 1960, my first job was making $60 a week as a book publicist for Prentice Hall. The company was a major publisher of all kinds of titles — nonfiction, self-help, biographies, business and salesmanship books and an occasional novel. My main assignment was to write press releases on new titles to accompany the pre-publication copies of the books being sent out to book reviewers. Their purpose was to excite reviewers so they would want to cover it — either as a listing announcement or, ideally, with a full-dress review.

A successful publicity release captures the reader's attention. The headline and copy must make the book sound so irresistible it is immediately placed in the reviewer's "A" pile of titles likely to get coverage.

In the 10 months I was at Prentice Hall, I became very good at this.

Galleys
Six or more sets of galley proofs were printed. These were two-foot-long sheets of raw type printed out before the book was turned into pages. Sets of galleys were distributed to management, sales, the author, editor and proofreader for final editing, corrections and changes. I got the sixth set. In my final months at Prentice Hall, I could be handed the galleys of a nonfiction book and produce a two-page press release in two hours flat.

My press release highlighted the most compelling elements of the book to make the reviewers' job easier.

Read a book in two hours? Okay, how'd I do it?
I developed a kind of system for speed-reading enabling me to gobble up those long galley proofs. I spent some time on the introduction, foreword and first chapter to see where the author was going.

Thereafter, I would carefully scan every galley sheet and when something caught my eye, I would slow down and start reading. If a section seemed usable, I would circle it, turn the page sideways and move on. It would take roughly 30 minutes to 45 minutes to know what was in the book. I would mark up all the stories, characters, pithy quotes and observations to grab the reader's attention and maybe, with luck, make news.

When I finished the book, I would have 15 to 25 sideways galley proofs, whereupon I would carefully read over what I had circled. The release would begin to take shape in my mind and I would start writing. The finished release was essentially "the best of ..." and filled with the juiciest goodies.

Because I had done the research, I did not have to "open a vein and bleed it out, drop by drop." I had plenty of material to work with and the writing came easily.

How an advertising legend worked

David Ogilvy (1911-1999) was one of the seminal figures in 20th century advertising. His memoir, *Ogilvy on Advertising*, I believe is essential reading for every person who wants to communicate well. I mean everybody — journalists, executives, lawyers, academics and bloggers — all who make a living with the English language.

The Rolls-Royce Silver Cloud—$13,995

"At 60 miles an hour the loudest noise in this new Rolls-Royce comes from the electric clock"

What makes Rolls-Royce the best car in the world? "There is really no magic about it—it is merely patient attention to detail," says an eminent Rolls-Royce engineer.

1. "At 60 miles an hour the loudest noise comes from the electric clock," reports the Technical Editor of THE MOTOR. Three mufflers tune out sound frequencies—acoustically.

2. Every Rolls-Royce engine is run for seven hours at full throttle before installation, and each car is test-driven for hundreds of miles over varying road surfaces.

3. The Rolls-Royce is designed as an *owner-driven* car. It is eighteen inches shorter than the largest domestic cars.

4. The car has power steering, power brakes and automatic gear-shift. It is very easy to drive and to park. No chauffeur required.

5. The finished car spends a week in the final test-shop, being fine-tuned. Here it is subjected to 98 separate ordeals. For example, the engineers use a *stethoscope* to listen for axle-whine.

6. The Rolls-Royce is guaranteed for *three years*. With a new network of dealers and parts-depots from Coast to Coast, service is no problem.

7. The Rolls-Royce radiator has never changed, except that when Sir Henry Royce died in 1933 the monogram RR was changed from red to black.

8. The coachwork is given five coats of primer paint, and hand rubbed between each coat, before *nine* coats of finishing paint go on.

9. By moving a switch on the steering column, you can adjust the shock-absorbers to suit road conditions.

10. A picnic table, veneered in French walnut, slides out from under the dash. Two more swing out behind the front seats.

11. You can get such optional extras as an Espresso coffee-making machine, a dictating machine, a bed, hot and cold water for washing, an electric razor or a telephone.

12. There are three separate systems of power brakes, two hydraulic and one mechanical. Damage to one will not affect the others. The Rolls-Royce is a very *safe* car—and also a very *lively* car. It cruises serenely at eighty-five. Top speed is in excess of 100 m.p.h.

13. The Bentley is made by Rolls-Royce. Except for the radiators, they are identical motor cars, manufactured by the same engineers in the same works. People who feel diffident about driving a Rolls-Royce can buy a Bentley.

PRICE. The Rolls-Royce illustrated in this advertisement—f.o.b. principal ports of entry—costs **$13,995.**

If you would like the rewarding experience of driving a Rolls-Royce or Bentley, write or telephone to one of the dealers listed on opposite page. Rolls-Royce Inc., 10 Rockefeller Plaza, New York 20, N. Y. CIrcle 5-1144.

Ogilvy had the incredible ability to make his copy every bit as interesting and readable as the articles and stories in newspapers and magazines surrounding his ads. From *Ogilvy on Advertising*:

> You don't stand a tinker's chance of producing successful advertising unless you start by doing your homework. I have always found this extremely tedious, but there is no substitute for it.
>
> First, study the product you are going to advertise. The more you know about it, the more likely you are to come up with a big idea for selling it. When I got the Rolls-Royce account, I spent three weeks reading about the car and came across a statement that "at sixty miles an hour, the loudest noise comes from the electric clock." This became the headline, and it was followed by 607 words of factual copy.
>
> If you are too lazy to do this kind of homework, you may, occasionally, luck into a successful campaign, but you will run the risk of skidding about on what my brother Francis called "the slippery surface of irrelevant brilliance."

Doing homework is not only essential for successful advertising, but also for all prose — reports, memos, e-mails, letters, proposals, articles or a full-length book.

"Good ideas don't come from smoking joints and wearing funny clothes," wrote Ogilvy's associate Drayton Bird. "It's just hard work and discipline. I do not believe the mysterious qualities of flair and originality are nearly as important as relevant knowledge."

David Ogilvy's Rolls-Royce ad

A prime example of meticulous homework is one of the most famous automobile ads in the history of advertising — Ogilvy's 1958 full page for Rolls-Royce.

According to the Ogilvy agency, this ad ran in only two newspapers and two magazines. Yet it sold a shipload of Rolls-Royce cars.

The secret: Ogilvy's copy, based on exhaustive research, outshone the content of the publication readers paid to receive. The text of the ad:

At 60 miles an hour the loudest noise in this new Rolls-Royce comes from the electric clock.

What makes Rolls-Royce the best car in the world?
"There is really no magic about it — it is merely patient attention to detail," says an eminent Rolls-Royce engineer.

> "At 60 miles an hour the loudest noise comes from the electric clock" reports the Technical Editor of THE MOTOR. Three mufflers tune out sound frequencies — acoustically.
>
> Every Rolls-Royce engine is run for seven hours at full throttle before installation, and each car is test-driven for hundreds of miles over varying road surfaces.

The Rolls-Royce is designed as an owner-driven car. It is eighteen inches shorter than the largest domestic cars.

The car has power steering, power brakes and automatic gear-shift. It is very easy to drive and to park. No chauffeur required.

The finished car spends a week in the final test-shop, being fine-tuned. Here it is subjected to 98 separate ordeals. For example, the engineers use a stethoscope to listen for axle-whine.

The Rolls-Royce is guaranteed for three years. With a new network of dealers and parts-depots from coast to coast, service is no problem.

The Rolls-Royce radiator has never changed, except that when Sir Henry Royce died in 1933 the monogram RR was changed from red to black.

The coachwork is given five coats of primer paint, and hand rubbed between each coat, before nine coats of finishing paint go on.

By moving a switch on the steering column, you can adjust the shock-absorbers to suit road conditions.

A picnic table, veneered in French walnut, slides out from under the dash. Two more swing out behind the front seats.

You can get such optional extras as an Espresso coffee-making machine, a dictating machine, a bed, hot and cold water for washing, an electric razor or a telephone.

There are three separate systems of power brakes, two hydraulic and one mechanical. Damage to one will not affect the others. The Rolls-Royce is a very safe car-and also a very lively car. It cruises serenely at eight-five. Top speed is in excess of 100 m.p.h.

The Bentley is made by Rolls-Royce. Except for the radiators, they are identical motor cars, manufactured by the same engineers in the same works. People who feel diffident about driving a Rolls-Royce can buy a Bentley.

Price. The Rolls-Royce illustrated in this advertisement — f.o.b. principal ports of entry — costs $13,995.

If you would like the rewarding experience of driving a Rolls-Royce or Bentley, write or telephone to one of the dealers listed on the opposite page. Rolls-Royce Inc., 10 Rockefeller Plaza, New York 20, N.Y. Circle 5-1144.

....

When Ogilvy presented his copy to Rolls-Royce management in New York, the senior engineer said, "We really must do something to improve our clock."

Compare Ogilvy's Rolls-Royce ad to this 1959 Edsel effort
A year after David Ogilvy's Rolls-Royce ad ran, Ford took the Edsel account away from Foote, Cone & Beldng and assigned it to Kenyon & Eckhardt.

Named after Henry Ford's son who died at age 49 in 1943, the Edsel was called "one of the cruelest tributes ever paid a man." The author of this line was Pulitzer Prize-winning *Los Angeles Times* automotive critic Dan Neil. In his delicious 2007 round-up for *Time* magazine, "The 50 Worst Cars of All Time," the Edsel was the lead illustration. Neil wrote:

> That's why we're all here, right? To celebrate E Day, the date 50 years ago when Ford took one of the autodom's most hilarious pratfalls. But why? It really wasn't that bad a car. True, the car was kind of homely, fuel thirsty and too expensive, particularly at the outset of the late '50s recession. But what else? It was the first victim of Madison Avenue hyper-hype. Ford's marketing mavens had led the public to expect some plutonium-powered, pancake-making wondercar; what they got was a Mercury. Cultural critics speculated that the car was a flop because the vertical grill looked like a vagina. Maybe. America in the '50s was certainly phobic about the female business. How did the Edsel come to be synonymous with failure? All of the above, consolidated into an irrational groupthink and pressurized by a joyously catty media. Interestingly, it was Ford President Robert McNamara who convinced the board to bail out of the Edsel project; a decade later, it was McNamara, then Secretary of Defense, who couldn't bring himself to quit the disaster of Vietnam, even though he knew a lemon when he saw one.

I was an NBC page at New York's Hudson Theater in 1958 when late-night host Jack Paar wisecracked, "The Edsel looks like an Oldsmobile sucking a lemon."

Below is a full-page magazine ad for the sad-sack Edsel cooked up on Madison Avenue. Flowery language and minimal research by the "Mad Men" resulted in the typical Mad Ave. claptrap.

"Every time we get creative," RCA Record Club CEO Ed McCabe told me, "we lose money."

> **1959 EDSEL**
>
> **High in distinction-but low in price!**
>
> **Makes history by making sense.**
>
> **Exciting new kind of car! Luxury without going overboard. Power without gulping gas. Full-size, six-passenger comfort. And priced with the most popular three.**
>
> This is a new breed of car. A car with looks, features, power and price that make sense. It's styled with beauty and grace you usually find only in expensive cars. It's soundly engineered. Edsel's compact 120-inch wheelbase makes parking a pleasure. Yet there's room for six adults to ride comfortably.

You get your choice of four new Edsel engines including a thirsty six and a new economy V-8. Plus practical luxury features like contour seats and self-adjusting breaks. The 1959 Edsel is actually priced with the most popular three — Plymouth, Chevrolet and Ford!
EDSEL DIVISION • FORD MOTOR COMPANY

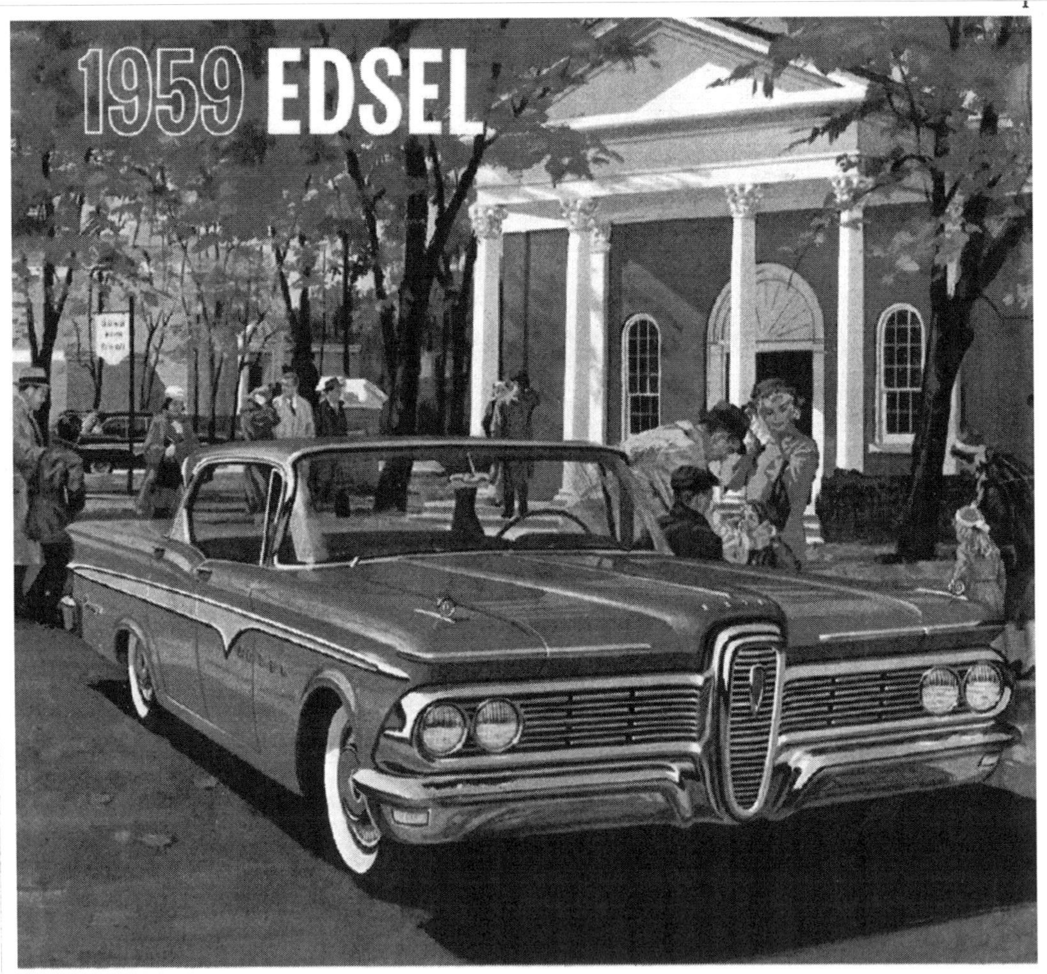

High in distinction–but low in price!

Makes history by making sense

Exciting new kind of car! Luxury without going overboard. Power without gulping gas. Full-size, six-passenger comfort. And priced with the most popular three!

This is a new breed of car. A car with looks, features, power *and price* that make sense. It's styled with beauty and grace you usually find only in expensive cars. It's soundly engineered. Edsel's compact 120-inch wheelbase makes parking a pleasure. Yet there's room for six adults to ride *comfortably*. You get your choice of four new Edsel engines including a thrifty six and a new *economy* V-8. Plus practical luxury features like contour seats and self-adjusting brakes. Price? *The 1959 Edsel is actually priced with the most popular three—Plymouth, Chevrolet and Ford!*

EDSEL DIVISION • FORD MOTOR COMPANY

....

In your research, vacuum up specifics
"Specifics sell," said copywriter Andrew J. Byrne. "Generalities don't."

For example, Procter & Gamble made a fortune with the slogan for the purity of its Ivory soap. Not "very" pure. Not "oh-so-pure."

> *"99 and 44/100% pure."*

Specifics are fun and actionable. You come away with something to drop at dinner parties or sprinkle in memos and reports to dazzle your colleagues and management.

Generalities lie on the page like a lox.

Finally, in terms of advertising, Ogilvy was the pro while others were slobs. The writer of this Edsel ad did minimal research. Compare this lame copy with the myriad statistics and factoids of Ogilvy.

What's more, because of the invitation to drive a Rolls, responses could be counted, conversions to sales could be determined, dollar revenues totaled and then tracked back to the original ads.

Rolls-Royce and Ogilvy knew the precise return on investment (ROI) of the campaign, while the Edsel shop never had a clue as to whether the ad generated sales.

Which means these clowns were, ipso facto, failures.

Brilliant ad copy unwittingly crafted by a *New York Times* obit writer
On July 12, 2013, *The New York Times* ran the obituary of Amar G. Bose. He was the inventor of the Acoustic Wave Music System, noise cancelling headphones and myriad audio high tech audio systems for consumers and businesses. Bose advertising has always fascinated me.

Many years ago my first novel was bought for the movies (no film was ever made, alas) and Peggy and I blew the option money on a Bang & Olufsen Beomaster 2400 stereo rig. Included were the magnificent receiver/amplifier, giant speakers and turntable. The B&O line is not only eye candy so elegant it was exhibited at New York's Museum of Modern Art, but also produces a rich, gorgeous sound.

The Bose Conundrum
The copy message was upbeat and effusive. But not believable:

> **Our best all-in-one music system that delivers**
> **room filling performance no matter what you play!**
> Advanced audio technologies fine-tune the sound for clarity and consistency even at loud volume levels, in large rooms.

In all the years I read Bose ads, I never bought into the copy. It was impossible, I thought, this a little piece of plastic could deliver concert hall quality sound. For starters, it did not have external speakers. The sound had to be ordinary at best. I would have happily bought a Bose rig for the office if it lived up to the copy.

HEAR THE RADIO THAT WOKE UP AN ENTIRE INDUSTRY.

Bose presents the Wave radio. It's the one radio acclaimed by leading audio critics. Because it's the one radio that delivers big, rich, lifelike stereo sound *plus* a small, convenient size.

Wired magazine said it has a "clean, sweet sound that will have your friends wondering where you've hidden your fancy speakers." But you have to hear the Wave radio for yourself to believe it.

While our B&O was continually delighting us, I kept coming across ads for Bose radios. These looked to me like the kind of slick plastic junk offered during — and just after — World War II.

World class ad copy by accident!

What follows are the most powerful two paragraphs of advertising copy ever created for Bose Corporation. It was not written by an agency copywriter. Rather it was from Amar G. Bose's obituary by Glenn Rifkin in The New York Times. It is the work of a superb journalist who whose job is to relate who, what, where, when and how. Rifkin s riff was far more informative than the tons manure generated by Madison Avenue over the years:

> A perfectionist and a devotee of classical music, Dr. Bose was disappointed by the inferior sound of a high-priced stereo system he purchased when he was an M.I.T. engineering student in the 1950s. His interest in acoustic engineering piqued, he realized that 80 percent of the sound experienced in a concert hall was indirect, meaning that it bounced off walls and ceilings before reaching the audience.
>
> This realization, using basic concepts of physics, formed the basis of his research. In the early 1960s, Dr. Bose invented a new type of stereo speaker based on psychoacoustics, the study of sound perception. His design incorporated multiple small speakers aimed at the surrounding walls, rather than directly at the listener, to reflect the sound and, in essence, recreate the larger sound heard in concert halls.

For me, this was an epiphany — a "holy shit" revelation that unlocked the secret of how the Bose system worked.

Of course no giant speakers were needed. This little wonder blew sound all over the room. The walls and ceiling became speakers! Bloody brilliant!

Where was Glenn Rifkin when Dr. Bose needed him most?

I give David Ogilvy the last word here:

> I do not regard advertising as entertainment or an art form, but as a medium of information. When I write an advertisement, I don't want you to tell me that you find it "creative." I want you to find it so interesting that you buy the product. When Aeschines spoke, they said, "How well he speaks." But when Demosthenes spoke, they said, "Let us march against Philip!"

Check your sources: the Internet can make you a chump — forever!
When I started out as a copywriter, novelist and nonfiction writer, doing research meant endless clipping of newspapers and magazine articles. I had to schlep down to a local library to spend hours chasing down leads in books, magazines and scrolling through endless microfilm reels of old newspapers.

Today, what took five days at the library can be accomplished in an hour on any computer in the world with Internet access.

Trouble is, the Internet is rife with misinformation. If you get caught advertently or inadvertently propagating its nonsense in a report, memo, article, letter, ad or book, you will look like a chump. If your careless work finds its way onto the Internet, it will follow you to the grave and beyond.

In the world of research, separating the bogus from the true takes work.

A personal digression: My Alhambra nightmare
Unlike my goody two-shoes classmates in elementary school who did their weekend homework on Friday nights, I always waited until late Sunday afternoon to start it.

In the early autumn of my tenth year, I was assigned to show up on Monday morning with a paper on the Alhambra. I didn't have a clue what the Alhambra was or what it meant. We were still in the beach house with no encyclopedia and miles away from a library — which would have been closed on Sunday anyway.

"The-dog-ate-my-homework" excuse would not have cut it. The teacher would have said, "That's okay. Tell the class what you learned about the Alhambra over the weekend."

I was in a panic and near tears — maybe in tears. My parents called all the neighbors. An hour later they came up with the "A" volume of an encyclopedia, which saved my bacon.

Fast-forward 60 years. Click on Google and enter "Alhambra, Granada," and you have at your fingertips 816,000 entries. One of the first listings for the Alhambra is the Wikipedia article of 5,110 words, glorious illustrations and a ton of internal and external hyperlinks.

All of this in one-quarter of a second!

One rule for research: beware of provenance
There's this guy I know in Denver — a political extremist, who forwards to me the most scurrilous, inflammatory stories to validate his pet hates. His e-mails are laced with comments such as, "OMG!" or "See, I told you so!"

Trouble is, when I put a phrase from his diatribe in quotation marks and paste it into Google, I get a bunch of cuckoo entries. Bloggers, screamers and nut cases have picked up the story and repeated it verbatim to and from each other. The busy little Google spiders capture this fiction and add it to the vast maw of data in the ether. A couple of Google entries, and it fogs the mirror. With six entries it grows legs. Fifteen Google entries turn it into a living, breathing monster that becomes harder and harder to disprove.

Can it be found on the website of a legitimate newspaper, broadcast station, wire service or commentator? Nah.

Eventually it may show up on the Annenberg Public Policy Center's factcheck.org. This website is honchoed by widely respected gumshoe journalist Brooks Jackson, who will do in-depth research and expose the story for what it is — a load of hooey.

By then it's too late. It will have made its way into the speeches and writings of the extreme Left or extreme Right, nobody having bothered to check it out.

"A lie told often enough becomes truth," wrote Vladimir Lenin and later quoted by Joseph Goebbels, Hitler's minister of propaganda.

"A lie can travel halfway around the world while the truth is putting on its shoes," Mark Twain said.

It is the same principle as a forged Picasso painting. As it is bought and sold over the years, it acquires a longer and longer pedigree — so-called provenance in the art world. After years in the marketplace, it becomes the real thing, no questions asked, even though it's an out-'n'-out fake.

The Wikipedia trap

School and college students are constantly being nailed for turning in papers with erroneous facts (and frequently plagiarized copy) lifted verbatim from the highly touted Wikipedia. This online source of all knowledge describes itself thusly:

> Since its creation in 2001, Wikipedia has grown rapidly into one of the largest reference websites, attracting 470 million unique visitors monthly as of February 2012.[1] There are more than 77,000 active contributors working on over 22,000,000 articles in 285 languages. As of today, there are 4,139,188 articles in English. Every day, hundreds of thousands of visitors from around the world collectively make tens of thousands of edits and create thousands of new articles to augment the knowledge held by the Wikipedia encyclopedia. (See the statistics page for more information.)

Trouble is, many of the volunteer editors and writers have their own agendas and are dishonest propagandists. For example:

> **Limbaugh Taken In: The Judge Was Not Loaded for Bear**
> PENSACOLA, Fla. — Anyone listening to Rush Limbaugh's radio show Tuesday could be forgiven for thinking that Judge Roger Vinson has the federal government dead in his sights … Apparently, Mr. Limbaugh had fallen prey to an Internet hoax … On Sunday night, and again Monday morning, someone identified only as "Pensacolian" edited Judge Vinson's Wikipedia entry to include the invented material. The prankster footnoted the entry to a

> supposed story in The Pensacola News Journal. The article — like its stated publication date of June 31, 2003 — does not exist. The same person who posted the information removed it on Tuesday afternoon, Wikipedia logs show. *—Kevin Sack, The New York Times*

Below are three of the entries in the dossier of Wikipedia flimflam entries in my private archive:

> 1. "Sleuthing into the accuracy of the open-source web encyclopedia known as Wikipedia has led to the door of its founder, Jimmy Wales. Public edit logs reveal that Wales has changed his own Wikipedia bio 18 times, deleting phrases describing former Wikipedia employee Larry Sanger as a co-founder of the site." *—Evan Hansen, wired.com*
>
> 2. "Political operatives are covertly rewriting – or defacing – candidates' biographical entries to make the boss look good or the opponent look ridiculous." *—Shannon McCaffrey, Associated Press*
>
> 3. "WikiScanner revealed that CIA computers were used to edit an entry on the U.S.-led invasion of Iraq in 2003. A graphic on casualties was edited to add that many figures were estimated and were not broken down by class. Another entry on former CIA chief William Colby was edited by CIA computers to expand his career history and discuss the merits of a Vietnam War rural pacification program that he headed." *—Randall Mikkelsen, Reuters*

The list of misinformation and disinformation uncovered in Wikipedia is lengthy and embarrassing. In 2007, the Middlebury College History Department banned the citing of Wikipedia as a research source.

Wikipedia as a starting point

Because Wikipedia is constantly churning out new information, it is one of the most frequently surveilled sites on the Internet by the robot crawlers of Google and other search engines. This also means it is frequently the top entry in data searches.

I have found Wikipedia can give you the basics of a story and often contains many links to related entries. In short, Wikipedia is a good place to start. But it is imperative to search out other sources — ideally ones with impeccable provenance — the websites of major newspapers, magazines and books. Think of Wikipedia as a wiring diagram.

Otherwise, you can get caught with your pants down as Rush Limbaugh did.

Not a pretty image.

One real plus in Wikipedia

Hyperlinks. When doing research and starting with Wikipedia, you'll see many bits of type in blue. In the articles themselves, these hyperlinks send the reader off to other entries in Wikipedia. However, at the bottom of Wikipedia entries are links to other sources — "Cited Sources," "Other Sources" and "External Links." These can get you out of Wikipedia and on to your own research.

Takeaways to Consider

• During your research, if you come across a story or quotation used by another writer, stop right there and Google it, so you get to the original source.

• "You don't stand a tinker's chance of producing successful advertising unless you start by doing your homework. I have always found this extremely tedious, but there is no substitute for it." *—David Ogilvy*

• "I do not regard advertising as entertainment or an art form, but as a medium of information. When I write an advertisement, I don't want you to tell me that you find it 'creative.' I want you to find it so interesting that you buy the product. When Aeschines spoke, they said, 'How well he speaks.' But when Demosthenes spoke, they said, 'Let us march against Philip!'" *—David Ogilvy*

• "Good ideas don't come from smoking joints and wearing funny clothes. It's just hard work and discipline. I do not believe the mysterious qualities of flair and originality are nearly as important as relevant knowledge." *—Drayton Bird*

• "Every time we get creative, we lose money." *—Ed McCabe*

• "Specifics sell. Generalities don't." *—Andrew J. Byrne*

• Procter & Gamble made a fortune with the slogan for the purity of its Ivory soap. Not "very" pure. Not "oh-so-pure."

• Check your sources. The Internet can make you a chump — forever!

• In the world of research, separating out the bogus from the true takes work.

• One rule for research: beware of provenance.

• "A lie told often enough becomes the truth." *—Vladimir Lenin*

• "A lie can travel halfway around the world while the truth is putting on its shoes." *—Mark Twain*

• Use Wikipedia as a starting point, never as a primary source.

• If you ever want to know the precise source of a quote, story or statistic, chances are it will turn up on Google. Simply enter the line into Google and the answer will be on-screen in less than a second.

• Never rely on a single source for your research (unless it is certifiably an original document).

CHAPTER 7

What You Own and What You Can Lose

"Egypt plans to copyright the Pyramids, the Sphinx and various museum pieces and use the royalties from copies to pay for the upkeep of its historic monuments and sites, *The Guardian* of London reported." —*Lawrence Van Gelder, The New York Times*

....

Quite simply, 4,000-year-old edifices are in public domain. How could Egypt enforce the copyright? It cannot. The entire concept is preposterous.

What is not preposterous is what you can copyright: Section 8 of the U.S. Constitution states that Congress has the power "to promote the Progress of Science and useful Arts, by securing for limited Times to Authors and Inventors the exclusive Right to their respective Writings and Discoveries."

U.S. copyright law

Copyright law can be boiled down to seven short paragraphs:

• You own outright every original thought, idea and verbiage the minute it comes out of your head and is committed to the written word. (Or music notes, art and design, a photograph, etc.) This is inviolate.

• The exception: anyone on salary that produces copy, design, music or film relating to the job does not own that material unless a special agreement exists with the employer.

• An employee who writes a novel or symphony on the side that has no relation to salaried work should own that copyright.

• A fact cannot be copyrighted. An arrangement and presentation of facts can.

• When a non-salaried person is engaged by another person or corporation to create something and signs a "Work Made for Hire" agreement, the employer owns that work.

• You can use copyrighted creative work if you give full credit. This is known as "fair use." Example: you can take a portion of someone's copyrighted work; give full credit to the author, composer or designer; and then critique it.

• If you reprint the entire work without credit to the original copyright owner, you are a plagiarist.

• If you register a work with the Copyright Office, and you catch a plagiarist, it's possible to sue and get money. If the work is not registered, you can tell a plagiarist to cease and desist, but cannot sue for damages.

How long does a copyright last?

The term of copyright for a particular work depends on several factors, including whether it has been published, and, if so, the date of first publication. As a general rule, for works created after January 1, 1978, copyright protection lasts for the life of the author plus an additional 70 years. For an anonymous work, a pseudonymous work, or a work made for hire, the copyright endures for a term of 95 years from the year of its first publication or a term of 120 years from the year of its creation, whichever expires first. For works first published prior to 1978, the term will vary depending on several factors. To determine the length of copyright protection for a particular work, consult chapter 3 of the Copyright Act (title 17 of the *United States Code*). More information on the term of copyright can be found in Circular 15a, *Duration of Copyright*, and Circular 1, *Copyright Basics. —U.S. Copyright Office*

A potential rip-off

Many years ago I was hired to write and design a mailing for a regular client who marketed book series to consumers. I already had four winning mail packages for his products. These were generating orders at a nice profit. The marketing manager — for whom I had done many successful jobs over the years when he was at various companies — quit suddenly. He was replaced by a new guy. I had known this full-of-himself new fellow many years back in the world of book publishing. He did not know how to work with freelancers.

The guy had not thought through this new project. It was a work in progress. I would create draft copy and thumbnails and my designer would create rough layouts, whereupon the guy would change the product and want a new version.

My artist was running up bills — for which I was liable, and I was spending a lot of time on the project. Finally the idea was scrapped. I sent a bill for our work — the artist's and mine — and it was not paid. I sent two more reminders and nothing happened. If I did not do something, I was going to be out-of-pocket several thousand dollars to my artist with zero income for me.

Mad as hell, I sent a copy of the bill to the president of the company — with a copy to the controller — along with a letter stating the following:

- I was the author and designer of four successful mailings that were currently generating revenue — and I listed them.

- The new guy's predecessor hired me on a handshake — with no work-made-for-hire contract on any of the assignments.

- Therefore, I own all the rights to those mailings.

- If the enclosed bill were not paid immediately, I would withdraw the company's rights to use all prior mailings and would take them all to court in order to enforce the action.

I received a check for the full amount within a week.

The copyright thieves

Back in 1998 when he was just 18, Shawn Fanning dreamed up a computer program called Napster. The scheme enabled him to share electronic music files with his pals in the freshman dorm at Northeastern University in Boston. And Harvard, Oxford University in England and all over the world.

All the hotshot young kids who were setting the direction of the Internet believed everything online should be free. Napster was the logical extension of that warped philosophy.

A huge outcry

None of these kids had ever written music and borrowed money from their parents to produce a CD for sale. Had they done so, it would have become immediately obvious that music lovers had no reason to buy their CD. With Napster, it could be traded all over the Internet around the world with nary a penny going into the owners' pockets.

The recording and motion picture industries went ballistic. If Napster remained on the scene, copyright protections would go up in smoke. Trillions of dollars were in jeopardy.

According to *The New York Times'* Saul Hansell, this digital piracy caused album sales to drop 30 percent from the prior year. In addition, "10 times as many songs are downloaded from file-sharing services as are bought from paid series like iTunes."

Make no mistake, this was outright theft of "intellectual property" with the same criminality and financial consequences as a bank heist. The numbers were staggering:

> At the end of June, just before [Napster] went off line, 120,000 users were typically logged on to the system; and, in all, 140 million songs were downloaded during the month, according to Webnoize, a digital music news and research service.
>
> That traffic represents a startling drop since February, the peak of Napster's use. At that time, Webnoize reported the service had 1.5 million simultaneous users, with 2.79 billion songs being exchanged altogether during the month. *—Matt Richtel, The New York Times*

If allowed to stand, the sales of motion picture VCRs and DVDs would soon tank as well.

Judge Marilyn Patel of the United States District Court for the Northern District of California ordered Napster shut down. It was to remain blacked out until the royalty situation could be resolved and the artists could be properly paid for their work.

Theft in the Far East

Piracy is rampant all over the world. Included in the thefts: music, films, books, software and products. The prime thieves are the Chinese. Not only do the buy American products and reproduce them for sale all over the world, they hack into our corporations and steal plans, business models and marketing memos.

Where is this illegal stuff sold? Everywhere from Hong Kong's Stanley Market to the most sinister worldwide criminal fencing operation in the history of humankind — eBay.

In many instances copyright doesn't mean squat
My father, Alden Hatch, was a historian and biographer who produced more than 40 books in his lifetime. In 1945, he published the first biography of Franklin D. Roosevelt to come out after the President's death. It included a great deal of original material, since he interviewed many of the players in the high drama of Roosevelt's life.

One day in prowling the Internet I came across a copy of my father's biography for sale by a company called Kessinger Publishing in Whitefish, Montana. It was out-and-out theft of copyright. No contract existed. No member of the family was ever contacted. No royalties were paid to the copyright owner (my stepmother).

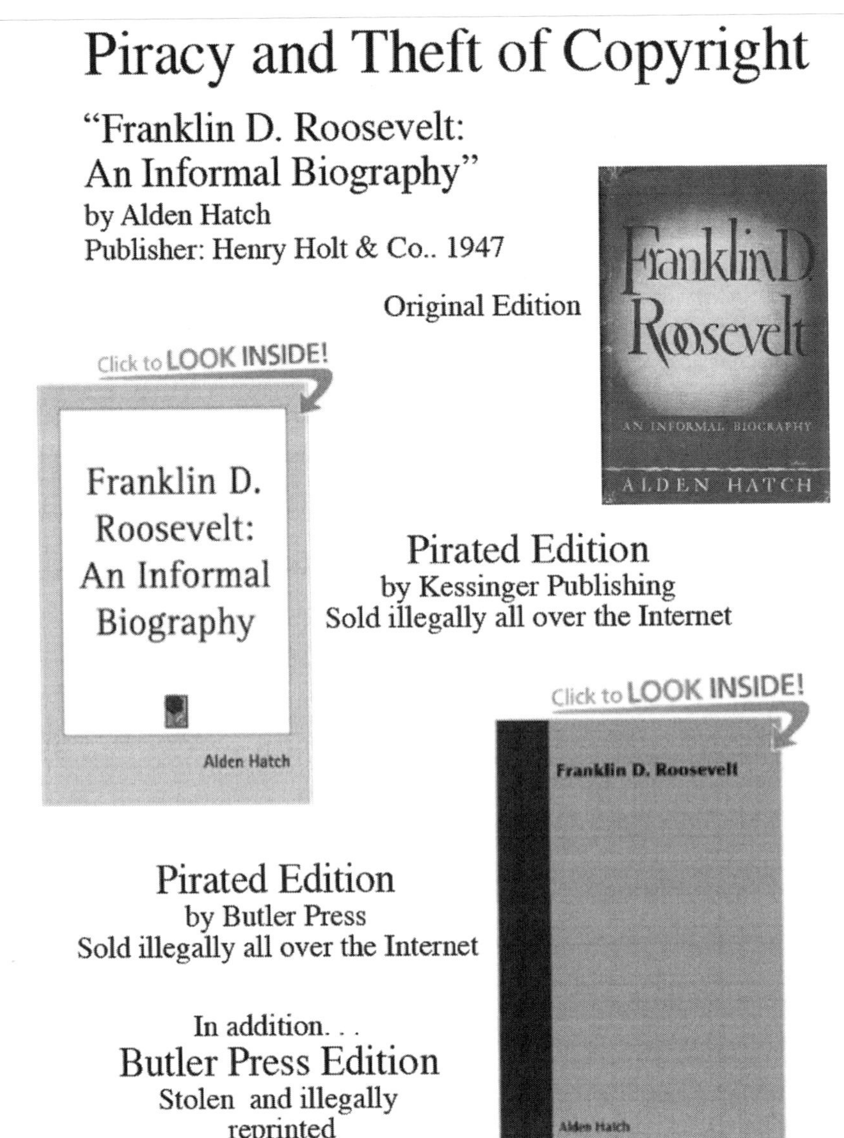

Piracy and Theft of Copyright
"Franklin D. Roosevelt:
An Informal Biography"
by Alden Hatch
Publisher: Henry Holt & Co.. 1947
Original Edition
Franklin D. Roosevelt
AN INFORMAL BIOGRAPHY
ALDEN HATCH
Click to LOOK INSIDE!
Franklin D. Roosevelt: An Informal Biography
Alden Hatch
Pirated Edition
by Kessinger Publishing
Sold illegally all over the Internet
Click to LOOK INSIDE!
Franklin D. Roosevelt
Alden Hatch
Pirated Edition
by Butler Press
Sold illegally all over the Internet
In addition. . .
Butler Press Edition
Stolen and illegally
reprinted
by Google Books

The Kessingers photographed the pages, created a cover and added it to their list. Suddenly it appeared for sale all over the Internet including amazon.com and barnesandnoble.com.

I raised hell. The Kessingers' response: Oops, we did not realize the book was still in copyright.

The "oops" excuse was bullshit. Using the Internet, it is possible to research the copyright status of any title in print in 30 seconds. Simply data-enter "copyright renewal" into Google and follow the digital breadcrumbs.

The Kessingers promised to withdraw the title. But seven years later if you go to their website, data-enter "Alden Hatch," you will immediately be sent to amazon.com, where the edition is for sale.

On all counts, the Kessingers are boldfaced liars and thieves.

Several months later I found another pirated edition of the book for sale on Amazon and Barnes & Noble. The publisher is Butler Press — impossible to find anywhere on the Internet.

In addition, Google Books copied this Butler Press edition into its massive database of stolen literary works — again in flat violation of copyright law.

The Roosevelt biography also turned up on something called "The Internet Archive" — an online theft operation that was giving a digital edition of the book away free along with five other of my father's titles. My father's stolen books had been downloaded — free — by nearly 2,000 readers before I blew the whistle.

Takeaways to Consider

• Generally speaking you own what you create, unless you are a salaried employee or sign a work-made-for-hire agreement.

• Your ownership of anything is no guarantee it will not be stolen and sold all over the world with not a penny going into your pocket.

• Is it worth it to spend money tracking these thieves down? Probably not. They'll tell the court, "Oops," and temporarily delete it from their lists, until you go away or die. Whereupon it will be back on the market again — either as before or under a new imprint.

• You can stop the unauthorized use of your material. However, you cannot sue for damages unless that material has been registered with the U.S. Copyright Office.

• If you hire freelancers, it is wise to have a contract that includes a work-made-for-hire agreement, specifics on what is expected including revisions, and kill-fee policies.

CHAPTER 8

The Perils of Plagiarism

Advertent and inadvertent plagiarism
Plagiarism is appropriating someone else's words, music or design and claiming authorship and, by extension, ownership.

Plagiarism also occurs when an author forgets to credit a source. When a plagiarist's theft of copyright material is discovered, it's not only embarrassing but also actionable. It's rare when two prominent authors crash and burn on the same day — May 3, 2006. Both were found guilty of plagiarism and both severely punished:

> **Raytheon board cuts CEO pay after book flap**
> ARLINGTON, VA — Raytheon Co.'s board said on Wednesday that it cut its chief executive's compensation in response to what others have called plagiarism in a management booklet, a penalty that one person familiar with the matter said could cost him $1 million. *—Jim Wolf, Bill Rigby and Kevin Drawbaugh, Reuters, May 3, 2006*

William H. Swanson, 56, CEO of military contractor Raytheon — ranked 97 in the Fortune 500 — produced a 76-page booklet, *Swanson's Unwritten Rules of Management.* Raytheon and Swanson — so in love with these unwritten rules — gave away 300,000 copies. *Business 2.0* featured it on its July 2005 cover.

In response to a *USA Today* story on Swanson's book, San Diego chemical engineer and blogger/whistleblower Carl Durrenberger wrote:

> However, it should be mentioned to your readers that nearly all of these "unwritten rules" have indeed been written — by another author in fact, 60 years ago. Mr. Swanson has plagiarized from the little-known book *The Unwritten Laws of Engineering* by W.J. King (1944, American Society of Mechanical Engineers), trying to pass off others' work as his own.

> **Young Harvard author's book deal canceled**
> NEW YORK — A Harvard University sophomore's debut novel has been permanently withdrawn by the book's publisher and her two-book deal canceled after allegations of literary borrowing piled up against her. *—Hillel Italie, Associated Press*

In creating *How Opal Mehta Got Kissed, Got Wild, and Got a Life*, 19-year-old Harvard sophomore Kaavya Viswanathan lifted 40 passages practically verbatim from two novels by Megan McCafferty. The young author was ordered to return her the six-figure advance and Steven Spielberg canceled the film deal.

"I remember by reading," the disgraced novelist told Dinitia Smith of *The New York Times*. "I never take notes." It might have happened because she claimed to have a photographic memory.

It matters not whether the plagiarism is inadvertent and the result of sloppy research. The consequences of being caught with your hand in the literary cookie jar can be devastating.

Google's long memory

A plagiarist's misdeeds will remain in cyberspace for years, long after the person has been rehabilitated.

For example, on Google's Advanced Search I entered the names of 11 well-known writers, academics plus a vice president of the United States. I surrounded their names with quotation marks and added the word "plagiarism." The results (shown here in alphabetical order) are thousands of entries for each name:

- Stephen Ambrose, historian, author
- Mike Barnicle, newspaper columnist, TV commentator
- Joseph Biden, U.S. senator, vice president
- Jayson Blair, *New York Times* reporter
- Ward Churchill, professor, University of Colorado
- T.S. Eliot, Nobel Laureate
- Doris Kearns Goodwin, Pulitzer Prize-winning biographer
- Jonah Lehrer, writer for *The New Yorker* and *Wired*
- William Swanson, CEO, Raytheon
- Nina Totenberg, legal affairs correspondent, NPR
- Laurence Tribe, professor, constitutional law, Harvard
- Kaavya Viswanathan, novelist

How did this happen?

Nina Totenberg's first job was with a short-lived publication, *The National Observer* (1962-1977). She reportedly lifted some copy from *The Washington Post* sans attribution. As a young journalist, she didn't know copyright or fair use. Nonetheless she was fired. Her reported comment many years later: "I have a strong feeling that a young reporter is entitled to one mistake and to have the holy bejeezus scared out of her to never do it again."

The stories of Stephen Ambrose and Doris Kearns Goodwin — both world-renowned historians — are more complex. Apparently they assigned freelancers to do some research. The material the authors received was picked up from original sources. But alas, since it was not attributed to others, the writers assumed it was their own and used the text verbatim. These were embarrassing errors.

It can pay to plagiarize

In 2012, Jonah Lehrer, 31, was thrown off *The New Yorker* staff for fabricating quotes by Bob Dylan. He was also fired by *Wired.* A year later he submitted a 65-page book proposal to Jonathan Karp, publisher of Simon & Schuster, and it was accepted. He was also paid $20,000 by the Knight Foundation to give a mea culpa talk about plagiarism to attendees at a Miami Journalism conference.

My bet: Lehrer's writing career is short-lived. A reputable publisher would be a fool to trust him.

Detecting copyright infringement

Prior to the Internet, catching a copyright thief was very difficult. Today it's easy. Simply type the sentence or paragraph — surrounded by quotes — into Google and see what turns up. Or Google "plagiarism software" and you'll find programs to offer immediate help.

Takeaways to Consider

• Plagiarism is to be avoided no matter what is being produced — article, memo, correspondence, e-mail, special report, whitepaper or full-length book.

• As a writer of nonfiction, I see myself as someone who absorbs vast amounts of information in order to connect dots. With this in mind, I always try to credit sources for two reasons. 1) A tip o' the hat to the wonderful minds working to clarify this confusing world. 2) To let the reader know I have done homework.

• I am scared to death someone else's work will slip into my prose sans attribution. I try to be vigilant.

• If a writer discusses another writer's work — or a report or a quote by somebody — it's a good idea to drop everything and find the original source of the information. You are then working from the same material, and your take will be original.

• Don't let deadlines deter you from homework, originality and your sacred honor.

• For Don Jackson's and my book, 2,239 Tested Secrets for Direct Marketing Success, I wrote to several hundred direct marketers asking for the rules they learned during their careers. Back came roughly 150 replies, which I categorized and data-entered.

• Everybody was credited. Jackson and I stuck in our two cents every so often, but we were not the stars of the show. Many of the quotes gave conflicting opinions and advice. Direct marketers loved it, because in an argument with a boss or client they can usually find support for their view by an industry giant.

• It is imperative to understand completely the concept of "Fair Use" — the right to reprint a certain amount of copyright material in order to discuss it.

• I cannot remember where I heard this rather simplistic explanation many years ago, but here it is. With Haiku, the Japanese poetry form of 17 syllables in three lines, quoting three syllables is Fair Use; to quote all 17 is a violation of copyright.

• Use the hyperlink. Rather than bogging down the flow of your work with long quotations (and risking copyright infringement), send the reader to the original source.

CHAPTER 9

Start Right or Suffer Writer's Block

"A writer who waits for ideal conditions under which to work will die without putting a word to paper." —*E.B. White*

....

Benchley's solution
If you are pondering a blank computer screen (or a blank piece of paper), you'll never get started.

I am reminded of the great wit, writer and actor of the 1930s and '40s, Robert Benchley (1889-1945), grandfather of Peter (*Jaws*) Benchley. One day under deadline and with a severe hangover, Benchley was sitting in his room at the Algonquin Hotel in New York. He stared and stared at a blank piece of paper in his typewriter. To get started he typed the word "The."

Benchley arose from his chair, walked to the window and glanced at his watch. The gang of regulars was assembling for a splendid lunch of booze and *bon mots* at the legendary Round Table downstairs. Among them: Dorothy Parker, Harpo Marx, George S. Kaufman, Alexander Woollcott, *New Yorker* editor Harold Ross and others.

Benchley returned to the typewriter and stared at "The" for a long time. In a burst of inspiration he completed the sentence. It read, "The hell with it."

Whereupon he took the elevator down to join the party.

A *New Yorker* writer's letter to a distraught former student
Here's a splendid bit of advice:

> Dear Joel: You are writing, say, about a grizzly bear. No words are forthcoming. For six, seven, 10 hours no words have been forthcoming. You are blocked, frustrated, in despair. You are nowhere, and that's where you've been getting. What do you do? You write, 'Dear Mother.' And then you tell your mother about the block, the frustration, the ineptitude, the despair. You insist that you are not cut out to do this kind of work. You whine. You whimper. You outline your problem, and you mention that the bear has a 55-inch waist and a neck more than 30 inches around but could run nose-to-nose with Secretariat. You say the bear prefers to lie down and rest. The bear rests 14 hours a day. And you go on like that as long as you can. And then you go back and delete the 'Dear Mother' and all the whimpering and whining, and just keep the bear. —*John McPhee, Draft No. 4, Replacing the words in boxes*

Ted Nicholas on getting started
Ted Nicholas (born Nick Peterson) is one of the great entrepreneurs, publishers, teachers and writers in the world of direct marketing. Here's his advice to copywriters and, by extension, to all writers:

1. Clear your mind. For some persons, this might mean lying down for a few minutes before going to work. For others, it could mean jumping in the pool or jogging around a track. Frolic, spend time with someone you love or go dancing. Do whatever comes naturally to you in order to have a clear mind for creative purposes.

2. Never write when you're tired. You're not going to try to drive or operate machinery when you're tired. Don't try to write if you're fatigued.

3. Never write when you're busy. If there are other demands pressing on you, tend to them first. I don't think anyone can write well when watching the clock. Don't try to write if you have appointments later in the day or errands to run.

4. Don't write in bits and pieces. Once you've turned on your creative energy, you need to keep it flowing. I don't stop until I complete a draft. I try not to stop even for meals. *—Ted Nicholas, The Golden Mailbox*

A kitchen timer

The late Gene Schwartz's powerful direct mail copy sold millions of dollars worth of books (many published by himself). His *Breakthrough Advertising* is must-read for direct response copywriters. Gene once told me to get a kitchen timer and set it on the desk next to me.

"Then hit 4-4-4-4. That's 44 minutes, 44 seconds. During that period, all you do is work — write, do research, deal with correspondence, design, whatever."

When the timer goes off, get up and shut the alarm sound off, he told me. Take a break. Walk around, stretch, get a cup of coffee, clear your head. When you're ready to go back to work, hit the 4-4-4-4 button again and dive in.

Hemingway on the mechanics of writing

Ernest Hemingway wrote standing at a high desk. When he finished writing a novel, he would stick the manuscript in a drawer and go deep-sea fishing, hunting in Africa or attend bullfights in Spain. On his return several weeks (or months) later, he would read the book with fresh eyes and immediately see where he went off the rails and what needed work.

Most of us under deadline do not have this kind of time. However, if you can lay aside a piece of writing for 12 or 24 hours or longer and then go back to it for edits and rewrites, it can be beneficial. In *A Moveable Feast*, Hemingway wrote:

> I always worked until I had something done and I always stopped when I knew what was going to happen next. That way I could be sure of going on the next day.

He added:

> I learned not to think about anything that I was writing from the time I stopped writing until I started again the next day. That way my subconscious would be

working on it and at the same time I would be listening to other people and noticing everything, I hoped; learning, I hoped; and I would read so that I would not think about my work and make myself impotent to do it.

Takeaways to Consider

• "A writer who waits for ideal conditions under which to work will die without putting a word to paper." *—E.B. White*

• Ted Nicholas on getting started

—Clear your mind.
—Never write when you're tired.
—Never write when you're busy.
—Don't write in bits and pieces. Once you've turned on your creative energy, you need to keep it flowing.

• Get a kitchen timer and punch in 4-4-4-4. That's 44 minutes and 44 seconds. That's when you write. When the buzzer goes off, stop. Move around. Have a cup of coffee. Then hit 4-4-4-4 again. *—Gene Schwartz*

• "I always worked until I had something done and I always stopped when I knew what was going to happen next. That way I could be sure of going on the next day." *—Ernest Hemingway*

CHAPTER 10

Conceptualizing and Using the Unique Selling Proposition (USP)

What makes your book, article, memo, special report, press release or résumé special? In marketing and advertising, the unique selling proposition (USP) is what differentiates a product or service from the competition and makes it stand out from the crowd.

The USP was first articulated by Rosser Reeves. A great copywriter, VP and later chairman of the board of Ted Bates and Company, Reeves was the author of *The Reality of Advertising* (1961, now out of print).

On his invaluable website, hardtofindseminars.com, Michael Senoff describes Reeves' concept of the Unique Selling Proposition. He defines a USP as having three parts:

- Each ad must make a proposition — "Buy this product and you get these benefits."

- The proposition must be unique — something your competitors do not, cannot or will not offer.

- The proposition must sell — it must be something prospects really want; it pulls them over to your product.

- In essence, a Unique Selling Proposition briefly and clearly explains a single quality about your product enabling it to stand out against the competition.

As the great copywriter Maxwell Sackheim said, "The greatest challenge to copywriters is to find something to say that will be worth the reader's while."

This is true for whatever you write — e-mail, memo, whitepaper, letter, article, business plan or book.

A huge disappointment
Back in the summer of 2008, I came across a *Wall Street Journal* book review of *Tupperware Unsealed: Brownie Wise, Earl Tupper, and the Home Party Pioneers.*

I was intensely interested. Here was the genesis of a revolutionary marketing technique — the Tupperware party. Women (mostly) would get together in a home. A sales rep would demonstrate plastic food containers, take orders and give the hostess a commission or thank-you gift. Who dreamed it up? What were the thought processes, the trials and the errors going into the final business model that became a national craze?

The "review" was an article about the history of Tupperware. It told the reader the entire story from beginning to the very sad ending. I knew exactly what was in the book and no longer had any reason to buy it. Reviewer Mark Lasswell had screwed me out of a reading experience, screwed the author, Bob Kealing, out a royalty payment and screwed the publisher — the University Press of Florida — out of a sale. This was the classic lazy man's way to fill a newspaper column. You steal somebody else's research, get paid for condensing it into 1,057 words, add nothing to the mix and feel immensely pleased at having done a good day's work.

What could Lasswell have brought to the party instead of a rehash? I would have called this a revolutionary new merchandising concept and a fascinating narrative. I would give the reader a quick backgrounder in marketing: the Greek agora, barter, door-to-door, off-the-page advertising, retail, direct mail, multi-level marketing (M-L-M), TV, e-commerce, etc. Anything to enhance the reading experience and impart information that might help in the purchase decision.

For a writer to simply regurgitate material available elsewhere is of no real service to anybody. To create value, it is imperative to come up with a new slant — something memorable, fun or useful adding to the reader's life and knowledge. A writer must become a master of the USP.

How a marketer determines the USP

All products and services are made up of features, and each feature has a benefit to the user. Many fledgling copywriters and marketers do not understand the difference between features and benefits.

For example, a great confusion between features and benefits occurs in the insurance industry. If you buy a $1 million life insurance policy, you are promised your heirs will receive a benefit of $1 million when you die.

Actually the $1 million payment is not a benefit. Rather it is the main *feature* of the policy.

The benefit: You can sleep soundly knowing if something happens to you, your family will be okay. They can keep the house, pay the bills and will always remember you with love and appreciation.

Here's how *MBA Magazine* described the difference between a feature and a benefit: "People want quarter-inch holes, not quarter-inch drills."

A formula for creating the USP

What follows applies to anything written. Quite simply, how do you make it special? Unique? Worth the reader's time?

Whenever I'm handed a copy assignment, I spend a lot of time researching the product or service, getting to know it intimately.

I also research competitors' versions of the product.

In the course of the research, I make a list of all possible features I can come up with.

Features are "it" copy (as opposed to "you" copy and "me" copy). "It" copy shows and describes "it" — a feature of the product or service.

After making a list of the features, I turn those features into benefit-oriented "you" copy.

In essence, what this feature will do for "you."

I then rank the benefits in order of importance and come up with the one I feel is the most exciting and has the most selling power.

This becomes the unique selling proposition — and the headline.

It is the theme around which the piece is centered.

Is it possible to come up with more than one unique selling proposition? Yes. But generally, not too many. Otherwise the writer might wander off course — followed by the reader.

The greatest unique selling propositions are so short and powerful they overcome the competition for attention and became inexorably linked to the brand name and the product in the consumer's mind.

For his client, M&M's® candies, Rosser Reeves came up with: "Melts in your mouth, not in your hand."

Examples of other memorable USPs
"Bags Fly Free." *—Southwest Airlines (GSD&M, 2010)*
"A diamond is forever." *—De Beers (N.W. Ayer & Son, 1948)*
"We try harder." *—Avis (Doyle, Dane Bernbach, 1983)*
"99 and 44/100% pure." *—Ivory soap (Procter & Gamble, 1892)*
"Look sharp, feel sharp." *—Gillette (BBDO, 1940s)*
"The pause that refreshes." *—Coca-Cola (D'Arcy Co., 1929)*
"Tastes great, less filling." *—Miller Lite Beer (McCann-Erickson, 1974)*
"Does she…or doesn't she?" *—Clairol (Foote, Cone & Belding, 1957)*
"Mmm mmm good." *—Campbell Soup (BBDO, 1930s)*
"When it rains it pours." *—Morton salt (N.W. Ayer & Son, 1912)*
"We'll leave the light on for you." *—Motel 6 (Richards Group, 1988)*
"The skin you love to touch." *—Woodbury soap, (J. Walter Thompson Co. 1911)*
"Breakfast of Champions." *—Wheaties, Blackett-Sample-Hummert, 1930s)*

How David Ogilvy came up with his Rolls-Royce USP
Let's go back to the 1958 Rolls-Royce ad in Chapter 6.

Here are Ogilvy's words to describe three of the features and the resulting benefit:

Ogilvy's "it" feature: *"The car has power steering, power brakes and automatic gear-shift."*

Ogilvy adds the "you" benefit: *"It is very easy to drive and to park. No chauffeur required."*

Ogilvy's "it" feature: *"The Rolls-Royce is guaranteed for three years."*

Ogilvy adds the "you" benefit: *"With a new network of dealers and parts-depots from Coast to Coast, service is no problem."*

Ogilvy's "it" feature: *"There are three separate systems of power brakes, two hydraulic and one mechanical. Damage to one will not affect the others."*

Ogilvy adds the "you" benefit: *"The Rolls-Royce is a very safe car — and also a very lively car. It cruises serenely at eight-five. Top speed is in excess of 100 m.p.h."*

Ogilvy also described features, leaving the benefits to the reader's imagination.

Ogilvy's "it" feature: *"Every Rolls-Royce engine is run for seven hours at full throttle before installation, and each car is test-driven for hundreds of miles over varying road surfaces."*

Implied "you" benefit: *Your Rolls-Royce is not temperamental; every car has thrived on harder driving and abuse than you will ever give it.*

Ogilvy's "it" feature: *"A picnic table, veneered in French walnut, slides out from under the dash. Two more swing out behind the front seats."*

Implied "you" benefit: *Great for long trips and elegant seductions. Think of Cary Grant and Grace Kelly parked overlooking the Mediterranean in Hitchcock's To Catch a Thief.*

Ogilvy's "it" feature: *"By moving a switch on the steering column, you can adjust the shock-absorbers to suit road conditions."*

Implied "you" benefit: *Unmatched driving comfort, no matter where you take it.*

Ogilvy's "it" feature: *"The coachwork is given five coats of primer paint, and hand rubbed between each coat, before nine coats of finishing paint go on."*

Implied "you" benefit: *Guaranteed to look like new for many, many years with minimum upkeep.*

After weighing all the features in his mind, Ogilvy chose quietude as the ultimate benefit:

Ogilvy's "it" feature: *"Three mufflers tune out sound frequencies — acoustically."*

Here was Ogilvy's USP benefit-to-you headline:

At 60 miles an hour the loudest noise in this new Rolls-Royce comes from the electric clock.

Imagine! A car so quiet you can hear the electric clock! This has to be one magnificent machine — from the inside out! What a unique selling proposition!

The headline is so famous it generates 123,000 entries when entered into Google within quotation marks. The line reportedly secured Ogilvy a place in *The Oxford Dictionary of Quotations.*

Ogilvy closes his ad with an invitation to test drive a Rolls-Royce. A number of prospects made appointments to test-drive a Rolls, perhaps just to see if it was really as quiet as the promise. When it turned out to be true, they parted with $13,995 to own one. (2013 price new: $300,000+)

The backstory of the electric clock headline
A great researcher assembles as much material as possible from many sources. Ogilvy went far beyond relying solely on the information Roll-Royce spoon-fed him.

Instead, he swiped the headline from an ad used by Pierce-Arrow in a 1932 newspaper.

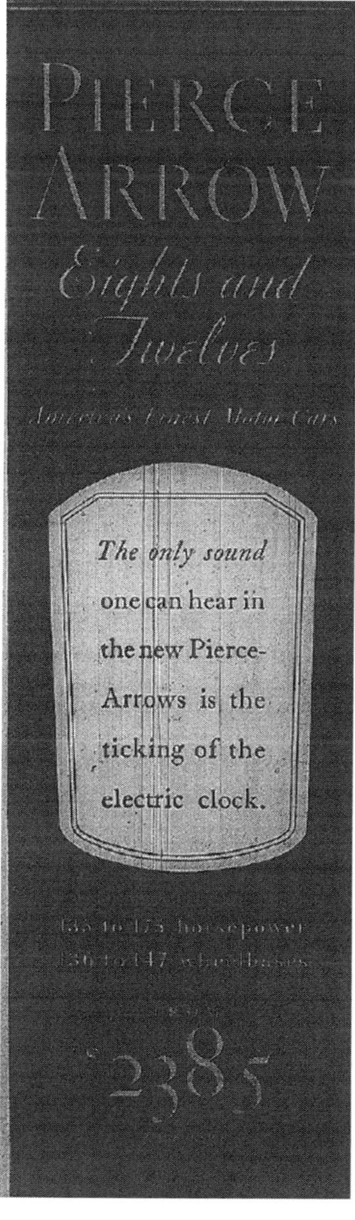

Did David Ogilvy steal the headline attributed to Clyde Bedell (1898-1985), a titan in the world of advertising from the 1930s to the 1960s? Yes.

Usually it's not a good idea to be light-fingered with other people's words without attribution. *(See Chapter 8 on Plagiarism.)* This is especially true in this Internet age where plagiarism can be quickly detected. Worldwide humiliation will follow a thieving author to the grave. Not to mention your competitor's schadenfreude — sheer delight in your misfortune.

In this case, Pierce-Arrow went out of business in 1938, some 20 years prior to Ogilvy's ad. Back in 1958, the Internet was unimaginable. What's more, on the slim chance some nerdy little researcher found the forbear to the Roll-Royce version, how could the word be spread and who would care?

The lesson here: do not rely on a single source for your research if more than one is available, and if you find something you can use, *steal smart.*

Finally, the greatest USP in advertising history
This is strictly my opinion. I believe the single most powerful line of copy ever written was not crafted by a copywriter. More likely it was the work of a lawyer, perhaps in concert with a physician. It was not even in the advertisements themselves, but rather a throwaway in the disclaimers. But it is riveting. This single line proves the product works and is responsible for billions in revenue. It became the USP:

> For an erection lasting more than four hours, seek immediate medical attention.

Takeaways to Consider

- "The greatest challenge to copywriters is to find something to say that will be worth the reader's while." *—Maxwell Sackheim*

- If you are writing a press release, a newspaper story, pitching a book or article or creating a business plan, it's a good idea to have a Unique Selling Proposition. You want to give the reader focus.

- For a writer to simply rehash, rewrite and regurgitate material available elsewhere is of no real service to anybody. To create value, it is imperative to come up with a new slant — something memorable, fun or useful adding to the reader's life and knowledge.

- The difference between a feature and a benefit: "People want quarter-inch holes, not quarter-inch drills." *—MBA Magazine*

- Whenever I'm handed a copy assignment, I spend a lot of time researching the product or service, getting to know it intimately.

- I also research competitors' versions of the product. In the course of the research, I make a list of all possible features I can come up with.

- Features are "it" copy (as opposed to "you" copy and "me" copy). "It" copy shows and describes "it" — a feature of the product or service.

- After making a list of the features, I turn those features into benefit-oriented "you" copy. In essence, what this feature will do for "you."

• I then rank the benefits in order of importance and come up with the one I feel is the most exciting and has the most selling power.

• This becomes the USP — unique selling proposition — and the headline.

• And perhaps the theme around which the piece is centered as well as maybe the title.

• Do not rely on a single source for your research if more than one is available, and if you find something you can use, *steal smart.*

CHAPTER 11

Takeaways: Don't Leave Your Reader Without Them

In 2005, I came up with the idea for an e-zine based on marketing (specifically direct marketing), business and life.

My wife, Peggy, president of the Target Marketing Group and publisher of the new e-zine, suggested including takeaways.

These were to be bulleted one- and two-liners or short paragraphs at the end of each column. They capture the main points of the piece and summarize for the reader why a particular column might be worth reading.

When the e-zine was delivered, it arrived either as HTML or in a text format designed to save the reader time.

With one click on the inbox announcement of the current issue, the reader received:

- Title and subtitle of the story.
- "In the News" — the story on which the column was based.
- A short lead showing where the thing was headed.
- Takeaways to Consider

Following the lead paragraph was the hyperlink: "Click to Continue." This took the reader to my column's landing page on the Target Marketing website.

I assume readers are very busy. I don't want to waste anybody's time.

Readers of *Business Common Sense* with no interest in the day's subject could be out of there in less than 20 seconds, maybe with a useful takeaway or two, maybe not.

Or they could click to continue and see where the thing was heading.

***The Wall Street Journal*'s editor problem**
For years I subscribed to *The Wall Street Journal* and found one or two stories a day worth downloading into my archive.

Until the redesign of *The Wall Street Journal* a number of years ago, the front page always had three main news stories on the front page. In the center column — known as the A-hed — the articles were often lightweight and amusing. For example, on Monday, Sept. 25, 1989, I was the subject of the A-hed with a piece titled, "You Call It Junk, But Denison Hatch Sees Gold in It." Her lede:

> STAMFORD, Conn — Imagine a guy who sits in his basement 12 hours a day, poring over junk mail the way Frank Perdue scrutinizes chickens. That's Denison Hatch.

This lighthearted story did provide value to businesspeople. Peggy and I were the pioneers in analyzing direct mail — the medium in which the most advertising dollars were spent at the time. We created a research system to discover which direct mail efforts were winners and what made them successful.

Our cranky little newsletter *WHO'S MAILNG WHAT!* was a breakthrough product. It helped a great many people work smarter — specifically advertisers, marketers, mailers, copywriters, designers and suppliers to the direct marketing community.

Today, *The Wall Street Journal* continues to clutter its front page with A-hed frippery. This forces busy people to search elsewhere for vital information. We exist in an economic mess. Unemployment, yo-yoing markets, record foreclosures, bankruptcies, government surveillance, seemingly endless wars and squirrelly weather are rampant. The business community is scared to death. Out-of-work consumers are scared worse.

What follows are some samples from front pages of *The Wall Street Journal* — stories I filed in my giant archive under the heading, "WSJ Stoopid Shit":

- **In Maine, a Rivalry Boils Up On the Lobster-Boat Racing Circuit.**
  To Catch Mr. Alley's Speedy Vessel, Mr. Johnson Tries a Pontiac; Prizes of Cash, Bait *—Robert Tomsho, Aug. 25, 2009*

- **Boing! Boing! Boing! Boing! Boing! Boing! Boing!**
  'Extreme' Pogoers Do Backflips, Hop Minivans; In This Sport, Bounces Per Second Matter *—Kris Maher, Aug. 28, 2009*

- **Snow-Shovel Racing Went Downhill, But It's Getting a Second Chance.**
  Speed Demons Really Dig It; The Shovelmeister Waxes Nostalgic *—Miguel Bustillo, Feb. 8, 2010*

- **Slaw and Order: Hot-Dog Stand in Chicago Triggers a Frank Debate.**
  'Felony Franks' Is Staffed by Ex-Cons, but Some Neighbors Don't Relish the Name *—Julie Jargon, Oct. 13, 2009*

- **When It Comes to Butter Carving, There's No Margarine for Error.**
  State Fair Winners Get Their Likenesses Carved; Making Cookies, Saving the Nose *—Jilian Mincer, Aug. 26, 2010*

- **Chill of Victory, Agony of the Feet: The Art of Snowshoe Racing.**
  Newfangled Gear, an Element of Danger and No Time to Savor the Scenery — *Barry Newman, Mar. 7, 2009*

Amusing, yes.

Are they worth taking up front-page real estate in the leading financial newspaper in the world? Nah.

Rupert Murdoch and his cutesy-poo, self-indulgent editors do not have their priorities straight.

Quite simply, no takeaways exist for any of this fatuous drool.

Murdoch's people were saying, "Spend time on this stuff and then it's up to you to figure out why such drivel was worth reading."

I decided not to renew the print edition of the *Journal* and strictly read it online. This means every year I am saving roughly 70 pounds of newsprint and the cost of three dinners with Peggy at an okay restaurant in Philly. I have not looked back. My paid online subscription is adequate.

If *The Wall Street Journal* made it mandatory for many of the stories to have takeaways, I might have stuck around. Takeaways serve two purposes:

- They force the writer to focus on the key points of the story.
- And they crystallize the story in the mind of the reader, making it memorable.

"Excellent column today!" a reader once wrote me. "Love your succinct 'takeaway point.' Joins others from previous columns above my desk!"

Every now and then a reader would write me and ask if I ever were planning to publish a collection of the takeaways. I said thanks for the suggestion (I personally answer all e-mail correspondence) and put the idea on the back burner.

In 2010, I resurrected the idea and published *Career-Changing Takeaways: Quotations, Rules, Aphorisms, Pithy Tips, Quips, Sage Advice, Secrets, Dictums and Truisms in 99 Categories of Marketing, Business and Life.*

Takeaways to Consider

- Whenever I write anything, in the back of my mind are the possible takeaways — the down-'n'-dirty one-liners or short paragraphs to help the reader remember the main points of what I'm trying to convey.

- Takeaways also force the writer to focus on the key points of the story.

- Knowing I have to create takeaways keeps me from wandering too far off course.

CHAPTER 12

Headlines, Titles and Teasers, Oh My!

"Writing headlines is one of the greatest journalist arts." —*Claude Hopkins*

"Headlines, subject lines, teasers and titles are the hot pants on the hooker." —*Bill Jayme*

....

In the world of advertising, they are called **headlines.**

Newspaper journalists call them **heds.**

On book covers, special reports, whitepapers, articles, short stories, blogs and press releases they are called **titles.**

On memos and e-mails they are **subject lines.**

On a direct mail envelope it's the **teaser.**

Whatever the medium, the headline, title or teaser is the first thing the reader sees.

John Caples on headlines

John Caples (1900-1990), one of the seven greatest copywriters of all time, wrote extensively on the art and science of direct marketing copy:

> Headlines make ads work. The best headlines appeal to people's self interest, or give news. Long headlines that say something outpull short headlines that say nothing.
>
> Remember that every headline has one job. It must stop your prospects with a believable promise. All messages have headlines. In TV, it's the start of the commercial.
>
> In radio, the first few words. In a letter, the first paragraph. Even a telephone call has a headline. Come up with a good headline, and you're almost sure to have a good ad. But even the greatest writer can't save an ad with a poor headline.
>
> You can't make an ad pull unless people stop to read your brilliant copy.

A hugely successful two-word headline

I used to know Sheldon Hearst, whose business was putting racks of 5½″ x 8″ take-one brochures in checkout areas of supermarkets. A marketer had a fraction of a second to catch the busy shopper's eye with a headline.

"The headline selects the reader," said the great direct marketing guru Axel Andersson. A great example of Axel's rule was one of Sheldon's clients who published a special report on nocturnal enuresis — involuntary bed wetting during the night. This condition afflicts millions of adults and children. The powerful headline was printed in giant type and dominated the rack full of little 5″ x 8″ cards on the supermarket wall: **WET BED?**

Sometimes it was printed with a question mark. Other times not. But it was used with great success for many years. Any shopper — victim or family member looking for help in this area — would reach for that card.

David Ogilvy on headlines

• **The headline is the ticket on the meat.** Use it to flag down readers who are prospects for the kind of products you are advertising. If you are selling a remedy for bladder weakness, display the words BLADDER WEAKNESS in your headline; they catch the eye of anyone who suffers from this inconvenience. If you want mothers to read your advertisement, display MOTHERS in your headline. And so on. Conversely do not say anything in your headline likely to exclude any readers who might be prospects for your product.

• **Headline.** "On the average, five times as many people read the headline as read the body copy. When you have written your headline, you have spent eighty cents out of your advertising dollar."

• **Benefited headline.** Headlines that promise benefits sell more than those that don't.

• **News and headlines.** Time after time we have found that it pays to inject genuine news into headlines. The consumer is always on the lookout for new products or new improvements in an old product, or new ways to use an old product. Economists – even Russian economists – approve of this. They call it "informative" advertising. So do consumers.

• **Simple headlines.** Your headline should telegraph what you want to say – in simple language. Readers do not stop to decipher the meanings of obscure headlines.

• **Localize headlines.** In local advertising, it pays to include the name of the city in your headline.

• **Typography.** The more typographical changes you make in your headline, the fewer people will read it.

• **Capital letters.** Set your headline, and indeed your whole advertisement, in upper-lower case. CAPITAL LETTERS ARE MUCH HARDER TO READ, PROBABLY BECAUSE WE LEARN TO READ IN LOWER CASE. People read their books, newspapers and magazines in upper-lower case.

• **Surprinting.** Never deface your illustration by printing your headline over it. Old-fashioned art directors love doing this, but it reduces the attention value of the advertisement by an average of 19 percent. Newspaper editors never do it. In general, imitate the editors; they form the reading habits of your customers.

• **Quotes.** When you put your headline in quotes, you increase recall by an average of 28 percent.

• **Blind headlines.** Some headlines are "blind." They don't say what the product is or what it will do for you. They are about 20 percent below average in recall.

The non sequitur headline
On the morning of June 12, 2013 I turned to the Opinion page of *The New York Times* and the following headline hit me in the face:

"The Price of the Panopticon" by James B. Rule

Having never heard of a panopticon, I was hooked.

The column was about the 2013 massive leak to the media detailing worldwide U.S. National Security Agency surveillance program — and subsequent uproar.

Astonishingly, nowhere in the column was the word "panopticon" used or defined. The headline was a bizarre non sequitur.

An Amusing Sidebar
The panopticon designer was eccentric British philosopher Jeremy Bentham (1748-1832), who spent 40 years writing about the law. In death the preserved Bentham is seated and fully dressed on display in a glass case at University College London, where he was "spiritual founder." Every 50 years he is carted into the meeting of the college council. When Bentham's name is called during the roll, someone answers, "Present but not voting."

At left: Panopticon cell house, Illinois State Penitentiary. All cells are in full view of the wardens in the central station. At right: Jeremy Bentham preserved behind glass at University College London.

It niggled me that *The New York Times* headline could highlight a panopticon and yet not mention panopticon anywhere in the story. Five months later I discovered the modus operandi of these weird dudes at the *Times.*

How a rogue New York Times headline sabotaged Mitt Romney

Being a political junkie, I bought *DOUBLE DOWN: Game Change 2012* — the riveting saga of the 2012 presidential election by Mark Halperin and John Heilemann.

When he was considering a run for the presidency, Mitt Romney decided to burnish his credentials as a strategic thinker and an expert in business. Since his late father had been chairman and CEO of American Motors from 1954-1962, Mitt felt a personal connection to the auto industry. Mitt submitted a think piece to *The New York Times* opinion page editor David Shipley.

The thrust of Romney's idea was not to hand Detroit millions of dollars in bailout cash. He wrote:

> The American auto industry is vital to our national interest as an employer and as a hub for manufacturing. A managed bankruptcy may be the only path to the fundamental restructuring the industry needs. It would permit the companies to shed excess labor, pension and real estate costs. The federal government should provide guarantees for post-bankruptcy financing and assure car buyers that their warranties are not at risk.

Shipley liked publishing op-eds at variance with the editorial board's views and accepted Romney's piece with glee. However, it was a house rule never to publish anything without receiving a final sign-off from the author. The project was turned over to Times editor Mary Duenwald, who had a few minor changes. From *DOUBLE DOWN:*

> A few seconds later, Romney was on the line, accepting the changes uncomplainingly or proposing his own. *What a nice guy*, Duenwald thought.
>
> The headline — LET DETROIT GO BANKRUPT — was the only thing, per long-standing *Times* tradition, that the author didn't see beforehand.
>
> Shipley's view was that it captured the essence of Romney's argument and fit the space. The Timesman understood that a structured bankruptcy was a specific thing; even so, he thought, *a bankruptcy is a bankruptcy.*

"LET DETROIT GO BANKRUPT" caused uproar — especially in Ohio and Michigan where the auto industry is a major player in those fragile economies. The liberal mantra on Romney as CEO of Bain Capital was his pattern of buying companies, firing workers and reaping millions of dollars. "I like being able to fire people," Romney told a Nashua, New Hampshire breakfast crowd in January, adding to the perception of his ruthlessness.

Shipley's unfair headline was thrown up in Romney's face over and over during the campaign. Not surprisingly, he lost the swing states of Michigan and Ohio to Obama.

The sad aspect of this story is that the headline was at variance with Romney's reasoned, logical argument for a "managed" or carefully "structured" bankruptcy.

> Shipley's view [of the headline] was that it captured the essence of Romney's argument and fit the space.
>
> *Fit the space?*
>
> "All the news that fits we print," goes an old parody of the *Times* motto.

Skewed headlines by outsiders

Suddenly the strange panopticon headline for James Rule's op-ed piece made sense. The *Times* is so mistrusting of its authors' competence they are not permitted to write their own headlines. Hence confusion from a boiler room of hotshot wordsmiths who put their own warped spin on a writer's story, while management delights in cleverness.

As David Ogilvy pointed out, on average five times as many people read the headline as the body copy. Thus the headline represents 80 percent of the writer's salary. Quite simply, the headline is the most important element of any story. "It is the headline that gets people into the copy," the great freelancer Vic Schwab said. "The copy doesn't get them into the headline."

Worse, under the preposterous system, the *Times* forces writers to sign off on words that are not their own. This means the entire editorial page is not only filled with unreadable gray walls of type, but is also a series of lies.

Same thing at *The Wall Street Journal*

I wrote the above on Nov. 19, 2013. Below are three smartypants blind headlines from that day's *Wall Street Journal:*

- New Beef Over Food Rules
- Despite Defaults, USDA Sweetens the Pot
- Chinese Couples — and Investors — Are Pregnant with Anticipation

You have to be nuts to write for *The New York Times* or *The Wall Street Journal*, where writers are not permitted to control of their headlines and the bon mot trumps information.

These publishers and editors are talking to themselves, not the reader — yet another reason why the loudest noise to come out of major newspaper offices is the death rattle.

Three of the most powerful 20th century headlines

The following three headlines sold a ton of product over many years:

"Can he really play?" a girl whispered. "Heavens no!" Arthur exclaimed. "He never played a note in his life."

They Laughed When I Sat Down At the Piano But When I Started to Play!—

ARTHUR had just played "The Rosary." The room rang with applause. I decided that this would be a dramatic moment for me to make my debut. To the amazement of all my friends, I strode confidently over to the piano and sat down.

"Jack is up to his old tricks," somebody chuckled. The crowd laughed. They were all certain that I couldn't play a single note.

"Can he really play?" I heard a girl whisper to Arthur.

"Heavens, no!" Arthur exclaimed. "He never played a note in all his life. . . But just you watch him. This is going to be good."

I decided to make the most of the situation. With mock dignity I drew out a silk handkerchief and lightly dusted off the piano keys. Then I rose and gave the revolving piano stool a quarter of a turn, just as I had seen an imitator of Paderewski do in a vaudeville sketch.

"What do you think of his execution?" called a voice from the rear.

"We're in favor of it!" came back the answer, and the crowd rocked with laughter.

Then I Started to Play

Instantly a tense silence fell on the guests. The laughter died on their lips as if by magic. I played through the first few bars of Beethoven's immortal Moonlight Sonata. I heard gasps of amazement. My friends sat breathless — spellbound!

I played on and as I played I forgot the people around me. I forgot the hour, the place, the breathless listeners. The little world I lived in seemed to fade — seemed to grow dim—unreal. Only the music was real. Only the music and visions it brought me. Visions as beautiful and as changing as the wind blown clouds and drifting moonlight that long ago inspired the master composer. It seemed as if the master musician himself were speaking to me—speaking through the medium of music—not in words but in chords. Not in sentences but in exquisite melodies!

A Complete Triumph!

As the last notes of the Moonlight Sonata died away, the room resounded with a sudden roar of applause. I found myself surrounded by excited faces. How my friends carried on! Men shook my hand — wildly congratulated me—pounded me on the back in their enthusiasm! Everybody was exclaiming with delight—plying me with rapid questions. . . "Jack! Why didn't you tell us you could play like that?". . . "Where *did* you learn?"—"How long have you studied?"—"Who *was* your teacher?"

"I have never even *seen* my teacher," I replied. "And just a short while ago I couldn't play a note."

"Quit your kidding," laughed Arthur, himself an accomplished pianist. "You've been studying for years. I can tell."

"I have been studying only a short while," I insisted. "I decided to keep it a secret so that I could surprise all you folks."

Then I told them the whole story.

"Have you ever heard of the U. S. School of Music?" I asked.

A few of my friends nodded. "That's a correspondence school, isn't it?" they exclaimed.

"Exactly," I replied. "They have a new simplified method that can teach you to play any instrument by mail in just a few months."

How I Learned to Play Without a Teacher

And then I explained how for years I had longed to play the piano.

"A few months ago," I continued, "I saw an interesting ad for the U. S. School of Music—a new method of learning to play which only cost a few cents a day! The ad told how a woman had mastered the piano in her spare time at home—and *without a teacher!* Best of all, the wonderful new method she used, required no laborious scales — no heartless exercises — no tiresome practising. It sounded so convincing that I filled out the coupon requesting the Free Demonstration Lesson.

"The free book arrived promptly and I started in that very night to study the Demonstration Lesson. I was amazed to see how easy it was to play this new way. Then I sent for the course.

"When the course arrived I found it was just as the ad said — as easy as A.B.C.! And, as the lessons continued they got easier and easier. Before I knew it I was playing all the pieces I liked best. Nothing stopped me. I could play ballads or classical numbers or jazz, all with equal ease! And I never did have any special talent for music!"

* * * *

Pick Your Instrument

Piano	'Cello
Organ	Harmony and Composition
Violin	Sight Singing
Drums and Traps	Ukulele
Banjo	Guitar
Tenor Banjo	Hawaiian Steel Guitar
Mandolin	Harp
Clarinet	Cornet
Flute	Piccolo
Saxophone	Trombone

Voice and Speech Culture
Automatic Finger Control
Piano Accordion

Play Any Instrument

You too, can now *teach yourself* to be an accomplished musician—right at home—in half the usual time. You can't go wrong with this simple new method which has already shown 350,000 people how to play their favorite instruments. Forget that old-fashioned idea that you need special "talent." Just read the list of instruments in the panel, decide which one you want to play and the U. S. School will do the rest. And bear in mind no matter which instrument you choose, the cost in each case will be the same—just a few cents a day. No matter whether you are a mere beginner or already a good performer, you will be interested in learning about this new and wonderful method.

Send for Our Free Booklet and Demonstration Lesson

Thousands of successful students never dreamed they possessed musical ability until it was revealed to them by a remarkable "Musical Ability Test" which we send entirely without cost with our interesting free booklet.

If you are in earnest about wanting to play your favorite instrument—if you really want to gain happiness and increase your popularity—send at once for the free booklet and Demonstration Lesson. No cost — no obligation. Right now we are making a Special offer for a limited number of new students. Sign and send the convenient coupon now — before it's too late to gain the benefits of this offer. Instruments supplied when needed, cash or credit. **U. S. School of Music, 1031 Brunswick Bldg., New York City.**

U. S. School of Music,
1031 Brunswick Bldg., New York City.

Please send me your free book, "Music Lessons in Your Own Home", with introduction by Dr. Frank Crane, Demonstration Lesson and particulars of your Special Offer. I am interested in the following course:

. . . .

Have you above instrument? . . . .

Name . . . .
(Please write plainly)

Address . . . .

City . . . . State . . . .

John Caples, 1925. This is one of the most famous ads in history. Copywriter (and musical comedy aficionado) Don Hauptman suspects this ad inspired lyricist Ira Gershwin to write, They All Laughed. ("They all laughed at Christopher Columbus when he said the world was round.")

HOW TO WIN FRIENDS AND INFLUENCE PEOPLE

"The Reader's Digest" devoted 10 pages to this volume because, in their words, "From Mr. Carnegie's extensive reservoir of experience has come the wealth of anecdote and common sense lessons in human relations in which HOW TO WIN FRIENDS AND INFLUENCE PEOPLE abounds."

JOHN D. ROCKEFELLER Sr. once said: *"The ability to deal with people is as purchasable a commodity as sugar or coffee. And I will pay more for that ability than for any other under the sun."*

Wouldn't you suppose every college would conduct practical courses to develop this "highest priced ability under the sun?" To our knowledge, none has.

How to develop that ability is the subject of Dale Carnegie's amazing new book.

A few years ago Chicago University and the United Y.M.C.A. Schools made a survey to find out the prime interest of adults. The survey took two years, cost $25,000. It indicated that their first interest is health and their second, how to understand and get along with *people*; how to make people like you; how to win others to your way of thinking.

Wouldn't you suppose that after the members of this survey committee had decided to *give* such a course, they could readily have found a practical textbook? They searched diligently yet could find none suitable.

The book they were looking for was recently published and overnight became a best seller. 36,000 copies were sold in three days of last week alone. More than 500,000 copies have been sold to date! IT IS OUT SELLING ANY OTHER BOOK IN AMERICA TODAY!

A New Book—and the Man Behind It

It is called *How to Win Friends and Influence People* and is written by the one man who is perhaps better qualified to write it than anyone else.

Dale Carnegie is the man to whom the big men of business come for practical guidance on the subject of getting along with people, dealing with them successfully, winning others to their own way of thinking. During the last 25 years he has trained more than 17,000 business and professional men and women among them some of the most famous in the country.

When he conducts his course on Public Speaking and How to Influence People in the ballroom of the Hotel Commodore or The Pennsylvania, or the Hotel Astor the second largest hall in New York the place is packed to capacity. Large organizations such as The New York Telephone Co., Westinghouse Electric and Manufacturing Company, and many others listed elsewhere on this page have had this training conducted by Mr. Carnegie in their own offices for their members and executives.

This new book, *How to Win Friends and Influence People*, grew and developed out of that vast laboratory of experience. As you can judge from the panel at the top of this advertisement, it is as practical as 24 years of actual successful experience with the problems of thousands of people in all walks of life can make it.

Consider the Case of Michael O'Neil

Michael O'Neil lives in New York City. He first got a job as a mechanic, then as a chauffeur.

When he got married he needed more money. So he tried to sell automobile trucks. But he was a terrible flop. He suffered from an inferiority complex that was eating his heart out.

On his way to see any prospect, he broke out into a cold sweat. Then, before he could get up enough courage to open the door, he often had to walk up and down in front of an office half a dozen times.

When he finally got in, he would invariably find himself antagonizing, arguing. Then he would get kicked out never knowing quite why.

THIS IS A BIG BOOK OF THIRTY-SEVEN CHAPTERS; INCLUDING:

The Big Secret of Dealing with People
Six Ways to Make People Like You Instantly
An Easy Way to Become a Good Conversationalist
A Simple Way to Make a Good First Impression
How to Interest People
Twelve Ways to Win People to Your Way of Thinking
A Sure Way of Making Enemies—and How to Avoid It
The Safety Valve in Handling Complaints
How to Get Cooperation
A Formula That Will Work Wonders for You
The Movies Do It. Radio Does It. Why Don't You Do It?
Nine Ways to Change People Without Giving Offense or Arousing Resentment
How to Criticize—and Not Be Hated for It
How to Spur Men on to Success
Making People Glad to Do What You Want
Letters That Produced Miraculous Results
Seven Rules for Making Your Home Life Happier

He was such a failure he decided to go back to work in a machine shop. Then one day he received a letter inviting him to attend the opening session of a Dale Carnegie course.

"It may do you some good, Mike. God knows you need it"

He didn't want to go he was afraid that he would be out of place that there would be a lot of college men. But his despairing wife made him, saying, "It may do you some good, Mike. God knows you need it."

He went to the meeting, and other meetings of the course. He lost his fear. He learned how to talk charmingly and convincingly, how to make people like him at once, how to win friends and influence others.

Today Michael O'Neil is a star salesman for one of the country's largest manufacturers of motor trucks. His income has mounted and skyrocketed. Last year at the Hotel Astor, he stood in front of 2500 people and told a rollicking story of his achievements. Few professional speakers could have equalled his confidence or his reception.

Only $1.96 if you decide to keep it!

Michael O'Neil is a salesman but his problem was exactly the same as that of thousands in other fields the fundamental one of *getting along with people*. The way it was solved is just one example of what Dale Carnegie's help has meant to more than 17,000 people in all types of endeavor. *What Dale Carnegie has done for them he can do for you.* Look at the chapter headings. They indicate the amount of hard-hitting, priceless information Dale Carnegie's book contains. But the subject is so intensely important that we say, look at this book without obligation. Then decide whether or not you want to own it.

DALE CARNEGIE

Dale Carnegie is the man the men of business come to for practical instruction in getting along with people. During the last 25 years, he has trained more than 17,000 business and professional men—more than any other living man.

Large organizations such as:

Westinghouse Electric Manufacturing Co.	Brooklyn Chamber of Commerce
New York Telephone Co.	Philadelphia Chamber of Commerce
Bell Telephone Co. of Pennsylvania	Philadelphia Electric Co.
American Institute of Electrical Engineers, New York	Philadelphia Gas Works Co.
McGraw-Hill Publishing Company, New York	Carrier Engineering Corporation
	Philadelphia Association of Life Underwriters

have had this training conducted in their own offices for their members and executives.

This new book is a direct result of Dale Carnegie's experience, the *only* working manual of its kind ever written to help people solve their daily problems in human relationships.

SEND NO MONEY

Try Dealing THIS WAY With People—for just FIVE Days!

This book has been published for only a short time. Yet it is now outselling *any other book*—fiction or non-fiction—in America! The presses are now running continuously to turn out 5,000 copies daily.

When you get your copy simply *read* it; there are no "exercises" to be practiced. Then try for five days Dale Carnegie's simple method of dealing with people. Judge for yourself, in your daily social or business life, how easily whatever you do, say, or write can win the friendship and the hearty cooperation of others—instead of arousing resentment, friction, and either a negative response or no action at all.

It is not necessary to send any money now. You may pay for "*How to Win Friends and Influence People*" when it is delivered—with the definite understanding that its price of only $1.96 will be refunded to you if you wish it. If this book does what we claim, it will mean more to you *than ANY book you have ever read*. If it doesn't we do not want you to keep it. Mail this coupon at once.

SIMON and SCHUSTER, Dept. C-628, 386 Fourth Ave. New York

SIMON and SCHUSTER, *Publishers*
Dept. C-628, 386 Fourth Ave., N. Y. C.

Please send me *How to Win Friends and Influence People*. I will pay postman only $1.96 plus few cents postage charges. It is understood that I may read it for 5 days and return it for refund if I then feel that it does not in every way live up to the claims made for it.

Name

Address

City *State*

Check here if you prefer to enclose $1.96 plus 4c New York Sales Tax WITH this coupon, in that case WE will pay the postage charges. The same refund privilege applies of course.

NOTE: If resident of New York City add 4c for City Sales Tax.

Vic Schwab, 1936-1939. This ad sold one million copies. "It is the headline that gets people into the copy," Schwab said. "The copy doesn't get them into the headline."

Do You Make These Mistakes in English?

Sherwin Cody's remarkable invention has enabled more than 100,000 people to correct their mistakes in English. Only 15 minutes a day required to improve your speech and writing.

MANY persons use such expressions as "Leave them lay there" and "Mary was invited as well as myself." Still others say "between you and I" instead of "between you and me." It is astonishing how often "who" is used for "whom" and how frequently we hear such glaring mispronunciations as "for MID able," "ave NOO," and "KEW pon." Few know whether to spell certain words with one or two "c's" or "m's" or "r's" or with "ie" or "ei," and when to use commas in order to make their meaning absolutely clear. Most persons use only common words—colorless, flat, ordinary. Their speech and their letters are lifeless, monotonous, humdrum.

Why Most People Make Mistakes

What is the reason so many of us are deficient in the use of English and find our careers stunted in consequence? Why is it some cannot spell correctly and others cannot punctuate? Why do so many find themselves at a loss for words to express their meaning adequately? The reason for the deficiency is clear. Sherwin Cody discovered it in scientific tests which he gave thousands of times. *Most persons do not write or speak good English simply because they never formed the habit of doing so.*

What Cody Did at Gary

The formation of any habit comes only from constant practice. Shakespeare, you may be sure, never studied rules. No one who writes and speaks correctly thinks of *rules* when he is doing so.

"Stepping Stone To Advancement"

"The Course was a stepping stone for me. Soon after I enrolled I was promoted to Chief Clerk. Later the Course was invaluable in helping me pass the bar examinations; 67% failed. Also aided me in passing a number of Civil Service examinations." Albert F. Nebelsick, Route 2, Sunman, Indiana.

"Great Help and Benefit"

"Your Course is quite the most interesting way I have ever studied English. I feel that it will be of great help and benefit to me in my secretarial work, and to me it is money well spent." Mrs. Reba Shields, 620 Ivy St., Jacksonville, Fla.

"Money Spent Wisely"

"To anyone seeking a knowledge of English I recommend the Course most heartily. I really enjoy writing letters now, because I express myself more effectively. I can truly say that I spent my money wisely." Mrs. Martha S. Marlowe, 3350 Grace St., Chicago, Ill.

Overcomes Inferiority Complex

"It has helped me a great deal, and it has given me an added sense of security when addressing other persons. It is surprising to find how lax one becomes in the use of English, especially when one has been out of school for some years. My mind and ambition had become somewhat stagnant, and I suffered from an inferiority complex. Mr. Cody's lessons have been of great help to me in overcoming these weaknesses, for which I am thankful." Mrs. Verne Cunningham, 608 W. Emerson, Monterey Park, Calif.

Here is our mother-tongue, a language that has built up our civilization, and without which we should all still be muttering savages! Yet our schools, by wrong methods, have made it a study to be avoided—the hardest of tasks instead of the most fascinating of games! For years it has been a crying disgrace.

In that point lies the real difference between Sherwin Cody and the schools! Here is an illustration: Some years ago Mr. Cody was invited by the author of the famous Gary System of Education to teach English to all upper-grade pupils in Gary, Indiana. By means of unique practice exercises *Mr. Cody secured more improvement in these pupils in five weeks than previously had been obtained by similar pupils in two years under old methods.* There was no guesswork about these results. They were proved by scientific comparisons. Amazing as this improvement was, more interesting still was the fact that the children were "wild" about the study. It was like playing a game!

SHERWIN CODY

The basic principle of Mr. Cody's new method is habit-forming. Anyone can learn to write and speak correctly by constantly using the correct forms. But how is one to know in each case what is correct? Mr. Cody solves this problem in a simple, unique, sensible way.

100% Self-Correcting Device

Suppose he himself were standing forever at your elbow. Every time you mispronounced or misspelled a word, every time you violated correct grammatical usage, every time you used the wrong word to express what you meant, suppose you could hear him whisper: "That is wrong, it should be thus and so." In a short time you would habitually use the correct form and the right words in speaking and writing.

If you continued to make the same mistakes over and over again, each time patiently he would tell you what was right. He would, as it were, be an everlasting mentor beside you—a mentor who would not laugh at you, but who would, on the contrary, support and help you. The 100% Self-Correcting Device does exactly this thing. It is Mr. Cody's silent voice behind you, ready to speak out whenever you commit an error. It finds your mistakes and concentrates on them. You do not need to study anything you already know. There are no rules to memorize.

Only 15 Minutes a Day

Nor is there very much to learn. In Mr. Cody's years of experimenting he brought to light some highly astonishing facts about English.

For instance, statistics show that a list of sixty-nine words (with their repetitions) *make up more than half of all our speech and letter-writing.* Obviously, if one could learn to spell, use, and pronounce these words correctly, one would go far toward eliminating incorrect spelling and pronunciation.

Similarly, Mr. Cody proved that there were no more than one dozen fundamental principles of punctuation. If we mastered these principles, there would be no bugbear of punctuation to handicap us in our writing.

Finally he discovered that twenty-five typical errors in grammar constitute nine-tenths of our everyday mistakes. When one has learned to avoid these twenty-five pitfalls, how readily one can obtain the facility of speech which denotes the person of breeding and education!

When the study of English is made so simple, it becomes clear that progress can be made in a very short time. *No more than fifteen minutes a day is required.* Fifteen minutes, not of study, but of fascinating practice! Mr. Cody's students do their work in any spare moment they can snatch. They do it riding to work or at home. They take fifteen minutes from the time usually spent in profitless reading or amusement. The results really are phenomenal.

Sherwin Cody has placed an excellent command of the English language within the grasp of everyone. Those who take advantage of his method gain something so priceless that it cannot be measured in terms of money. They gain a mark of breeding that cannot be erased as long as they live. They gain a facility in speech that marks them as educated people in whatever society they find themselves. They gain the self-confidence and self-respect which this ability inspires. As for material reward, certainly the importance of good English in the race for success cannot be over-estimated. Surely, no one can advance far without it.

FREE — Book on English

It is impossible in this brief review, to give more than a suggestion of the range of subjects covered by Mr. Cody's new method and of what his practice exercises consist. But those who are interested can find a detailed description in a fascinating little book called "How You Can Master Good English in 15 Minutes a Day." This is published by the Sherwin Cody School of English in Rochester. It can be had by anyone, free upon request. There is no obligation involved in writing for it. The book is more than a prospectus. Unquestionably, it tells one of the most interesting stories about education in English ever written.

If you are interested in learning more in detail of what Sherwin Cody can do for you, send for the book "How You Can Master Good English in 15 Minutes a Day."

Merely mail the coupon, a letter or postal card for it now. No agent will call. SHERWIN CODY SCHOOL OF ENGLISH, 8811 B. & O. Building, Rochester 4, N. Y.

SHERWIN CODY SCHOOL OF ENGLISH
8811 B & O Building, Rochester 4, N. Y.

Please send me, without obligation on my part, your new free book "How You Can Master Good English in 15 Minutes a Day." No agent will call.

Name ....

Address ....

City .... Zone No. *(If any)* .... State ....

☐ *If 18 years or under, check here for Booklet A*

Maxwell Sackheim, 1919 — 1959. This ran for 40 years without change. It has been called the greatest off-the-page advertisement in history.

These headlines were not slapped together as afterthoughts. For master copywriter Claude Hopkins, copy was secondary to headlines. He often spent:

> ... hours on a single headline. Often scores of headlines are discarded before the right one is selected. For the entire return from an ad depends on attracting the right sort of readers. The best of salesmanship has no chance whatever unless we get a hearing.
>
> The vast difference in headlines is shown by keyed returns... The identical ad run with various headlines differs tremendously in its returns. It is not uncommon for a change in headlines to multiply returns from five or 10 times over.

Hopkins' observation directly relates to all other writing. A poorly written headline, subject line, teaser or title guarantees poor readership.

Copy wizard John Caples echoes the wisdom of Claude Hopkins on the importance of headlines:

> What do people see of advertising? Headlines! What do you yourself see of advertising as you glance through a newspaper or magazine? Headlines! What decides whether or not you stop a moment and look at an advertisement, or even read a little of it? The headline!
>
> Now, I spend hours on headlines — days if necessary. And when I get a good headline, I know that my task is nearly finished. Writing the copy can usually be done in a short time if necessary. And that advertisement will be a good one — that is, if the headline is really a "stopper."
>
> What good is all the painstaking work on copy if the headline isn't right? If the headline doesn't stop people, the copy might as well be written in Greek.
>
> If the headline of an advertisement is poor, the best copywriters in the world can't write copy that will sell the goods. They haven't a chance. Because if the headline is poor, the copy will not be read. And copy that is not read does not sell goods. On the other hand, if the headline is a good one, it is a relatively simple matter to write the copy.

When John Caples explained to copywriters how to create headlines for advertisements, his teachings apply to all kinds of writing:

> **3 Classes of Successful Headlines**
> Advertisers ... find the majority of their most successful headlines can be divided into three classes:
>
> **1. Self-interest**
> The best headlines are those that appeal to the reader's self-interest, that is, headlines based on reader benefits. They offer readers something they want — and can get from you. For example:

• ANOTHER $50 RAISE
• RETIRE AT 55

2. News
The next-best headlines are those that give news. For example:
• NEW FEATURES OF THE FORD TRUCK
• DISCOVERED — A NEW KIND OF HAND CLEANER

3. Curiosity
The third-best headlines are those that arouse curiosity. For example:
• LOST: $35,000
• ARE YOU PLAYING FAIR WITH YOUR WIFE?

However, the effectiveness of the average curiosity headline is doubtful. For every curiosity headline that succeeds in getting results, a dozen will fail.

Why is it that self-interest headlines are best and the curiosity headlines only third best? You can answer this question for yourself. Suppose you are looking through a newspaper. You see a headline that arouses your curiosity. You will read the copy if you have time. But suppose you see a headline that offers you something you want. You will make time to read the copy.

The deck
Often a headline or a title needs further explanation — a deck or subhead above or below the main headline. It amplifies and clarifies what the reader can expect. For example, here is Max Sackheim's headline:

Do You Make These Mistakes in English?

This headline falls into John Caples's "curiosity" category. By itself it is intriguing, but doesn't say precisely what's coming. So Sackheim inserted this three-line deck.

Sherwin Cody's remarkable invention has enabled more than 100,000 people to correct their mistakes in English. Only 15 minutes a day required to improve your speech and writing.

Here is a bold promise of self-improvement and adds both self-interest and news (100,000 people took advantage of Sherwin Cody's system). The result is a powerhouse of an ad with a life span of 40 years. It is considered by many to be the greatest "off-the-page" ad ever written.

Headlines should break naturally and evenly
Headlines should look tidy and be immediately easy to scan. Below is the University of Kansas "Two-x" rule for headlines:

Do not have one line of a multi-line head too short. Exceptions can be made on some headlines with narrow specifications (such as one-column heds). Note: The two-"x" rule for this class and the Kansan; it is not a rule that is universally followed. Some publications allow greater leeway; most do not, some requiring you to come even closer. Nevertheless, the two-"x" rule is a good one to follow.) Examples:

Lincoln, Douglas to debate
at new KU Dole Centerxxx *(not acceptable — almost 3 Xs short)*

Lincoln, Douglas to debate
at KU's new Dole Centerxx *(OK — fewer than two Xs short)*

Lincoln-Douglas
debate todayxxx *(acceptable in narrow, multi-line headlines)*
at Dole Center

When to write the headline, subject line or decide on a title

One suggestion: Don't start with the headline. First get familiar with the nuts-'n'- bolts. Understand the basics of this thing you are working on, who you are talking to and what you want to tell these readers.

The great freelance direct mail writer Chris Stagg once told me whenever he got a writing assignment, the first thing he created was the order form.

"Huh?" I mumbled.

"The order form — or coupon on the ad — is the reprise. It's the last thing most people read. It crystalizes everything going before. It tells the prospect exactly what will be received and when, as well as the price.

"Once I have this information written down in the form of an order mechanism," Stagg said, "only then can I begin to begin to combine everything I learned about the product and the audience and everything I know about how to get my head inside their heads and make them want to order."

John Caples also suggested you probably should hold off writing headline:

> **When Not to Write the Headline First**
>
> Of course, writing the headline first is based on your knowing what you are selling so well that the copy will flow naturally no matter where you begin. When that is not the case, begin by learning about the product or service.
>
> Then, before starting on possible headlines, write a first draft of the copy to help organize what you now know. Somewhere in that copy you are likely to find the key selling point on which to base your headline — not its words, but the concept on which your headline will be based. Now spend all the time you need to get the best headline possible, then rewrite and polish your copy to flow naturally from final headline to the logo.

How the Internet plays havoc with headlines

For centuries, headlines were designed to not only capture the reader's attention, but also as an aid in knowing whether what follows will be of interest and worth pursuing. "The headline is the ad for the ad," said retail marketing consultant Murray Raphel.

Double duty

With the rise of the Internet, headlines have taken on another dimension. Not only are they designed with the reader in mind, but they also must do double duty. Headlines must capture the attention of the search engine robotic spiders continually crawling through the Internet to pick up keywords. This guarantees the material will appear in the correct subject categories. In fact, many headlines are written for search engines first and the reader second. This is the art and science of search engine optimization (SEO). As David Carr wrote in *The New York Times*:

> Headlines in newspapers and magazines were once written with readers in mind, to be clever or catchy or evocative. Now headlines are just there to get the search engines to notice. In that context, "Jon Stewart Slams Glenn Beck" is the beau ideal of great headline writing. And both Twitter and Facebook have become re-publishers, with readers on the hunt for links with nice, tidy headlines crammed full of hot names to share with their respective audiences.
>
> Keep in mind that all of the things that make headlines meaningful in print — photographs, placement and context — are nowhere in sight on the Web. Headlines have become, as Gabriel Snyder, executive editor of newsweek.com, called them, "naked little creatures that have to go out into the world to stand and fight on their own."

Jim Romenesko, former doyen of the poynter.org website, pointed out failure to use search engine-powered words in a headline will cause a website to lose traffic.

Romanesko's example was the crash of US Airways flight 1549 into the Hudson River on January 15, 2009. All the passengers were saved by the quick thinking and competence of Captain Chesley (Sully) Sullenberger.

The New York Times website broke the story, but lost the ratings race. The headline posted at 3:48 p.m.:

> "Updates from Jet Rescue in Hudson River."

Potential readers entered the term "plane crash," which was not in the title. The first instance of the word "crash" was in the eighth paragraph, some 559 words deep in the story.

How long should a headline be?

This question will guarantee disagreements among experts. "When writing headlines, stay under 15 words," counseled freelancer Harry B. Walsh:

> Before I got into mail order, my magazine ads were judged by the ratings they earned in Starch readership ad studies. At one point, Starch did a huge review of how the length of the headline affected the read-most rating. I was used to shooting for four- or five-word headlines, and was surprised to learn that headlines of up to 14 words were read equally as well as the short ones.

David Ogilvy on headline length

In headline tests conducted with cooperation from a big department store, it was found that headlines of 10 words or longer sold more goods than short headlines. In terms of recall, headlines between 8 and 10 words are most effective. In mail order advertising, headlines between 6-and-12 words get the most coupon returns. On the average, long headlines sell more merchandise than short ones — headlines like our "At 60 miles an hour, the loudest noise in this new Rolls-Royce comes from the electric clock."

Four additional rules of headlines

• **Put headlines below the illustration.** According to research conducted by Starch INRA Hooper, Inc., headlines in print ads should be placed below the illustration or photograph. This is because the eye naturally falls onto the illustrative area of an ad first. Should the headline be above the illustration, the eye must then fight gravity and go "uphill." By placing the headline below the illustration, the eye can fall effortlessly and begin reading. *—Drew Allen Miller*

• **"Don't use puns.** They rarely translate to the reader's context."*—George Duncan*

• **"Don't ask questions** in teasers and headlines that can be answered yes or no. That gives control of the communication to your reader." *—George Duncan*

• **"Avoid the 'hard-to-grasp' headline** — the headline that requires thought and is not clear at first glance." *—John Caples*

No headline? No title? No subject line?
David Ogilvy wrote, "The wickedest of all sins is to run an advertisement without a headline."

Check out this full-page ad from *Fortune* with no headline.

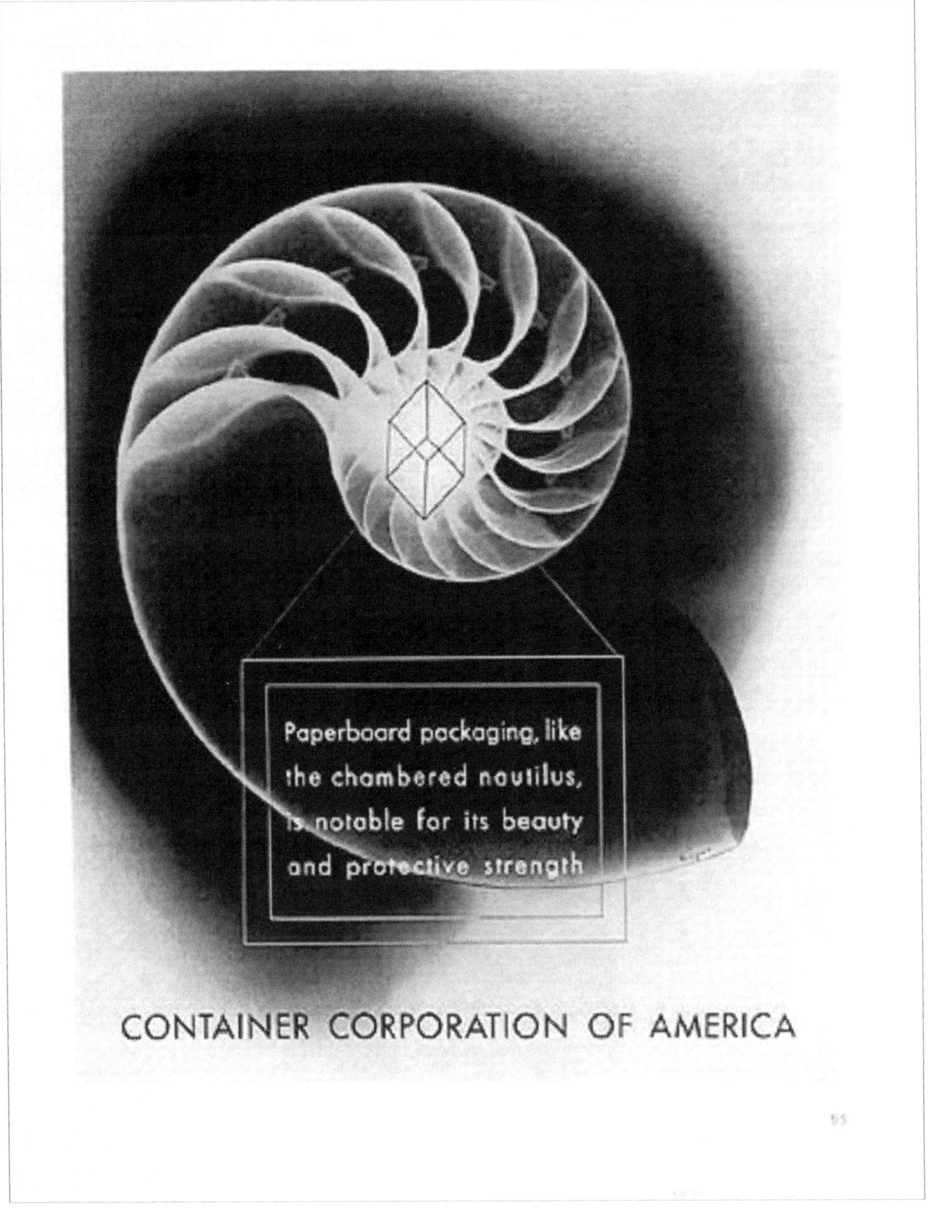

This headless Container Corporation ad is elegant, arresting and pleasing to the eye. But with no headline, it's not immediately obvious to whom this message is addressed or what is being advertised.

In this case, it is aimed at an extreme business niche: packagers who should consider using paperboard. With no headline, it is not immediately obvious to packagers and a waste of time for everyone else.

Creating an arresting, elegant advertisement with no headline is like peeing in blue serge: it makes you feel warm all over and nobody notices. Same thing with a memo, article, e-mail or special report.

Who designs your booth for a business conference?
The annual Direct Marketing Association Conference and Exhibition in San Francisco several years ago was all about size. In the vast exhibit hall you could fire a cannon in any direction and not hit anybody.

It was the polar opposite of Direct Marketing Days New York at the Hilton where the aisles were narrow and booths jammed cheek-by-jowl. It was intimate and fun. You were part of a giant human pinball machine helplessly bumping into old friends and making new ones.

Walk the interstate-sized aisles of any Direct Marketing Association exhibit hall, and the booths are as sterile as the atmosphere. Check out the signage as you wander.

The company name and logo are featured in massive type. What follows should be the unique selling proposition — a punchy burst or slogan telegraphing what the company does. What makes these folks different from all the others, and what is the reason for stopping by?

These slogans are the equivalent of the headline on the ad, the teaser on the envelope and the subject line of the e-mail. Alas, the headlines on the booth signage at the DMA exhibition all say the same things — nothing. I jotted some down:

- Media Solutions
- Web Applications
- Performance Driven Marketing
- Database Solutions
- More Relevance
- The Power of Partnership
- Full Service Solutions
- Recharge Your Marketing

These are neither unique nor selling nor propositions. It's the bland leading the bland.

Takeaways to Consider

- "What good is all the painstaking work on copy if the headline isn't right? If the headline doesn't stop people, the copy might as well be written in Greek." *—John Caples*

- Writing headlines is one of the greatest journalist arts. *—Claude Hopkins*

- I would urge all writers to be responsible for creating their own headlines and titles. If written by someone else, a headline could be so clever it misses the point and confuses the reader.

• "Headlines, subject lines, teasers and titles are the hot pants on the hooker." *—Bill Jayme*

• "The headline selects the reader." *—Axel Andersson*

• "It is the headline that gets people into the copy. The copy doesn't get them into the headline." *—Vic Schwab*

• "Your headline should telegraph what you want to say — in simple language. Readers do not stop to decipher the meanings of obscure headlines." *—David Ogilvy*

• "On the average, five times as many people read the headline as read the body copy. When you have written your headline, you have spent 80 cents out of your advertising dollar." *—David Ogilvy*

• "Now, I spend hours on headlines — days if necessary. And when I get a good headline, I know that my task is nearly finished. Writing the copy can usually be done in a short time if necessary." *—John Caples*

• One suggestion: Don't start with the headline. First off get familiar with the nuts-'n'-bolts. Understand the basics of what this thing you are working on are, whom you are talking to and what you want to tell these readers.

• Many headlines are written for search engines first and the reader second. This is the art and science of search engine optimization (SEO).

• Jim Romenesko, former doyen of the poynter.org website, pointed out failure to use search engine-powered words in a headline will cause a website to lose traffic.

• "Don't use puns. They rarely translate to the reader's context." *—George Duncan*

• "Don't ask questions in teasers and headlines that can be answered yes or no. That gives control of the communication to your reader." *—George Duncan*

• "Avoid the hard-to-grasp headline — the headline that requires thought and is not clear at first glance." *—John Caples*

• "The wickedest of all sins is to run an advertisement without a headline." *—David Ogilvy*

• Creating an arresting, elegant advertisement with no headline is like peeing in blue serge: It makes you feel warm all over and nobody notices.

CHAPTER 13

Your All-Important Lede and Your First 10 Words

"Your first 10 words are more important than the next 10,000." —Elmer "Sizzle" Wheeler

lede ***noun*** \ lēd \
Definition of LEDE
the introductory section of a news story that is intended to entice the reader to read the full story

Origin of LEDE
alteration of *²lead*
First Known Use: 1976
—*Merriam-Webster Dictionary*

....

I first became aware of the word "lede" fairly recently — three or four years ago. It's the journalist's spelling of "lead" and describes "the lead sentence or lead paragraph."

This odd spelling makes good sense. "Lead" (when pronounced "led") is also the heavy metal used to make plumbing pipes and fishing sinkers. A lead paragraph would indicate heavy going.

News people also refer to a paragraph as a "graf."

Early on I suggested all writers are in the business of selling. The reader must be sold on going on to the next sentence, the next paragraph and all the way to the end of whatever is being written.

This is true of every literary form — e-mail, letter, résumé, memo, white paper, business plan, article, advertisement, nonfiction book or novel.

The place to start selling is the lede
Many writers start off by clearing their throats, rolling up their sleeves and rubbing their hands together. By then the reader is on Page 2, with nothing to show for the time spent.

Create a lousy lede and chances are the reader will go no further into your copy.

In a *Capitol Weekly* column, titled, "Please just give us the news and spare us the anecdotal lead," Will Shuck wrote:

> I am sick to death of the anecdotal lead, that annoying habit of news writers to start a straightforward story by painting a quaint little picture of everyday life.
>
> If the story is about a bill requiring pet owners to spay or neuter their dogs (just to pick an imaginary example), the anecdotal lead first tells us how much

Janey Johnson loves Missy, her cocker spaniel.

No doubt Janey and Missy are a lovely pair, but a lot of us have jobs and kids and commutes and precious little time to muse about Missy's reproductive potential.

A sampling of dreadful ledes
Since 1982 the English Department at San Jose State University has sponsored the Bulwer-Lytton Fiction Contest. This whimsical literary competition challenges entrants to compose the opening sentence to the worst of all possible novels.

Named for a minor Victorian novelist, the contest memorializes — and expands upon — the iconic lede sentence made famous in the 20th century by Charles Shultz. Here is Snoopy starting his novel. The actual lede is one very long, 59-word sentence:

"It was a dark and stormy night; the rain fell in torrents - except at occasional intervals, when it was checked by a violent gust of wind which swept up the streets (for it is in London that our scene lies), rattling along the housetops, and fiercely agitating the scanty flame of the lamps that struggled against the darkness." *—Edward George Bulwer-Lytton, Paul Clifford (1830)*

Recent winners of the Bulwer-Lytton contest
Theirs was a New York love, a checkered taxi ride burning rubber, and like the city their passion was open 24/7, steam rising from their bodies like slick streets exhaling warm, moist, white breath through manhole covers stamped "Forged by DeLaney Bros., Piscataway, N.J." — *Garrison Spik, Washington, D.C. (2008)*

For the first month of Ricardo and Felicity's affair, they greeted one another at every stolen rendezvous with a kiss — a lengthy, ravenous kiss, Ricardo lapping and sucking at Felicity's mouth as if she were a giant cage-mounted water bottle and he were the world's thirstiest gerbil. *—Molly Ringle, Seattle, WA (2010)*

Cheryl's mind turned like the vanes of a wind-powered turbine, chopping her sparrow-like thoughts into bloody pieces that fell onto a growing pile of forgotten memories. *—Sue Fondrie, Oshkosh, WI (2011)*

As he told her that he loved her she gazed into his eyes, wondering, as she noted the infestation of eyelash mites, the tiny deodicids burrowing into his follicles to eat the greasy sebum therein, each female laying up to 25 eggs in a single follicle, causing inflammation, whether the eyes are truly the windows of the soul; and, if so, his soul needed regrouting. *—Cathy Bryant, from Manchester, England (2012)*

She strutted into my office wearing a dress that clung to her like Saran Wrap to a sloppily butchered pork knuckle, bone and sinew jutting and lurching asymmetrically beneath its folds, the tightness exaggerating the granularity of the suet and causing what little palatable meat there was to sweat, its transparency the thief of imagination. *—Chris Weiloch, Brookfield, WI (2013)*

The greatest copywriting team of the 20th century
In the late years of the 20th century when a fledgling young publisher wanted to launch a magazine, the first step was to send out a subscription mailing to see if anyone would sign up. This was called a dry test — the offer for a product not yet in existence.

For 25 years, the masters of this genre were copywriter Bill Jayme and his Finnish-born partner, designer Heikki Ratalahti. With their copy, design and offer of a free trial issue (no obligation to subscribe), they made the prospective magazine irresistible.

Bill Jayme and Heikki Ratalahti

Readers of their mailings signed up in droves. Venture capitalists were impressed with the results. Investment dollars flowed in to start the magazine.

Jayme-Ratalahti helped start a slew of magazines.

Five wonderful ledes by Bill Jayme

***Bon Appetit* (1975)**

First, fill a pitcher with ice.

Now pour in a bottle of ordinary red wine, a quarter cup of brandy and a small bottle of club soda.

Sweeten to taste with a quarter to a half-cup of sugar, garnish with slices of apple, lemon, orange.

... then move your chair to a warm sunny spot. You've just made yourself Sangria — one of the great glories of Spain, and the perfect thing to sit back with and sip while you consider this invitation.

***Worth* (1993)**

It was Scott Fitzgerald who observed, "The rich are different from us."

It was Ernest Hemingway who then shot back, "Yes, they have more money."

But money isn't all that the rich have more of. They also have more worries... so before you accept this invitation to move up higher financially, you may want to consider some of the pros and cons.

***Elle* (1987)**

You're waiting at the corner for the light to turn green.

On your right is a woman who'd love to look like you. To possess your vitality. To have you skin, your hair, your eyes.

On your left is a schoolgirl who yearns to own everything you have on. The gold. The cashmere. The leather. The fragrance...

...and looking at you from across the street is a really good-looking guy who'd give almost anything to * ... or something equally R-rated.

***Utne Reader* (1985)**

If you believe that exercise will help you live longer... that small companies are better to work for than big ones...and that you can't possibly make money while maintaining your principles...

... then there's something you should know. It won't. They aren't. You can. And if revelations like these contradict axioms you learned at your mother's knee, there are more surprises to come. Just open the Utne Reader to any page. Overturned truisms. Shattered shibboleths. Debunked bromides. Truth.

Andy Warhol's *Interview* (1983)
When you find yourself seated at dinner next to someone unusual like Bette Midler, you've got two choices.

You can ask what her brother Danny is up to, why she worships Bobby Darin, whether they really paid her in gold for her recent round-the-clock world tour, why she thinks that Paloma Picasso should design clothes, where her favorite hot dog stand is in L.A. and how she feels about Barbra Streisand.

Or... you can say, "Excuse me. Can you please pass the salt?"

....

With these ledes, Bill Jayme is selling two ways:

• Selling subscriptions to magazines.
• Selling the reader on going on to the next sentence, the next paragraph, the next page and all the way to the order form at the end.

My no-buy decision based on a Barbara Walters lede
A number of years ago I bought the first iteration of Amazon's Kindle e-reader and was (and am) hooked. Apart from being able to carry a library of many hundreds of books in my jacket pocket, I can change the size of the type. What's more, before spending a dime on a Kindle title, I can receive a free sample of the prose.

I always liked Barbara Walters. She knows everybody worth knowing in the world. Over the years she developed into a first-class interviewer. In 2008, Walters published *Audition: A Memoir* in hardcover and Kindle.

I immediately sent for a free sample, hoping for a delicious dishing of dirt about her world of celebrities — a cascade of grand, old-fashioned gossip. Here's what arrived:

Prologue

Sister.

I thought for a while that is what the title of this memoir should be because it was my older and only sister, Jacqueline, who was unwittingly the strongest influence in my life. Jackie was three years older than I, but all our lives she appeared younger. My sister was mentally retarded, as the condition was called then, though only mildly so. Just enough to prevent her from attending regular school, from having friends, from getting a job, from marrying. Just enough to stop her from having a real life.

I found this depressing as hell and took a pass on ponying up cash. Compare Walters's lede with Dan Brown's opening in his mega best seller:

PROLOGUE

LOUVRE MUSEUM, PARIS

10:46 P.M.

> Renowned curator Jacques Saunière staggered through the vaulted archway of the museum's Grand Gallery. He lunged for the nearest painting he could see, a Caravaggio. Grabbing the gilded frame, the seventy-six-year-old man heaved the masterpiece toward himself until it tore from the wall and Saunière collapsed backward in a heap beneath the canvas. *—Dan Brown, The Da Vinci Code*

I once sent the first couple of chapters of a novel to former colleague Bob Scott *(See Chapter 20)* with a check for a small sum of money and asked him for a critique. In the 1970s, we had been book club directors at Macmillan. For the start of this novel I thought I had created some very well written prose to set the scene. However, I had a lurking fear it might be boring. My fears were justified. Bob's suggestion:

> What you should do with your lede is upset a bucket of gore in the reader's lap and spend the rest of the time cleaning it up.

Dan Brown absolutely followed Bob Scott's dictum with his lede for *The Da Vinci Code.* David Ogilvy told of a Harvard history professor who walked into the first day of class and silenced the room with just 22 words:

> Cesare Borgia murdered his brother-in-law for the love of his sister, who was the mistress of their father — the Pope.

Two deal-killer ledes

The Barbara Walters lede above was a conscious decision on her part. She wanted to involve (presumably) women in the life drama of dealing with a mentally handicapped sister. I wanted gossip. Walters was not writing for me.

The Da Vinci Code was a hell of a book. But when I went to amazon.com to have a look at the promised preview of Dan Brown's new *Inferno*, I found a writer blathering to himself.

What first hit my screen were two pages of "Acknowledgments." Dan Brown's lede — the very first words I saw:

> My most humble and sincere thanks to:
>
> As always, first and foremost, my editor and close friend, Jason Kaufman, for his dedication and talent . . . but mainly for his endless good humor.
>
> My extraordinary wife, Blythe, for her love and patience with the writing process ... blah, blah, blah.

Hey, Dan, I don't give a damn about Jason Kaufman, wife Blythe or dozens and dozens of people who made your career possible. I wanted to find out if *Inferno* is worth investing $12.99 and seven hours of my time.

Acknowledgments belong at the end of the book — when the reader is dazzled and spent. At that point it's fascinating to know who helped make this work of genius possible.

When I got to the Prologue, here's what I found:

> *I am the Shade.*
>
> *Through the dolent city, I flee.*
>
> *Through the eternal woe, I take flight.*
>
> Along the banks of the river Arno, I scramble breathless . . . turning left on to Via dei Castellani, making my way northward, huddling in the shadows of the Uffizi.
>
> And still they pursue me.
>
> Their footsteps grow louder now as they hunt with relentless determination.
>
> For years they have pursued me. Their persistence has kept me underground . . . forced me to live in purgatory . . . laboring between the earth like a chthonic monster.
>
> *I am the Shade.*

Huh?

I have never used — or even seen — the word "dolent." I am not alone. When I went to look it up, Merriam-Webster added this footnote:

> [Dolent] doesn't usually appear in our free dictionary, but the definition from our premium Unabridged Dictionary is offered here on a limited basis. Note that some information is displayed differently in the Unabridged.

What is a "chthonic monster"?

What does *"I am the Shade"* mean?

Here were three interruptions of the thread in the first 100 words.

Clearly Dan Brown isn't writing for me. This thing was above my pay grade.

With one click Dan Brown was oblivion.

"Get to the point," said copywriter Richard Jordan:

It may once have been that you had plenty of time to develop a creative story line in a direct mail piece; not so today. You have to get to the point and let readers know where you're taking them — and you have to do it quickly.

Most readers — with the possible exception of devotees of "thought magazines" — simply won't stay with you through a leisurely development of a creative idea. They're the Type A people behind your car at the stoplight; they beep their horns the minute the light turns from red to green.

A Gallery of Great Advertising Copywriters

Claude Hopkins

John Caples

Rosser Reeves

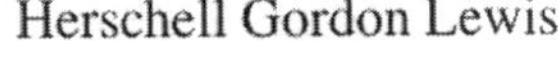

Herschell Gordon Lewis

Drayton Bird

Elmer "Sizzle" Wheeler

Frank Johnson

Maxwell Sackheim

Mel Martin

Pat Friesen

Ted Nicholas

Elmer "Sizzle" Wheeler

In 1960 I went to work for Prentice Hall book publishers as apprentice flack. One of the leading authors was Elmer "Sizzle" Wheeler, who had created a mystique by billing himself as "America's Number One Salesman."

Wheeler's most famous book, *The Fat Boy's Book: How Elmer Lost 40 Pounds in 80 Days*, was published in 1950. We used to joke about Wheeler, but had to take him seriously. He sold many thousands of books on salesmanship — and the language of selling — to a regular following who bought every title of his published by Prentice Hall.

Since all writers are in the business of selling ourselves in print, Wheeler's words are worth noting:

> **Four Wheelerpoints**
>
> **1. Don't Sell the Steak — Sell the Sizzle!** What we mean by the "sizzle" is the BIGGEST selling point in your proposition — the MAIN reasons why your prospects will want to buy. The sizzling of the steak starts the sale more than the cow ever did, though the cow is, of course, very necessary. [This paragraph resulted in Elmer Wheeler's adopted middle name, "Sizzle."]
>
> **2. "Don't Write — Telegraph."** "DON'T WRITE — TELEGRAPH" means: get the prospect's IMMEDIATE and FAVORABLE attention in the fewest possible words. If you don't make your first message "click," the prospect will leave you mentally, if not physically.
>
> **3. Your first 10 words are more important than the next 10,000**. You have only ten short seconds to capture the fleeting attention of the other person, and if in those ten short seconds you don't say something mighty important, he will leave you — either physically or mentally!
>
> **4. Don't Ask If — Ask Which!** By "DON'T ASK IF — ASK WHICH" I mean you should always frame your words (especially at the close) so that you give the prospect a choice between something and something, never between SOMETHING and NOTHING.
>
> We were given this assignment by the Schulte-United stores for their restaurants. There were 36 possible methods of asking a customer if he would care for some ice cream on his pie.
>
> Finally, we reverted to the old principle and had the waitresses ask, "Would you care for an order of vanilla or chocolate ice cream on your pie?"
>
> The mind of the customer would fluctuate between vanilla and chocolate, not between ice cream and no ice cream. Whichever he decided upon meant a happier customer — and a richer restaurant proprietor.
>
> "Which" is a stronger word than "if." It is better to use a question mark to "hook" your proposition securely on to a prospect than an exclamation mark to "club" him into responding.
>
> The hook is more potent than the crow bar!

Takeaways to Consider

• Do not repeat your headline in your lede. A powerful headline captures the reader's attention. If the lede is the same as the headline, the reader will say, "I've seen this before," and go elsewhere. Instead, a riveting headline plus a potent lede are a lethal combination.

• "Your first ten words are more important than the next ten thousand." *—Elmer "Sizzle" Wheeler*

• "I am sick to death of the anecdotal lead, that annoying habit of news writers to start a straightforward story by painting a quaint little picture of everyday life." —*Will Shuck, Capitol Weekly*

• "What you should do with your lede is upset a bucket of gore in the reader's lap and then spend the rest of the time cleaning it up." *—Bob Scott*

• "Your best lede is usually to be found somewhere on the second page of your first draft." *—Pat Friesen*

• "Most readers — with the possible exception of devotees of 'thought magazines' — simply won't stay with you through a leisurely development of a creative idea. They're the Type A people behind your car at the stoplight; they beep their horns the minute the light turns from red to green." *—Richard Jordan*

• "'DON'T WRITE — TELEGRAPH' means: get the prospects IMMEDIATE and FAVORABLE attention in the fewest possible words. If you don't make your first message 'click,' the prospect will leave you mentally, if not physically." *—Elmer "Sizzle" Wheeler*

CHAPTER 14

How to Keep Your Reader's Eyes Moving: Part 1

Bad design can hurt good copy
What separates the great advertising copywriter from ordinary authors is a laser-like focus on grabbing attention and keeping the eye moving all the way to the end.

If enough readers of an ad, a direct mail piece or an online sales pitch lose interest and never reach the order coupon, the advertiser loses money. What's more the copywriter won't get any more work.

Success and failure in direct marketing copy and design are precisely measured in dollars and cents — right down to a gnat's eyebrow.

"You cannot bore people into buying your product," David Ogilvy wrote. "You can only interest them in buying it."

Same thing with a letter, e-mail, memo, news story or article. If the reader gets bored in the middle and never reaches the end — the punch line or coda — the writer has failed.

However, even the very best copywriters and authors don't always create prose so powerful and involving as to make readers hang on every word. Help is needed, so if a bland, boring patch turns up, something is needed to catch the reader's eye and get it back on track.

With the exception of a novel or a nonfiction book, the worst thing for a reader is to be hit in the face with piles of solid text.

For example, imagine settling into your chaise longue in the garden on a summer morning with your Sunday *New York Times* and a second cup of coffee.

You come across this page in Times' magazine, complete with a depressing funereal black border top and bottom. It violates one of David Ogilvy's basic rules of design:

> "Avoid gray walls of type."

fter more than 4,000 years — almost since the dawn of recorded time, when Utnapishtim told Gilgamesh that the secret to immortality lay in a coral found on the ocean floor — man finally discovered eternal life in 1988. He found it, in fact, on the ocean floor. The discovery was made unwittingly by Christian Sommer, a German marine-biology student in his early 20s. He was spending the summer in Rapallo, a small city on the Italian Riviera, where exactly one century earlier Friedrich Nietzsche conceived "Thus Spoke Zarathustra": "Everything goes, everything comes back; eternally rolls the wheel of being. Everything dies, everything blossoms again. ..."

Sommer was conducting research on hydrozoans, small invertebrates that, depending on their stage in the life cycle, resemble either a jellyfish or a soft coral. Every morning, Sommer went snorkeling in the turquoise water off the cliffs of Portofino. He scanned the ocean floor for hydrozoans, gathering them with plankton nets. Among the hundreds of organisms he collected was a tiny, relatively obscure species known to biologists as Turritopsis dohrnii. Today it is more commonly known as the immortal jellyfish.

Sommer kept his hydrozoans in petri dishes and observed their reproduction habits. After several days he noticed that his Turritopsis dohrnii was behaving in a very peculiar manner, for which he could hypothesize no earthly explanation. Plainly speaking, it refused to die. It appeared to age in reverse, growing younger and younger until it reached its earliest stage of development, at which point it began its life cycle anew.

Sommer was baffled by this development but didn't immediately grasp its significance. (It was nearly a decade before the word "immortal" was first used to describe the species.) But several biologists in Genoa, fascinated by Sommer's finding, continued to study the species, and in 1996 they published a paper called "Reversing the Life Cycle." The scientists described how the species — at any stage of its development — could transform itself back to a polyp, the organism's earliest stage of life, "thus escaping death and achieving potential immortality." This finding appeared to debunk the most fundamental law of the natural world — you are born, and then you die.

One of the paper's authors, Ferdinando Boero, likened the Turritopsis to a butterfly that, instead of dying, turns back into a caterpillar. Another metaphor is a chicken that transforms into an egg, which gives birth to another chicken. The anthropomorphic analogy is that of an old man who grows younger and younger until he is again a fetus. For this reason Turritopsis dohrnii is often referred to as the Benjamin Button jellyfish.

Yet the publication of "Reversing the Life Cycle" barely registered outside the academic world. You might expect that, having learned of the existence of immortal life, man would dedicate colossal resources to learning how the immortal jellyfish performs its trick. You might expect that biotech multinationals would vie to copyright its genome; that a vast coalition of research scientists would seek to determine the mechanisms by which its cells aged in reverse; that pharmaceutical firms would try to appropriate its lessons for the purposes of human medicine; that governments would broker international accords to govern the future use of rejuvenating technology. But none of this happened.

Some progress has been made, however, in the quarter-century since Christian Sommer's discovery. We now know, for instance, that the rejuvenation of Turritopsis dohrnii and some other members of the genus is caused by environmental stress or physical assault. We know that, during rejuvenation, it undergoes cellular transdifferentiation, an unusual process by which one type of cell is converted into another — a skin cell into a nerve cell, for instance. (The same process occurs in human stem cells.) We also know that, in recent decades, the immortal jellyfish has rapidly spread throughout the world's oceans in what Maria Pia Miglietta, a biology professor at Notre Dame, calls "a silent invasion." The jellyfish has been "hitchhiking" on cargo ships that use seawater for ballast. Turritopsis has now been observed not only in the Mediterranean but also off the coasts of Panama, Spain, Florida and Japan. The jellyfish seems able to survive, and proliferate, in every ocean in the world. It is possible to imagine a distant future in which most other species of life are extinct but the ocean will consist overwhelmingly of immortal jellyfish, a great gelatin consciousness everlasting.

But we still don't understand how it ages in reverse. There are several reasons for our ignorance, all of them maddeningly unsatisfying. There are, to begin with, very few specialists in the world committed to conducting the necessary experiments. "Finding really good hydroid experts is very difficult," says James Carlton, a professor of marine sciences at Williams College and the director of the Williams-Mystic Maritime Studies Program. "You're lucky to have one or two people in a country." He cited this as an example of a phenomenon he calls the Small's Rule: small-bodied organisms are poorly studied relative to larger-bodied organisms. There are significantly more crab experts, for instance, than hydroid experts.

But the most frustrating explanation for our dearth of knowledge about the immortal jellyfish is of a more technical nature. The genus, it turns out, is extraordinarily difficult to culture in a laboratory. It requires close attention and an enormous amount of repetitive, tedious labor; even then, it is under only certain favorable conditions, most of which are still unknown to biologists, that a Turritopsis will produce offspring.

In fact there is just one scientist who has been culturing Turritopsis polyps in his lab consistently. He works alone, without major financing or a staff, in a cramped office in Shirahama, a sleepy beach town in Wakayama Prefecture, Japan, four hours south of Kyoto. The scientist's name is Shin Kubota, and he is, for the time being, our best chance for understanding this unique strand of biological immortality.

Many marine biologists are reluctant to make such grand claims about Turritopsis' promise for human medicine. "That's a question for journalists," Boero said (to a journalist) in 2009. "I prefer to focus on a slightly more rational form of science."

Kubota, however, has no such compunction. "Turritopsis application for human beings is the most wonderful dream of mankind," he told me the first time I called him. "Once we determine how the jellyfish rejuvenates itself, we should achieve very great things. My opinion is that we will evolve and become immortal ourselves."

I decided I better book a ticket to Japan.

One of Shirahama's main attractions is its crescent-shaped white-sand beach; "Shirahama" means "white beach." But in recent decades, the beach has been disappearing. In the 1960s, when Shirahama was connected by rail to Osaka, the city became a popular tourist destination, and blocky white hotel towers were erected along the coastal road. The increased development accelerated erosion, and the famous sand began to wash into the sea. Worried that the town of White Beach would lose its white beach, according to a city official, Wakayama Prefecture began in 1989 to import sand from Perth, Australia, 4,700 miles away. Over 15 years, Shirahama dumped 745,000 cubic meters of Aussie sand on its beach, preserving its eternal whiteness — at least for now.

Shirahama is full of timeless natural wonders that are failing the test of time. Visible just off the coast is Engetsu island, a sublime arched sandstone formation that looks like a doughnut dunked halfway into a glass of milk. At dusk, tourists gather at a point on the coastal road where, on certain days, the arch perfectly frames the setting sun. Arches are temporary geological phenomena; they are created by erosion, and erosion ultimately causes them to collapse. Fearing the loss of Engetsu, the local government is trying to restrain it from deteriorating any further by reinforcing the arch with a harness of mortar and grout. A large scaffold now extends beneath the arch and, from the shore, construction workers can be seen, tiny flyspecks against the sparkling sea, paving the rock.

This *New York Times Magazine* page is neat and orderly. And boring as dirt.

To keep the reader's eye moving, the prose had better be riveting. It ain't. Here's the lede paragraph:

> After more than 4,000 years — almost since the dawn of recorded time, when Utnapishtim told Gilgamesh that the secret of immortality lay in a coral found on the ocean floor — man finally discovered eternal life in 1988. The discovery was made unwittingly by Christian Sommer, a German marine-biology student in his early 20s. He was spending the summer in Rapallo, a small city on the Italian Riviera, where exactly one century earlier Friedrich Nietzsche conceived "Thus Spoke Zarathustra": "Everything goes, everything comes back; eternally rolls the wheel of being. Everything dies, everything blossoms again...."

Let's say in the course of reading this dense prose the phone rings or your tummy rumbles. You lay things aside to take care of immediate business. When you return to this page, where do you restart? You are forced to stumble around until you find the right place. Your time has been wasted.

What are needed: visual touch-points

My second job after I got out of the U.S. Army in 1960 was with Grolier Enterprises, marketers of the Dr. Seuss books by mail. My new boss and mentor Lew Smith sat me down for a one-hour lecture — Direct Marketing Copy and Design 101. Lew's first maxim is etched in memory:

> "Neatness rejects involvement."

If an advertisement, a letter, a special report, a memo or an article is too neat, Lew explained, it is not visually involving. It's up to the author (and designer) to break the visual monotony.

"Ugly works," said Seattle direct marketing wizard Bob Hacker. It is the explanation why direct mail is generally ugly and why it works. If the reader's mind drifts off message, there's always something up ahead — or to one side — to catch the eye and refocus attention.

Here is a classically ugly ad by Fred Breismeister of Greystone Press for a set of books, *The Made Simple Self-Teaching Library.* Note the hand holding the bottom of the book, the arrow screaming "FREE" and the burst, "Yes ... Take it FREE!" This is ugly stuff. But all these devices and interruptions move the eye around.

David Ogilvy on moving the eye

The following concepts apply to virtually any printed communication, with the exception of a short story or novel.

1. A display subhead of two or three lines between your headline and your body copy will heighten the reader's appetite for the feast to come.

2. If you start your body copy with a large initial letter, you will increase readership by an average of 13 percent.

3. After two or three inches of copy, insert your first crosshead, and thereafter pepper crossheads throughout. They keep the reader marching forward. Make some of them interrogative, to excite curiosity in the next run of copy.

4. An ingenious sequence of boldly displayed crossheads can deliver the substance of your entire pitch to glancers who are too lazy to wade through the text. —*Confessions of an Advertising Man*

In *Ogilvy on Advertising* is this full-page broadsheet newspaper advertisement. Created in the 1950s for Merrill Lynch by the late Louis Engel, former managing editor of *Business Week*, it is a textbook example of Ogilvy's philosophy.

Note the design and layout — upper deck, headline, lower deck and subhead in the box — all designed to telegraph the importance of the message and preview what is coming.

What everybody ought to know . . .

About This Stock And Bond Business

Some plain talk about a simple business that often sounds complicated.

WHY WE ARE PUBLISHING THIS INFORMATION

How to Buy and Sell Securities

"WHAT'S THIS? . . . WHAT'S THAT?"

Copies of this advertisement in pamphlet form are available on request. No charge, no obligation. Just write or phone . . .

MERRILL LYNCH, PIERCE, FENNER & BEANE

10 Post Office Square
BOSTON 9

Ogilvy's text-heavy full-page newspaper advertisement

Forcing the reader's eye to keep moving

In addition, Louis Engel strategically inserted three subheads, a call-out and no less than 18 crossheads to introduce individual paragraphs and sections. If interest flags for a moment anywhere in the piece, the reader's eyes will flick to a crosshead nearby and interest is recaptured.

Further, if the reader is interrupted by a phone call or doorbell, touch-points throughout make it easy to see where to resume reading.

Running 6,450 words, this copy-heavy ad was a single insertion in *The New York Times*. It pulled 10,000 responses, and — as David Ogilvy pointed out — it didn't even have a coupon.

In my opinion, all writers should consider using the visual techniques of copywriting professionals such as this ad by Louis Engel to make their prose more inviting and readable. And I'm talking all writers:

- Presidential press secretaries, academics, lawyers and judges.
- Businesspeople creating memos, reports, letters and whitepapers.
- Journalists, writers of articles, nonfiction and maybe even fiction.
- Out-of-work professionals polishing their résumés.

Ed Elliott on readability and design

These 16 devices can turn a skimmer into an interested reader

- Table of contents.
- Headlines and subheads.
- Photography, especially of people and action.
- Tables, charts, graphs.
- trations clarifying or reinforcing the text.
- Captions under every visual. People read captions as they skim.
- A word or subhead which is bigger, bolder, blacker or has a different color than other elements on the page.
- Enlarged numbers, possibly followed by an enlarged or bold lede.
- A word or line set off at an angle or in a box or a burst.
- Text inside an arrow or a ruled box.
- Anything that interrupts a page-by-page pattern of columns.
- Text with a light screen behind it.
- Pull quotes.
- A paragraph set off in bold or with a double indent.
- Handwritten indications.
- Bulleted text, especially with bullets that are larger or different from other bulleted text.

3 ways to get maximum readership

- **Text Size:** 10- or 11-points is optimum for readability; maybe one point larger for older readers.

- **Column Width:** 35 to 55 characters is a good target range. 10- or 11-point is generally most readable on a column width of about a third of a page. Larger than eleven point should probably be about a half page wide. Columns wider than a half page are not quickly read.

- **Alignment:** Rag right is often better than justified. It creates a text shape that allows an area for the eye to rest. It can also appear more inviting, less imposing, more personal.

6 design techniques to AVOID

• AVOID: text without sufficient contrast to its background. Examples:
  —A background screen that is too dark.
  —Paper color that is too dark.
  —Text that is too light, printed in a color other than black.

• AVOID: text printed over — or reversed out of — a busy or distracting background.

• AVOID: text reversed out of a dark color.

• AVOID: flush right or centered paragraphs.

• AVOID: text that is too condensed.

• AVOID: character spacing that is too tight.

Takeaways to Consider

• What separates the great advertising copywriter from other writers is a laser-like focus on achieving two aims — grabbing attention and keeping the eye moving all the way to the end.

• "You cannot bore people into buying your product. You can only interest them in buying it." *—David Ogilvy*

• "People will not be bored in print. They may listen politely at a dinner table to boasts and personalities, life history, etc. But in print they choose their own companions, their own subjects. They want to be amused or benefited. They want economy, beauty, labor savings, good things to eat and wear." *—Claude Hopkins*

• Same thing with a letter, e-mail, memo or article. If the reader gets bored in the middle and never reaches the punch line or coda, the writer has failed.

• "It takes hard writing to make easy reading." *—Robert Louis Stevenson*

• "Neatness rejects involvement." *—Lew Smith*

• "Ugly works." *—Bob Hacker*

• "Avoid gray walls of type." *—David Ogilvy*

• Major newspapers are mired in the 19th century design model. Gray walls of type are everywhere. Every page is daunting — a bore to look at. With poor attention spans, readers prefer the lively news and information of TV and the Internet.

• The coin of the realm in communications today is the 140-character tweet. Everybody from the literati to the kid with attention deficit disorder can read a tweet.

• All of us read tweets. We like tweets. Good tweets are tightly written and packed with information. As of November 2013, Twitter had 813 million accounts — two-and-a-half times the population of the United States.

• The message to print media designers is loud and clear. Break up the gray walls of type into manageable bites of text. Jar the reader. Move the eyes.

• "After two or three inches of copy, insert your first crosshead, and thereafter pepper crossheads throughout. They keep the reader marching forward. Make some of them interrogative, to excite curiosity in the next run of copy." *—David Ogilvy*

• "An ingenious sequence of boldly displayed crossheads can deliver the substance of your entire pitch to glancers who are too lazy to wade through the text." *—David Ogilvy*

• By failing to heed Ogilvy's advice, traditional print media — cumbersome and filled with gray walls of type — are dead meat.

• The exception: jazzy tabloids, which are a series of interruptions, loaded with illustrations and a lot of fun.

CHAPTER 15

How to Keep Your Reader's Eyes Moving: Part 2

Words, sentences and paragraphs
As a copywriter, I have always been acutely aware of the need to keep the reader's eye moving. Not only can eyes be manipulated by commonsense design, but also with type.

What follows is rather technical. Skip it if you get bored.

The en dash vs. the em dash
An *en dash* is a word connector. It is a short dash akin to the hyphen. It is called an en dash because it has the same width as the letter n.

The en dash is also the equivalent of the word "to," as in Dwight D. Eisenhower (1890 – 1969).

An *em dash* — a long dash with the width of the letter m — is used in sentences to separate thoughts. Herschell Gordon Lewis uses the example:

> The writer's talent — or lack of talent — combines elements of brightness and thoughtfulness

You can achieve the same meaning with parenthesis:

> The writer's talent (or lack of talent) combines elements of brightness and thoughtfulness

Where the parenthesis stops the eye for an instant, the em dash allows the eye to flick across it and keep moving. It's entirely your call — whatever you are comfortable with. I would urge, however, not using more than two em dashes per sentence and not in contiguous sentences.

> **Know the difference between hard and soft transitions**
> A dash (—) provides a hard transition.
>
> An ellipsis (...) provides a soft transition. Example:
>
> "The writer's talent — or lack of talent — combines elements of brightness and thoughtfulness ... joy and sadness ... leading the reader by an emotional leash." *—Herschell Gordon Lewis*

Lew Smith's leaping ellipsis
On my very first day of employment at Grolier Enterprises, Lew Smith — in his tutorial — talked about moving the reader's eye along. He used the example of the ellipsis as Herschell does above:

> brightness and thoughtfulness ... joy and sadness

Herschell's ellipsis has three dots — or periods — midway between two words with a space on either side of them.

Lew Smith said to move the reader's eye, the ellipsis should look like this:

> brightness and thoughtfulness ... joy and sadness

Lew's contention was no space before the ellipsis — coupled with a space following the ellipsis — forces the eye to leap ahead to the next word.

Admittedly, these are minor points of word placement and punctuation.

But let's say five or 25 of these bits of grammatical minutiae moved one more reader along to the order form — or the coupon at the end of the ad. If the result was one more order, it's worth the effort. Especially since no additional cost is involved.

Herschell Gordon Lewis' parentheses rules
Parentheses increase distance. Use parentheses when you want to downplay.

Don't use parentheses when you want immediate involvement. Example: Compare the dynamics of these two build-up questions:

> What are the eight signs you should start looking for another job? (See page 120.)
>
> What are the eight signs you should start looking for another job? See page 120.

Use parentheses to imply exclusivity
Original issue price for our preferred members just $99.50

— instead use —

Original issue price (for our preferred members) just $99.50

[Using brackets]
Let's say you are writing about writers' peculiarities and you want use this quote from Paul Reid and William Manchester's book on Winston Churchill:

> His valet warmed his brandy snifter over a neatly trimmed candle; his typists and secretaries kept more candles at the ready in order to light his cigars (Cuban Romeo y Julieta were his favorites). He had never ridden a bus.

It's okay to change the quote for clarity using brackets:

> [Winston Churchill's] valet warmed his brandy snifter over a neatly trimmed ...

In the off chance you are creating a parenthetical phrase within a parenthetical line, use [square] brackets within (round) brackets. Example: (Marx [1867] 1967, p. 90)

David Ogilvy on text for space ads (Consider these techniques for everything you write.)

1. Keep your opening paragraph down to a maximum of 11 words. A long first paragraph frightens readers away. All your paragraphs should be as short as possible; long paragraphs are fatiguing.

2. Type smaller than 9-point is difficult for most people to read.

3. "Widows" increase readership, except at the bottom of a column, where they make it too easy for the reader to quit. [A widow occurs when a line of copy is too long by a single word, with the result that the word shows up in the next line — and is the only word in that line.]

4. Break up the monotony of long copy by setting key paragraphs in boldface or italic.

5. Insert trations from time to time.

6. Help the reader into your paragraphs with arrowheads, bullets, asterisks and marginal marks.

7. If you have a lot of unrelated facts to recite, don't try to relate them with cumbersome connectives; simply number them, as I am doing here.

8. Never set your copy in reverse (white type on a black background) and never set it over a gray or colored tint. The old school of art directors believed that these devices forced people to read the copy; we now know that they make reading physically impossible.

9. If you use leading between paragraphs, you increase readership by an average of 12 percent.

Number of words in a sentence

I dug through my correspondence and found the following e-mail from Scott Huch in response to a column of mine on how to write:

> As an aspiring, young direct mail copywriter in the early 1990s, I clipped an item from my local newspaper. It has been taped to my desk — right next to my computer — ever since. It is now tattered and yellow. But I keep it there as a reminder anytime I'm writing. It says:

Tests have shown that a sentence of eight words is very easy to read; of 11 words, easy; of 14 words, fairly easy; of 17 words, standard; of 21 words, fairly difficult; of 25 words, difficult; of 29 or more words, very difficult; so this sentence with 54 words, counting numbers, is ranked impossible.

Tests have shown that a sentence of eight words is very easy to read; of 11 words, easy; of 14 words, fairly easy; of 17 words, standard; of 21 words, fairly difficult; of 25 words, difficult; of 29 or more words, very difficult; so this sentence with 54 words, counting numbers, is ranked impossible.

A mind-numbing 96-word single sentence from Paul Kennedy's *Engineers of Victory*
Once the immediate German invasion threat diminished, the various British countermoves — such as the maritime relief of Gibraltar, Malta, and Cairo, the preservation of the cape routes to the East, the military buildups (including dominion and empire forces) in Egypt, Iraq, and India, and the development of the early strategic bombing offensive against the Third Reich — were, while critically important, impossible to sustain unless a constant flow of foodstuffs, fuel, and munitions reached the home islands from across the seas and new British divisions and weaponry were carried from the home islands to Africa and India.

My W.G. Sebald problem
I spent a weekend at a friend's house in the country. On a side table was a paperback book I really wanted to read, On the Natural History of Destruction by W.G. Sebald. I am a student of World War II, and this was all about the philosophy and execution of strategic bombing by the Nazis, British and Americans. Below is the second sentence of the text:

> It is true that the strategic bombing surveys published by the Allies, together with the records of the Federal German Statistics Office and other official sources, show that the Royal Air Force alone dropped a million tons of bombs on enemy territory; it is true that of the 131 towns and cities attacked, some only once and some repeatedly, many were almost entirely flattened, that about 600,000 German civilians fell victim to air raids, and that three and a half million homes were destroyed, while at the end of the war seven and a half million people were left homeless, and there were 31.1 cubic meters of rubble for every person in Cologne and 42.8 cubic meters for every inhabitant of Dresden — but we do not grasp what it all actually meant.[1]

This 132-word sentence — followed by an interruptive [1] at the end — was a message to the reader:

> *"Fight your way through my turgid prose, chum, and then stop reading, so you can go hunting for the endnote to explain what I'm really trying to say."*

I figured Sebald was writing for a claque of loyal readers. Two hundred pages of this stuff were beyond the mental acrobatics I was prepared to do, and I turned to a Will Shortz Monday crossword book.

A member of Sebald's claque — my hostess
My friend's wife noticed the Sebald book on the table beside me. "You're going to love it!" she said.

"I gave up on it," I said. "I can't deal with long sentences and footnotes."

"Oh, but Sebald is a wonderful writer. He's just difficult."

"That is an oxymoron," I said.

Ignore all of the above ... if you can come up with a riveting 65-word lede sentence like this:

> Barbara Piasecka Johnson, whose rags-to-riches tale — an immigrant maid marries a multimillionaire and inherits all of his money, fending off the furious claims of his children — was at the center of what one writer called "the largest, costliest, ugliest, most spectacular and most conspicuous" probate battle in American history, died on Monday near Wroclaw, Poland, where she spent much of her childhood. She was 76. *—Bruce Weber, The New York Times*

Ideal width of a line on paper

> "Anything from 45 to 75 characters is widely-regarded as a satisfactory length of line for a single-column page set in a serifed text face in a text size. The 66-character line (counting both letters and spaces) is widely regarded as ideal." *—Robert Bringhurst, Elements of Typographic Style*

"To determine line length for optimum readability, a good guideline is between nine and 12 words for unjustified text. Fewer words may cause the sentence structure to break up, and may also result in too many hyphenations. Both of these reduce readability. Conversely, a line with more than 12 words can become tedious to read. Additionally, a reader can easily get lost when going from the end of one long line to the beginning of the next, and may inadvertently reread the same line, or miss a line or two." *—Ilene Strizver, founder, The Type Studio*

Takeaways to Consider

- You can keep the reader's eye moving with visual devices in the text.

- If you create sentences longer than 29 words, split 'em up.

- I have been through this text numerous times. I think (hope) no sentence of mine is longer than 29 words.

- If you find a sentence longer than 29 words, let me know and I'll do my best to change it for the second edition (if there is one).

- The 66-character line (counting both letters and spaces) is widely regarded as ideal.

- To determine line length for optimum readability, a good guideline is between 9 and 12 words for unjustified text.

- A wonderful writer who is difficult to read is an oxymoron.

CHAPTER 16

Why Johnny Can't Read: The Evils of Sans Serif Type in Print

This landmark article from *National Review* by Vrest Orton argues that sans serif type makes text unreadable.

DH NOTE: I clipped this article on Sept. 2, 1977, and carried it around with me for years. Written by a catalog industry pioneer, it is reprinted with permission from Vrest Orton's family. It appeared long before computers were widely used and is relevant to print media. *(For digital media, see Sara Quinn's discussion in Chapter 17.)*

MANY LEARNED books and papers have been written these last several years on the appalling inability of our public-education system to teach our children to read their own language. It seems that the more we spend building bigger and more luxurious schools and paying higher and higher salaries to teachers and administrators, the less Johnny can read.

Parents are disgusted with this puzzle and are voting down, all over the nation, requests for more money for schools. Yet they are seldom aware of a major reason why youngsters can pass through the primary system, and even graduate from high school, without the ability to read.

This reason has to do with printing. In the last ten years, American book and magazine publishers, ignorant of tradition and the true purpose of printing, have introduced into the printed page the most impossible type ever invented since movable type was first used over 525 years ago.

I refer to a bold, blunt, hard, stark, rigid style of type called sans serif. The best definition is given by the Oxford English Dictionary, which succinctly declares that sans serif is "a form of type without serifs, also called grotesque." Grotesque it certainly is.

> This paragraph is set in a sans serif typeface. A paragraph later in this article is set in Caslon type so that the reader may instantly get the point. And what is the point? It's simple. Type is a medium; it is not an end in itself. The purpose of printing, whether a book, magazine, or newspaper, is to make the text easy, pleasant and inviting to read. Years ago I was associated with one of America's most distinguished printers, Daniel Berkeley Updike, who wrote the modern history of printing in America. Mr. Updike expressed most concisely the aim of arranging type on a page by saying: "Typography should be invisible." If you pick up a book or a magazine and exclaim, "Oh, isn't this beautiful type!" the designer has failed. Any type that gets between the reader and the author is not doing its job.

Any type that makes the message difficult to read, that makes the printed page strident, brazen, and uncomfortable to the eye, is wrong, except for one purpose for which sans serif was designed by the Germans: advertising. For generations, sans serif was kept where it belonged: in display advertisements whose function was to shout at the reader.

The man who first sold the printers this type for use in anything but advertising should be accorded his proper place in history, which is a place of infamy. Thanks to him, many textbooks and a number of magazines are now printed in this style of type, which not only repels and insults the eye, but actually makes printed matter almost impossible to read. And I can think of only one reason why magazine designers would use sans serif. They don't want Johnny to read the text, they want him to read the advertisements. So by using a Look-Ma-no-hands type for both text and advertising, they have achieved the advertising man's fondest dream: you can't tell what is text and what is advertising.

> So, by contrast, why are types such as Caslon (the type you are now reading) the best and most legible? William Caslon first came out with a complete specimen sheet of his magnificent English type in 1734. At the same time, other similar typefaces were being designed: Baskerville, Bell, Janson and Garamond, to mention a few. All these performed the two proper functions of a typeface: 1) to make the printed page easy, agreeable and pleasant to read; 2) to create, by the harmonious relationship of type, a comfortable, inviting page of printing-all without the reader's knowing why! These classic types achieve that purpose because of their perfect proportions between thin and heavy tines, thin and heavy curves and the height and width of each letter. The letters fit together in such a way that the reader is never conscious of each letter, but only of word and sentence.

Sans serif type does just the opposite. Each letter stands alone and yells for attention. Each letter is the same width in all its parts; there are no contrasts. A page of sans serif type is like a landscape with two hundred hills in the distance, all exactly the same shape, size and height. The words for both are monotonous and unnatural.

Caslon and other historic types exude character and charm-while remaining always unobtrusive. And they have survived the test of time. The eye, for two centuries, has found these types agreeable, just as the eye of knowledgeable and educated people finds the aesthetic character of Georgian architecture comfortable and agreeable. In contrast, modern architects (who derive their inspiration from German masters) build cold, stark, impressive skyscrapers and cold, sterile, modern furniture, chromed and slick. We look at these and exclaim in awe at their boldness. But no one ever fell in love with them. They shout and startle, but they do not welcome the eye.

Same way with sans serif type.

It's a mongrel. It has no history, and it's there only to say: "Look at me!"

It's why Johnny can't read: The sheer effort of trying to read a crude type that was never, even by the Germans, made for reading is too much, and Johnny says the hell with it.

Johnny can't read, in large part, because printers and designers have kept him from reading.

Vrest Orton, author of many books and articles, was born Sept. 3, 1897, in Hardwick, VT. He founded The Vermont Country Store in 1946; that year he began publishing its catalog, The Voice of the Mountains. Orton died in 1986, at age 89, but the fourth and fifth generations — Lyman, Cabot, Gardner and Eliot Orton — are carrying on both The Vermont Country Store and The Voice of the Mountains catalog, which is still set, as it was from the beginning, in Times Roman type.

Takeaways to Consider

• If text is not easy to read, people won't read it.

• The best definition is given by the Oxford English Dictionary, which succinctly declares that sans serif is "a form of type without serifs, also called grotesque." Grotesque it certainly is.

• Any type that makes the message difficult to read, that makes the printed page strident, brazen, and uncomfortable to the eye, is wrong, except for one purpose for which sans serif was designed by the Germans: advertising. For generations, sans serif was kept where it belonged: in display advertisements whose function was to shout at the reader.

• Many textbooks and a number of magazines are now printed in this style of type, which not only repels and insults the eye, but actually makes printed matter almost impossible to read.

• Each letter stands alone and yells for attention. Each letter is the same width in all its parts; there are no contrasts. A page of sans serif type is like a landscape with two hundred hills in the distance, all exactly the same shape, size and height. The words for both are monotonous and unnatural.

• Caslon and other historic types exude character and charm — while remaining always unobtrusive. And they have survived the test of time. The eye, for two centuries, has found these types agreeable, just as the eye of knowledgeable and educated people finds the aesthetic character of Georgian architecture comfortable and agreeable.

• "Use sans serif type for headlines, not for body copy." —*Andrew J. Byrne*

• "Use serif type in body copy, not sans serif type; it's more readable and will bring a better response." —*Craig Huey*

• "Use serif typefaces for body copy; they're easier to read." —*Ted Kikoler*

• "Never, never use a sans-serif typeface in body copy." —*Ted Nicholas*

CHAPTER 17

In Search of the Best Online Reading Experience

Coming late in life to the computer, I was slow to pick up on the digital reading experience being different from print.

I was schooled primarily by Vrest Orton's screed on the evils of sans serif type in the preceding chapter — my bible for 30 years.

When I started *Business Common Sense* in 2005, a reader wrote me with a question about the ideal font for online readability. It set me off on a quest resulting in a long column on the subject.

The best quick discussion of online readability I found was by Sara Dickenson Quinn on poynter.org:

> The better news is that a few great typefaces have been designed specifically for reading large amounts of text on-screen — and there are more on the way for some computer systems. Verdana, a sans serif, Georgia, a serif, and Trebuchet ... have become standards for readability on the Web. They've been around for several years, and they are wonderful because they've been drawn with painstaking detail, just for the screen. They reproduce quite well in print, too.
>
> **Here's why they work**
> • Their lowercase characters are slightly larger than the average typeface. This larger "x-height" makes the character look bigger overall. The open spaces are slightly larger than average, so they don't seem to "fill in."
>
> • To limit jagged edges, the curves are reduced to a minimum in the open spaces of the letters.
>
> • The letters are spaced farther apart, in a more regular way, so they don't seem to touch.
>
> • Some combinations of letters that might normally bump or overlap, like "ft," "fi," and "fl," are specially drawn so that they have extra space between them.
>
> • Verdana, Georgia and Trebuchet are installed on both Windows and Apple operating systems, making them universally available for use on any Web page. Some people call these "Web-safe" fonts, because most users have them.
>
> • Commissioned by Microsoft, Verdana and Georgia were designed by Matthew Carter and hinted by Tom Rickner of Ascender Corporation. (A simple description of hinting is "a method of defining exactly which pixels

are turned on in order to create the best possible character … at small sizes and low resolutions.") Trebuchet was designed by Vincent Connare. *—Sara Dickenson Quinn, Updated March 2, 2011*

Takeaways to Consider

• Sans serif fonts are more readable on the Web.

• A few great typefaces have been designed specifically for reading large amounts of text on-screen — and there are more on the way for some computer systems. Verdana, a sans serif, Georgia, a serif, and Trebuchet … have become standards for readability on the Web.

CHAPTER 18

Prose: Organize It and Write It Right

The greatest copywriter in the world
Whenever I get burned out, I go to visit and watch the greatest copywriter in the world at work, under the portales in the Plaza de Santo Domingo in Mexico City. Oliverio, with his Olympia typewriter made in Brazil, is clearly a king among evangelists, the scribes who sit at card tables behind the old platen presses where you can have your wedding invitations printed while you wait.

Good, plain people who can't write letters for themselves come to Oliverio, and he is much closer to life than I'll ever get. He writes most eloquently about love waiting at home for sons and daughters to return and claim it.

Oliverio always writes from the heart, and his business letters ring with the same truth as his love letters, so people travel from miles around with their problems for Oliverio to solve with his clever typewriter.

Under his fingernails I see a permanent black edge from changing his ribbons. Back home, when I confront my antiseptic computer, I first look at my fingernails and if they are all clean I know my letter would be antiseptic, too.

I wish I could take Oliverio's place at his card table for just one hour, but that would turn into a bitter circus — his clients would believe I was mocking them, and I think they would be right about that. Mocking them or him is something I would never want to do, so I melt into the background and watch and listen while my friend works.

For my own work, the best thing I can do is try to keep Oliverio's human touch in mind every time I write. Lord knows I try. *—Bob Dolman, freelancer*

The classic arrangement — an inverted pyramid

Traditional news stories and press releases are created in the "inverted pyramid" format. The short lede paragraph describes who, what, where, when and how. This enables the reader to grasp the basics and decide whether or not to continue.

Subsequent paragraphs fill in details, from the most important down to the least important.

When an inverted pyramid story goes out over the wires or Internet, editors can pick up as much or as little as they want, depending on the space available. Even if all but the first two paragraphs are lopped off, readers still get the guts of the story.

When the pyramid is received, all the editor or reader needs to do is eyeball the first paragraph to know what's there and whether it may be of value.

The above technique is a viable concept for memos, press releases, white papers, new stories, reports, PowerPoint presentations and virtually any other nonfiction writing you create.

Violate the inverted pyramid at your peril

When I started reading *The New York Times* on Sunday, Aug. 30, 2009, my brain kept bumping into articles making no sense. Was I the problem, having just turned 74? Or was it poor writing and editing on the part of the *Times*?

After careful analysis, I discovered editorial excellence in *The New York Times* had deteriorated right along with its finances.

Poor writing in print media — memos, whitepapers, letters, reports, newspapers and books — is relatively harmless.

"Today's $1 newspaper is tomorrow's birdcage liner," wrote Doc Searls, blogger, columnist and one of the authors of *The Cluetrain Manifesto*.

Writers beware: if your written material — riddled with mistakes and non-sequiturs — makes it to the Internet, it can plague us all the way to the grave and beyond. From *The New York Times*:

> **Clash in Alabama Over Tennessee Coal Ash**
> UNIONTOWN, Ala. — Almost every day, a train pulls into a rail yard in rural Alabama, hauling 8,500 tons of a disaster that occurred 350 miles away to a final resting place, the Arrowhead Landfill here in Perry County, which is very poor and almost 70 percent black.
>
> To county leaders, the train's loads, which will total three million cubic yards of coal ash from a massive spill at a power plant in east Tennessee last December, are a tremendous financial windfall. A per-ton "host fee" that the landfill operators pay the county will add more than $3 million to the county's budget of about $4.5 million. *—Shaila Dewan, The New York Times*

As I started reading this 1,173-word story about the pernicious politics of coal ash disposal, my addled brain kept raising the following questions:

- What is coal ash?
- Where'd it come from?
- How's it stored?
- How'd the great spill occur?

If coal ash is anything like the ashes in my fireplace or charcoal grill, a spill means the wind would blow it all over the countryside.

After 324 words came the first clue. The coal ash was described as "heavy, mudlike ash." This raised another question: How'd it become mudlike?

Following word 510 is the line: "Most of the problems from coal ash, which contains toxins like arsenic and lead that have contaminated the water supply at more than 60 sites nationwide, come from wet, unlined ponds like the one that ruptured in Tennessee..."

- How did presumably dry ash get into wet, unlined ponds?
- Do the ponds occur naturally, or are they dug specifically to hold coal ash?

• How does a pond — presumably below ground level — rupture and spill coal ash?
• What caused the rupture?

Finally, 85 percent of the way through the story — at word 980 — came the definition: "the ash, a byproduct of burning coal to produce electricity..."

This was disorganized journalism on the part of Metro News reporter Shaila Dewan and her clueless copy editor who should have known better.

The Supremes: literary lightweights
When you think of the law — from briefs to court decisions — precise language is expected from everybody. This goes from prosecutors and defense attorneys all the way up to the Supreme Court of the United States. Alas, not so. From *The New York Times*:

> **Justices Are Long on Words but Short on Guidance**
> WASHINGTON — In June, the Supreme Court issued a decision on the privacy rights of a police officer whose sexually explicit text messages had been reviewed by his employer. Ever since, lower court judges have struggled to figure out what the decision means ...
>
> Justice Antonin Scalia went along with the decision, but he blasted his colleagues for "issuing opaque opinions" ...
>
> *Brown v. Board of Education*, the towering 1954 decision that held segregated public schools unconstitutional, managed to do its work in fewer than 4,000 words. When the Roberts court returned to just an aspect of the issue in 2007 in *Parents Involved v. Seattle*, it published some 47,000 words, enough to rival a short novel ...
>
> Critics of the court's work are not primarily focused on the quality of the justices' writing, though it is often flabby and flat. Instead, they point to reasoning that fails to provide clear guidance to lower courts, sometimes seemingly driven by a desire for unanimity that can lead to fuzzy, unwieldy rulings. — *Adam Liptak, The New York Times*

Is Supreme Court prose truly "flabby and flat"?
What follows is the lede paragraph of Chief Justice Roberts' *Parents Involved* opinion cited by Adam Liptak in his analysis above.

Take just a moment to recall the Scott Huch rule that sentences longer than 29 words are extremely difficult to comprehend. In the text below, the boldface numbers in parentheses **(are mine).** These are the word counts for the preceding sentence.

> *THE CHIEF JUSTICE delivered the opinion of the Court with respect to Parts I, II, III–A, and III–C, concluding:*
> Seattle argues that Parents Involved lacks standing because its current members' claimed injuries are not imminent and are too speculative in

that, even if the district maintains its current plan and reinstitutes the racial tiebreaker, those members will only be affected if their children seek to enroll in a high school that is oversubscribed and integration positive. **(57)** This argument is unavailing; the group's members have children in all levels of the district's schools, and the complaint sought declaratory and injunctive relief on behalf of members whose elementary and middle school children may be denied admission to the high schools of their choice in the future. **(48)** The fact that those children may not be denied such admission based on their race because of undersubscription or oversubscription that benefits them does not eliminate the injury claimed. **(29)** The group also asserted an interest in not being forced to compete in a race-based system that might prejudice its members' children, an actionable form of injury under the Equal Protection Clause, see, e.g., Adarand Constructors, Inc. v. Peña, 515 U. S. 200, 211. **(44)** The fact that Seattle has ceased using the racial tiebreaker pending the outcome here is not dispositive, since the district vigorously defends its program's constitutionality, and nowhere suggests that it will not resume using race to assign students if it prevails. **(41)** See Friends of Earth, Inc. v. Laidlaw Environmental Services (TOC), Inc., 528 U. S. 167, 189. **(16)** Similarly, the fact that Joshua has been granted a transfer does not eliminate the Court's jurisdiction; Jefferson County's racial guidelines apply at all grade levels and he may again be subject to race-based assignment in middle school. **(37)** Pp. 9–11. **(3)**

This convoluted claptrap runs for 77 pages. Whew!

Substantial Job Losses in 2008

Substantial job losses in 2008: weakness broadens and deepens across industries

Employment losses in 2008 accelerated by year's end as continued weakness in construction, manufacturing, and professional and business services spread into consumer-driven industries

Laura A. Kelter

As measured by the Current Employment Statistics (CES) survey, total nonfarm employment peaked at 138.2 million in December 2007, coinciding with the official start of the current recession.[1] This turning point marked the end of a nearly 3-year employment expansion totaling almost 5.4 million jobs. (See chart 1.) Job growth had slowed during 2007, and then employment fell by 3.1 million (or 2.2 percent) during 2008, with declines in most industry sectors. Furthermore, the job losses were more widespread and severe than during the previous two employment contractions.

Manufacturing, construction, financial activities, and professional and business services had begun seeing job losses or weakened employment growth in 2007, after which they experienced a worsening employment picture during 2008. Consumer-driven industries, such as retail trade and leisure and hospitality, started to cut workers in 2008, and employment declines accelerated during the last several months of the year. Only health care, mining, and government industries continued to add jobs.

Several economic issues that faced the Nation in 2008 contributed to the employment loss. Among such issues were continued housing market troubles, record-high oil and gas prices, rising costs of food, a financial crisis brought on by mortgage defaults, tightened credit, and weak retail sales.

Laura A. Kelter is a supervisory economist in the National Estimates Branch, Office of Employment and Unemployment Statistics, Bureau of Labor Statistics. E-mail: kelter.laura@bls.gov

Nonfarm job loss in perspective

Over the past three decades, the United States experienced three employment contractions.[2] Following a peak in August 1981, total nonfarm employment fell by 2.8 million through December 1982. Next, nonfarm employment fell by 1.6 million (or 1.5 percent) during the 11 months of the 1990–91 contraction. Finally, nonfarm employment reached a peak in February 2001 and then fell by 2.7 million over the next 30 months.

The current employment contraction ran through 2008 and has continued into 2009. Compared with the previous contractions, job losses in 2008 accelerated more rapidly. During the first 8 months of the year, job losses were relatively mild, averaging 137,000 per month; then, in September and October, losses accelerated to an average of 351,000 per month. A further acceleration took place during November and December, to an average of 639,000 jobs lost per month.

In 2008, the employment contraction, in terms of total nonfarm job loss, appears most similar to the employment contraction that started in July 1981. (See chart 2.) In both the 1990 and 2001 contractions, employment flattened out 10 months after its peak. In relative terms, both the 2008 contraction and the 1980 contraction saw

20 Monthly Labor Review • March 2009

Alas, unreadable, imprecise prose is found everywhere. Here is the first page of a 14-page report from the Bureau of Labor Statistics.

This first page of a report from the Bureau of Labor Statistics follows all the correct rules of design to move the reader's eyes — a headline, deck, crosshead and a series of short sentences. But let's take just a moment to parse the prose of the two lede sentences.

> As measured by the Current Employment Statistics (CES) survey, total nonfarm employment peaked at 138.2 million in December 2007, coincid-

> ing with the official start of the current recession.[1] This turning point marked the end of a nearly 3-year employment expansion totaling almost 5.4 million jobs. (See chart 1.)

The first two sentences — just 48 words — should grab my undivided attention and propel me onward. Instead the thread was broken by three interruptions.

Interruption No. 1:

" ... Current Employment Statistics (CES)"

Academic and technical writers are schooled to use abbreviations, such as CES above. This stops the reader cold. It says, "Remember what CES means, because I'm going to use again later."

In this case, the writer did use "CES" four more times in the endnote of this 14-page snoozer some 688 words later. But she had the good grace to define it again. Many academic and technical writers simply define an abbreviation or acronym once and assume the reader will remember it forever.

Interruption No. 2:

> " ... official start of the current recession.[1]"

The footnote [1] indicator is an interruption.

The author is telling you in order to understand what she talking about, go to the bottom of the page to find footnote.[1]

Not there? Oh, gee, it must be an endnote. Go to the last page and look for endnote.[1] Here's what you'll find:

> *[1] The Current Employment Statistics (CES) survey is a monthly survey of about 150,000 nonfarm business and government agencies represent¬ing approximately 390,000 individual worksites. For more information on the program's concepts and methodology, see "Technical Notes to Establishment Data Published in Employment and Earnings," in Economic News Release: Employment Situation (Bureau of Labor Statistics, Feb. 6, 2009), on the Internet at* ***www.bls.gov/web/empsit.supp.toc.htm#technote*** *(visited Feb. 6, 2009). CES data are presented in Current Employment Statistics—CES (National) (Bureau of Labor Statistics, no date), on the Internet at* ***www.bls.gov/ces*** *(visited Feb. 6, 2009). The CES data used in this article are seasonally adjusted unless otherwise noted. The beginnings and endings of recessions are determined by the National Bureau of Economic Research (NBER). (See details at* ***www.nber.org/cycles/dec2008.html*** *(visited Jan. 30, 2009).)*

Not only is the endnote unreadable gobbledygook, but also the [1] was ill-placed. It followed "current recession," to indicate the endnote will give details about the slumping economy.

The endnote[1] in fact deals with the CES monthly survey. The superscript [1] should have followed the word "survey" and not "recession."

Sloppy writing. Sloppy editing.

Interruption No. 3

"(See Chart 1.)"

So in the first 48 words, Laura Kelter has me on the run. I have look up an endnote and am threatened with a short-term memory test (CES). Now she tells me to stop reading and "See Chart 1."

Imagine trying to make sense out of the remaining 13.5 pages.

About abbreviations and acronyms in print media
Universally understood abbreviations are okay to use without explanation: U.N., ATM, FYI, NBC, CBS, PIN, D-Day, PR, P.S., etc.

With an unfamiliar term such as "CES" above, two thoughts:

- If all your readers are insiders and use the abbreviation or acronym every day when conversing with each other, then use it.

- If you are taking to non-insiders, it's rude to use an abbreviation then suddenly spring it on the reader 20 or 40 pages later. Always put yourself inside the head of the reader — as Laura Kelter did — and remind the reader what it stands for.

Writers who failed to think of their readers
Many World War II historians are oblivious to readers' possible lack of prior knowledge. For example, various campaigns were given code names. "Overlord," the massive invasion of Normandy in June 1944 is well known. But dozens more were gibberish. Among them:

- **NUNTON** (March 1944) allied cover and deception plan
- **OCTAGON** code name for the Quebec Conference, September 1944
- **OLIVE** (September 1944) attack on the Gothic Line in Italy
- **OLYMPIC** plan (not executed) for the March 1946 invasion of the island of Kyushu
- **ORANGE** pre-war plan within the RAINBOW matrix for unilateral conflict between the United States and Japan; ORANGE 1 was approved in 1938, ORANGE 3 in April 1941
- **PANTHER** British 10 Corps drive across the Garigliano River in Italy
- **PICADILLY** World War II code name for a drop site for the Chindits in Burma
- **PIGSTICK** World War II limited operation (cancelled) on the south Mayu Peninsula

In a number of WWII books, many pages would go by and suddenly one of these words would surface. The author knew them in his sleep, but the reader was interrupted and forced to go back through the book to find out what the author was talking about.

In *The Last Lion* — the riveting account of Churchill during World War II, authors William Manchester and Paul Reid were considerate. When one of these words surfaced out of the blue, the authors always reminded the reader what it stood for. That's class.

Bagration?
Here is one of Paul Kennedy's 44-word monstrosities in *Engineers of Victory*:

> Remarkably, all five separate though interconnected challenges were overcome between early 1943 and the summer of 1944 — roughly, between Casablanca and the quadruple successes of Normandy, the fall of Rome, the Marianas landings in the Central Pacific, and Operation Bagration on the Eastern Front.

What was Operation *Bagration* (fifth word from the end)? Paul Kennedy used Bagration 31 times in the book. Only in the 15th instance did the author get around to defining Bagration:

> ... the Red Army launched Operation Bagration, a massive assault upon the German-held central front that involved several times as many ground-based forces as the combined totals of all those involved in the Marianas and D-Day attacks. . . Appropriately, the operation was named by Stalin after imperial Russia's most aggressive general, Piotr Bagration, who died of his wounds while blocking Napoleon at the great Battle of Borodino.

This is an instance where the author is showing off to his peers — a coterie of World War II experts who knew all about *Bagration*. The rest of us (paying customers) were left to twist in the wind fourteen times before Kennedy got around to explaining Bagration.

To compound the incompetence of Paul Kennedy and his Random House editor, Bagration's first name is Pyotr — with a "y"' — not Piotr as written in the book.

A caveat: stop with the TMI
TMI is text-speak for too much information. I have a longtime colleague who cannot stick to what's important. He does massive research and cannot help himself from inserting all kinds of minutiae that 1) interests him and 2) he knows will impress the reader on how much research he did.

This stalls the narrative. It should either be left on the cutting room floor or turned into endnotes.

> **The ultimate organizer, Holland Taylor, turned 1 million words into a hit play**
> LOS ANGELES — The sun was setting in the Hollywood Hills as Holland Taylor whisked a visitor into a front room of her home, a window overlooking the public garden across the street. Golden in the fading light, the den was overflowing with stacks of videotapes, dusty transcripts, books and photographs.

> "This used to be a really serene guest room with nothing in it, and now this is all Ann," said Ms. Taylor, a veteran actress, referring to Ann W. Richards, the former governor of Texas. "All Ann. These papers are about Ann. These boxes are all full of Ann videos. These are speeches, pre- and post-governor. These are Larry King transcripts.
>
> "I'm not sure what this is." She paused before yet another pile, the raw material for what became her first play (and turned this guest room into an office). "Oh. Those are my transcripts of speeches that I have no written text for." She sighed. "I can no longer organize it. I'm past that point."
>
> As she would be the first to admit, the 70-year-old Ms. Taylor is obsessed with Richards, a woman she met only once, when the gossip columnist Liz Smith insisted that the actress join them for lunch in 2004 at Le Cirque. She has spent the better part of four years studying every aspect of Richards's life, interviewing her friends, her staff members and her four children, reviewing 150 hours of filmed appearances, listening to tapes of speech-writing sessions and absorbing the off-color candor and bawdy humor that made Richards anything but your average politician — a personality as suited for the stage as for "Meet the Press." *—Adam Nagourney, "Immersion Politics: Being Ann Richards," The New York Times*

You can imagine a room piled high with myriad videos, speeches, books, articles, tapes and transcripts of interviews acquired over four years and 150 hours of filmed appearances.

Talk about massive research! Talk about discipline — boiling many thousands of hours down to 120 minutes for *Ann: An Affectionate Portrait of Ann Richards*, a one-woman play written and starring Holland Taylor. This is the tedium of mining research and the joy of finding gold to share with readers or play goers.

NOTE: *New York Times* critic Charles Isherwood headlined his review "Fiery, Salty and Brash, This Rose of Texas" and gave the show a rave.

What's more, Holland Taylor was nominated for a Tony as Best Actress in a Play by The American Theater Wing. This was thrilling!

The value of pre-empting

If you can come up with original material — as Taylor Holland did — you own it.

Others can follow suit, expound on it, discuss it, praise it or slam it. But if you found it, you are the godparent. Your name will be forever associated with it.

Pre-empt!

One of the savviest (and most fun) Energizer bunnies in the world of marketing is West Coast wizard Jay Abraham. He is an elfin figure who sports a full head of black hair (current photos show him gray) plus a mustache and neatly trimmed beard.

Jay used to charge $25,000 per person to attend one of his marketing seminars and routinely sold them out. If you decided to leave after the first day, he'd give you all your money back. Few students took him up on it. He has made zillions for himself. Many in his legion of protégés are rich beyond the dreams of avarice. From Jay's website:

> **Stealth Marketing Strategy of "Preemptive Advertising"**
> Let me tell you a story. You may have heard it before, but it's a classic example of the power of preemptive advertising...
>
> Back in 1919, Schlitz beer was the #10 beer in the marketplace. Claude Hopkins, the classic marketing strategist after whom I've patterned my life, was called in to salvage the marketing of this #10 beer and lift it to success.
>
> When he walked into the brewery, the first thing he did was learn how the beer was made. He toured the facilities and he saw that Schlitz was located right on the banks of one of the Great Lakes. And even though they were right there with this unlimited water source, they had dug five, 4,000-foot artesian wells right next to Lake Michigan because they wanted pure water.
>
> The brewers showed Claude a mother yeast cell that was a result of about 2,500 different experiments that had been done to find the quintessential yeast to make the proper taste. They showed him five different, three-foot-thick, plate glass rooms where beer was condensed and redistilled and re-condensed for purity. They showed him the tasters that tasted the beer five different times. They showed him where the bottles were cleaned and re-cleaned 12 times. They showed him the whole process. At the end, he was incredulous.
>
> He said, "My God, why don't you tell people the process that your beer goes through?"
>
> And they said, "Because that's how ALL beer is made. It's nothing special; it's nothing unique."
>
> And he said, "Yes, but the first person who tells the public about this will gain preemptive advantage."
>
> He got Schlitz to the #1 position in about six months. By using preemptive advertising windfall profits are virtually assured.

What is pre-emptive advertising? As a result of his dogged research, Hopkins was able to create a series of ads for Schlitz beer based on its purity. One line of copy in the ad:

> Every bottle of Schlitz beer is sterilized, to insure freedom from germs.

All beer manufacturers sterilized their bottles. But Schlitz said it first and pre-emptively owned the concept of sterilized bottles. The best Schlitz competitors could say weakly was, "Uh … gee … Our bottles are also sterilized."

"When in doubt, do the obvious," said book publisher Franklin Watts.

John Caples on first drafts
Overwriting is the key. If you need a thousand words, write two thousand. Trim vigorously. Fact-packed messages carry a wallop. Don't be afraid of long copy. If your ad is interesting, people will be hungry for all the copy you can give them. If the ad is dull, short copy won't save it.

John Caples on humor
Avoid it. What's funny to one person isn't to millions of others. Copy should sell, not just entertain. Remember there's not one funny line in the two most influential books ever written: the Bible and the Sears catalog.

Put everything on the same subject in the same place
Two of the great reading experiences of my life were volumes one and two of William Manchester's biography of Winston Churchill. Both were brilliantly researched and gripping in their detail. I felt I knew Churchill personally and vicariously lived his extraordinary life. I salivated for the third volume about the World War II years. The volume never appeared.

In 1998 the research was done and the first 100 pages written. Sadly, William Manchester suffered two strokes and the wires in his brain became disconnected. "Language for me came as easily as breathing for 50 years," he told The New York Times, "and I can't do it anymore."

Shortly before he died in 2004, Manchester designated Paul Reid to write the third volume. The deal: a 50-50 split. Reid, a former writer for The Palm Beach Post, spent 8 years deciphering Manchester's cryptic notes and writing at the painfully slow rate of roughly one manuscript page per day. The result is a masterpiece, every bit as worthy as Manchester's first two volumes.

However, with the gap of a quarter century, few book buyers would have read the prior two volumes. For the majority of readers, this new work would be a standalone. Quite simply, new young readers did not know Churchill — his brilliance, quirks, nastiness, love of animals and encyclopedic knowledge of history. He had a fantastic memory and could quote long passages of Shakespeare, Macaulay and Noel Coward. So to help the reader play catch-up, Paul Reid crammed everything into a remarkable 50-page preamble to make Churchill's character come alive. Here is a sampling:

> In many ways, Churchill remained a nineteenth-century man, and by no means a common man. He fit the mold of what Henry James called in *English Hours* persons for whom the private machinery of ease has been made to work with extraordinary smoothness. His valet warmed his brandy snifter over a neatly trimmed candle; his typists and secretaries kept more candles at the ready in order to light his cigars (Cuban Romeo y Julieta were his favorites). He had never ridden a bus. The only time he availed himself of the London Underground was during the general strike in 1926. Clementine [his wife] dropped him off at South Kensington but Winston did not know how to navigate the system, the result was that "he went round and round not knowing where to get off, and eventually had to be rescued." He never carried cash, except to casinos and the occasional derby, where an aide

would take care of the business of procuring chips or placing bets on worthy steeds.

This long, intensely personal preamble brought the reader up to speed on Churchill's personality, rudeness, habits, health, foibles, eccentricities and leadership style. Thus, later in the narrative — when Winston did something seemingly weird or off-the-wall — no explanation was necessary. Readers knew all about Churchill's nuttiness and the story could proceed without an interruption, sidebar or endnote.

In contrast ...
Unlike William Manchester and Paul Reid, in Engineers of Victory, quirky author Paul Kennedy wants the reader to jump around the book like a jackrabbit in heat. Throughout the narrative I was told:

Phrase	**No. of Times**
see Chapter 3 [or 4 or 5]	(12)
as noted above	(6)
as suggested above	(1)
as the narrative above	(1)
as we have seen	(6)
as has been argued ... above	(1)
as we have argued	(2)
as we shall see	(10)
in the pages below	(1)
analyzed in more detail below	(1)
will be discussed below	(2)
see below	(1)
exceptions mentioned below	(1)
the conclusions below	(1)

When you think about it, nowhere does the author tell you, "where."

- Where exactly *above* do I look?
- Where *below*?
- Where *shall we see*?
- Where are the *exceptions mentioned below*?

Each one of these statements interrupts the thread of concentration. It causes the reader to continually wish the writer would simply go away.

In this 464-page book, these offending phrases — and versions of them — show up roughly once every five pages. In 70-plus years of reading books, I have never encountered anything quite like this.

Paul Kennedy teaches at Yale. The three-word career path in institutions of higher learning is "Publish or perish." Presumably in the rarefied environment of a university, woolly-brained and tenured academes are literary gods, who no longer need to think about their readers. They write to impress colleagues and trustees in order to validate their status. And their timid editors — even at hifalutin Random House — don't dare touch a tenured professor's deathless prose.

Disappear from the scene!
Ideally a writer should be invisible. This is true of all writing (with the possible exception of poetry). The reader should be completely unaware of the words on paper or online.

If the reader says, "Oh, how beautifully this author writes," the author has failed.

The objective for writers is to evaporate from the scene. The thoughts they choose to convey should leave their heads and bounce off a piece of paper or through a computer screen. From there they go seamlessly into the brain of the reader with no interruptions.

The writer as an actor
Perhaps the greatest American stage actress of our generation was the late Julie Harris. In 1951 she won the first of her six Broadway Tony awards as the free-spirited Sally Bowles in *I Am a Camera*. Playwright John Van Druten described Harris as being like a glass pitcher:

> "You pour in red wine, the pitcher looks red; pour in crème de menthe, it is green. When she's by herself, Julie's almost transparent, almost nonexistent."

With the possible exception of poetry, this should be the goal of every writer.

Understanding people
The most successful advertisement in the history of the world was Martin Conroy's "Two Young Men ... " letter for *The Wall Street Journal. (See chapter 40.)*

I once asked Marty the secret of his success, and he sent me the following:

> **If you're trying to find out what makes people tick, you might take a look at the Seven Deadly Sins from the old Baltimore Catechism.**
>
> Remember them? Pride, covetousness, lust, anger, gluttony, envy and sloth. Of course, the deadly sins are all bad and all extreme and all no-nos.
>
> But there's an unsinful, unextreme side to every one of them where you can see how good and honest people act and react.
>
> On the sunny side of sinful price, for example, nice people still take normal, unsinful satisfaction in what they are and what they have.
>
> Short of deadly covetousness, people have an understandable desire to possess some of the good things in life.
>
> Instead of sinful lust, there's good old love that makes the world go 'round. Without raging in anger, good people can still feel a reasonable annoyance with bad people and bad things.
>
> Without getting into gross gluttony, normal men and women can have a normal appetite for good food and drink.

Short of envy, there's a very human yen to do as well as the next guy. And as for sloth, who isn't' happy to learn an easier way to do things? The Seven Deadly Sins. If you want to know what makes people act like people, they're worth a look.

Takeaways to Consider

• Are you writing for yourself or for your reader?

• Ruthlessly self-edit, because most folks in business do not have professional editors to tidy up their work.

• Delete anything taking the reader off subject.

• Don't use an acronym, code word or abbreviation once and then have it appear 40 pages later and expect the reader to know what you're talking about.

• Are you giving useful background information, or are you showing off how much you know?

• "Writing is easy, all you have to do is cross out the wrong words." *—Mark Twain*

• K.I.S.S. — "Keep it simple, stupid." *—Kelly Johnson, lead engineer at the Lockheed Skunk Works. (from: Wikipedia — always suspect until proven otherwise.)*

CHAPTER 19

Words, Words, Words: All About 'em

And from the first declension of the flesh
I learnt man's tongue, to twist the shapes of thoughts
Into the stony idiom of the brain,
To shade and knit anew the patch of words
Left by the dead who, in their moonless acre,
Need no word's warmth.
—Dylan Thomas, "From Love's First Fever To Her Plague"

....

If you use a word the reader does not know, you have interrupted the flow of the writing. Further, you may have made the reader feel like a chump. The reader, who is interrupted to go look up a fancy-schmancy word, may never get back to your message.

In the world of marketing, when the prospective customer is interrupted and the ad or mailing is laid aside, chances are the order is lost.

The case for short words

When you speak and write, there is no law that says you have to use big words. Short words are as good as long ones, and short, old words — like sun and grass and home — are best of all. A lot of small words, more than you might think, can meet your needs with a strength, grace, and charm that large words do not have.

Big words can make the way dark for those who read what you write and hear what you say. Small words cast their clear light on big things — night and day, love and hate, war and peace, and life and death. Big words at times seem strange to the eye and the ear and the mind and the heart. Small words are the ones we seem to have known from the time we were born, like the hearth fire that warms the home.

Short words are bright like sparks that glow in the night, prompt like the dawn that greets the day, sharp like the blade of a knife, hot like salt tears that scald the cheek, quick like moths that flit from flame to flame, and terse like the dart and sting of a bee.

Here is a sound rule: Use small, old words where you can. If a long word says just what you want to say, do not fear to use it. But know that our tongue is rich in crisp, brisk, swift, short words. Make them the spine and the heart of what you speak and write. Short words are like fast friends. They will not let you down.

The title of this article and the four paragraphs that you have just read are wrought entirely of words of one syllable. In setting myself this task, I did not feel especially cabined, cribbed, or confined. In fact, the structure helped me to focus on the power of the message I was trying to put across. *—Dr. Richard Lederer, author of Word Wizard*

The 50 most frequently looked-up words by readers of *The New York Times*
Jan. 1, 2010 through May 26, 2010 (Alphabetically, not by number of look-ups)

Note: If you use any of these, chances are good your reader may leave you to look it up. The thread is interrupted and maybe you've lost a reader.

alacrity — antediluvian — apoplectic — apostates — atavistic — austerity — baldenfreude — canard — chimera — comity — crèches — cynosure — démarche — desultory — egregious — epistemic — ersatz — feckless — hegemony — hubris — incendiary — inchoate — Internecine — jejune — Kristallnacht — laconic — Manichean — mirabile dictu — nascent — obduracy — obstreperous — omertà — opprobrium — overhaul — peripatetic — polemicist — prescient — profligacy — profligate — provenance — putative — redoubtable — renminbi — sanguine — sclerotic — solipsistic — soporific — sui generis — ubiquitous — verisimilitude

Words and phrases bad writers love — common among large firms, politicians, journalists, top executives — and second-rate copywriters
This is by no means a complete list — and I am sometimes guilty myself.

- Wordsmith — bad copywriter
- Awesome — any thing or person quite good
- Thought-leader — someone smarter than most and good at bullshit
- Solution —— added pointlessly to words like "menu" or "recipe"
- Experience — similar to solution, e.g., "meal experience"
- State of the art — something fairly new
- Cutting edge — as above
- Innovative — as above
- Cutting it — succeeding
- Legendary — been around for a while without being found out
- Insightful — perceptive
- Mind-set — way of thinking
- Guru — someone fairly knowledgeable *—Drayton Bird*

"We are using the word 'guru' only because 'charlatan' is too long to fit into a headline." *—Peter Drucker*

John Caples on word power
"Simple words are powerful words. Even the best-educated people don't resent simple words. But they're the only words many people understand. Write to your barber or mechanic or elevator operator. Remember, too, that every word is important. Sometimes you can change a word and increase the pulling power of an ad. Once I changed the word 'repair' to 'fix' and the ad pulled 20% more!"

The 12 most evocative words of the English language

On my first day at Grolier Enterprises, my new boss Lew Smith pulled out a column from the old Saturday Review by radio personality Goodman Ace. Here were the 12 most powerful and evocative words in the English Language:

> You — Save — Money — Easy — Guarantee — Health — Proven — Safety — Discovery — New — Love — Results

To these 12, I added one more, a favorite of the late Dick Benson: "'Free' is a magic word."

In the early years of my career, I typed up this list and pasted it on the base of the lamp on every desk I ever had. The logic: if these are the most powerful and evocative words, my copy should be laced with them.

NOTE: "Free" is a dangerous word to use in the subject line of e-mail; it has been known to trigger spam filters.

> **Bob Hacker's list of selling words**
> comfort — deserve — discover — easy — free — fun — guarantee — happy — health — love — money — new — profit — proud — proven — results — right — safety — save — trust — truth — understand — value
>
> **Hacker's response killers — words to avoid**
> bad — buy — cost — contract — death — decision — difficult — fall — hard — hurt — liable — lose — loss — obligation — pay — price — sell — sign — sold — try — worry

Herschell Gordon Lewis, master of English

One the most fascinating copywriters in the world of direct marketing is Herschell Gordon Lewis, who started out making movies. His reputation as a filmmaker was based on delicious shockers. Known as "The Godfather of Gore," Herschell's film titles included *Blood Feast* (1963), *Color Me Blood Red* (1965) and *The Wizard of Gore* (1970).

Herschell went on to become a prolific author of such marketing masterpieces as:

- *Direct Mail Copy That Sells*
- *On the Art of Writing Copy — 4th Edition*
- *Sales Letters That Sizzle: All the Hooks, Lines and Sinkers You'll Ever Need to Close Sales*
- *Effective E-Mail Marketing: The Complete Guide to Creating Successful Campaigns.*

He even wrote a 144-page book devoted entirely to the envelope in direct mail: *Open Me Now: Direct Mail Envelopes That Work ... and Those That Don't.*

Herschell and Margo Lewis are intrepid world travelers. And he is an inveterate lecturer on copy and design and a world-renowned expert on the finer points — indeed, the minutiae — of how to supercharge the English language. For example:

The capital letters rule
For an extra octane-boost, use capital letters.

Original issue price (for our Preferred Members) just $99.50

Capitals suggest greater stature.

Words/phrases with automatic power
don't miss out — first time offered — free gift — good only until [date] — hot — I'll look for your order — limited time — not sold in stores — right now — surprise — try it at our risk

12 words with implicit weakness
administration — approximately — define — earn — facilitate — features — formulate — indeed — needs (as a noun) — product — respond — work

Use "try" rather than "examine"
"Try it at our risk" will pull more response than "Examine it at our risk," because "Try" is less of a commitment and suggests the need for less expertise or time commitment.

"Think" is more potent than "thought"
"If you think that..." is a more potent opening than "If you thought that ..." because present tense implies an immediate change of current attitude; past tense suggests that whatever follows will be a revision of history.

"When" vs. "if"
"When" is superior to "if" for suggesting something will happen.

"If" is superior to "when" for suggesting something will not happen.

Add sarcasm or ridicule to a negative
Replace "isn't" or "aren't" with "anything but." Example:

"Your message isn't subtle"

— becomes —

"Your message is anything but subtle."

Get rid of "in"
You don't need "in" between adjective and noun.

"The best in furniture"
"The newest in colors"
"The latest in fashions"

"Replacement"
A replacement is superior to a substitution. Replacement suggests upgrade; substitution suggests downgrade.

"Eager"
"Eager" is positive; "anxious" is negative.

"The same as"
establishes a closer relationship than "Identical to."

The quotation mark rule
Putting quotation marks around a word or phrase that may not be immediately recognized tells the reader we share the novelty of the idea, which helps the reader accept the unknown.

For example, a description of a fax machine included the statement:

Uses thermal paper.

Many who read this description interpreted "thermal" in its traditional sense — something hot. Clarity would have been improved by quotation marks:

Uses "thermal" paper.

A more powerful wordsmith would have combined quotation marks with an explanation:

Special "thermal" paper means you never have to change a ribbon.

Use of exclamation points
Note the difference between:

Easy to assemble: No tools needed.

— and —

Easy to assemble: No tools needed!

The exclamation point
It says to the reader: "I think this is worth exclaiming."

Using more than one exclamation point
The writer is unsure of his/her ability to convince the reader.

Think through the use of numbers

Accurate within five seconds per month

— or —

Accurate within 60 seconds per year

"Five seconds per month" wins, because it seems to be less time.

"Accurate within ten minutes over a 10-year span" would be a miracle of accuracy ... but the reader thinks, "Uh-oh, I'll be 10 minutes late and miss my plane."

Which phrase will sell more for you?
"2 percent a month"

— or —

"24 percent a year"

If you're writing about what someone pays, it's 2 percent a month; if you're writing about what someone gets, it's 24 percent a year.

Use "now"
What is the difference between ...?

Next month ...

— or —

A month from now ...

— and —

It's 3 o'clock. We leave at 4 o'clock.

— or —

It's 3 o'clock. We leave an hour from now.

Tying an event to now makes it more imminent. Eliminating the tie to now seems to stretch the time.

Sell results, not circumstances
Instead of:

BURIED? You're no longer buried under that avalanche of written memos.

— write —

BURIED? You're finally out from under that avalanche of written memos.

The writer can choose his/her persona.
Aggressive opening: *I want to add a personal note.*

Permission-asking opening: *May I add a personal note?*

Bubbling-over-with-enthusiasm opening: *I couldn't wait. I had to add my own personal note.*

When possible and logical, use the definite article, not the indefinite article
An example of the superiority of definite over indefinite:

The gem in each earring is a full carat.

— instead use —

The gem in each earring is one full carat.

"The" is stronger
"The" [whatever] is stronger than "a" [whatever] because it suggests: Whatever you're selling stands alone, above competitors.

Use *"one"*
Use "one" instead of "a" to establish superiority.

one full carat

— instead of —

a full carat.

The more a number departs from the anticipated rounded-off figure, the more credible it is
Which is more credible?

Take four minutes to read this.

— instead try —

Take 3 minutes and 24 seconds to read this.

— or —

I made $46,000 last month.

— instead try —

I made $46,738 last month.

"As soon as" is sooner than "when"
... ergo, more motivational. Which is the more motivational sentence?

When your referral deposit comes in, we'll credit your account an additional $5.

— or —

As soon as your referral deposit comes in, we'll credit your account an additional $5.

Shift "we" to "you"
Instead of
It'll take just 10 seconds for you to indicate on the card whether we should keep you on our mailing list.

— write —

Take 10 seconds to indicate on the card whether you want us to keep you on our mailing list.

Adding "Will you?" to a statement changes a cold imperative to a warm request
Instead of
Call me tomorrow with a progress report,

— for warmth ... which you may not want ...

Call me tomorrow with a progress report, will you?

"Have no ..." is more desperate than "don't have any ..."

They have no food

— is a more desperate circumstance than —

They don't have any food.

Use these words sparingly:
Therefore — However — Furthermore

....

Don't start with "There is" ...
"The writer always has a stronger way to begin a message than the neutral phrase 'There is'... or 'There are'..." *—Herschell Gordon Lewis*

"As my mentor used to remind me, 'A sentence starting with "There is" is a sentence that doesn't really have a subject.'" *—Scott Huch*

"I don't know the rules of grammar ... If you're trying to persuade people to do something, or buy something, it seems to me you should use their language, the language they use every day, the language in which they think. We try to write in the vernacular." *—David Ogilvy*

That pesky word "that"
I despise "that." First of all, it sounds ugly — a flat "a" as in crap. If you look up "that" in *The Associated Press Stylebook*, you'll find gibberish. I once made up a sentence on the subject of "that":

> *That that that that you see here — especially that fourth that — may be overkill, but that is grammatically correct.*

I go by the rule of Grolier Enterprises CEO, the late Elsworth Howell:

> "If you can take 'that' and shove it up your ass, you don't need it."

In polishing up this manuscript, I did a search for that and deleted dozens of them. Marvelous mental Metamucil! I use "that" as little as possible — although it's still too frequent.

Datum vs. data
Datum is singular. Data are plural.

Ending a sentence with a preposition
For generations puritanical Victorians railed against ending a sentence with a preposition. Story has it an editor clumsily moved a preposition from the end of a sentence to the middle in a Winston Churchill manuscript. Churchill reportedly changed it back and scrawled in the margin: This is the sort of English up with which I will not put.

Online text messaging and abbreviating words
NBC News reported text messaging celebrated its 20th anniversary on Dec. 3, 2012. The 18-34 crowd texts an average of 105 messages a day — more than 3,200 a month.

Because the majority of texting is done via smartphones with thumbs on a mini-keyboard, abbreviations are almost always used. The 20 most popular in order of frequency:

gtg (got to go)
lol (laughing out loud)
rotfl (rolling on the floor laughing)
btw (by the way)
sup (what's up)
wtf (what the fuck)
fyi (for your information)
asap (as soon as possible)
w/ (with)
bf (boy friend)
b4 (before)
cos (because)
gf (girlfriend)
jk (just kidding)
l8r (later)
omg (oh my god)
thx (thanks)
oxox (hugs and kisses)
zzzz (sleeping or bored)
cya (see ya)

Starting in grade school, kids use these 20 abbreviations you see here — plus more than 1,000 more — in their everyday texting correspondence. This is their written argot — the equivalent of "like" and "sort of" in their speech.

Text shorthand is okay for communicating with chums and buds. But beware of letting this stuff — along with winky-face emoticons — slip out in a professional environ ment. Danger lurks when you allow them to creep into printed letters, reports, business plans or any communication to be read by more than one person. From *The Wall Street Journal:*

> **Thx for the IView! I Wud ♥ to Work 4 U!! ;-)**
>
> **Young Job Candidates Find Too-Casual Tone of Textspeak Turns Off Hiring Managers**
> After interviewing a college student in June, Tory Johnson thought she had found the qualified and enthusiastic intern she craved for her small recruiting firm. Then she received the candidate's thank-you note, laced with words like "hiya" and "thanx," along with three exclamation points and a smiley-face emoticon.
>
> "That e-mail just ruined it for me," says Ms. Johnson, president of New York-based Women For Hire Inc. *—Sarah E. Needleman, The Wall Street Journal*

Takeaways to Consider

• "Broadly speaking, the short words are the best, and the old words best of all." *—Winston Churchill*

• "'What's all this business of being a writer? Just putting one word after another.' My reply was, 'Pardon me, Mr. [Irving] Thalberg — putting one right word after another.'" *—Lenore Coffee (1896-1984), American screenwriter, playwright, novelist*

• "Build a big vocabulary, but use it sparingly." *—Jack Maxson*

• "Hemingway has never been known to use a word that might send a reader to the dictionary." *—William Faulkner*

• "Poor Faulkner. Does he really think big emotions come from big words? He thinks I don't know the ten-dollar words. I know them all right. But there are older and simpler and better words, and those are the ones I use." *—Ernest Hemingway (A. E. Hotchner, Papa Hemingway)*

• If you use a word the reader does not know, you have broken the thread — interrupted the flow of the writing. Further, you may have made the reader feel like a chump. The reader who drops everything to go look up the word — and then is interrupted — may never get back to your message.

• The 12 most evocative words of the English language: You — Save — Money — Easy — Guarantee — Health — Proven — Safety — Discovery — New — Love — Results. *—Goodman Ace*

• "'Free' is a magic word." *—Dick Benson*

• "Never use a word you can't spell." *—Jim Pappas, Copy Chief, Bobbs Merrill Company*

CHAPTER 20

Gunning for Readability

By Robert Scott

You've spent long hours at your computer. Your eyeballs ache, your fingers hurt. You've put together an important piece for someone who wants it yesterday. You're sure the copy is good — the various elements read well. Unfortunately, you can't afford the luxury of letting the piece marinate by putting it aside for a day or two for leisurely review and touch-up revision.

In the early days, computers sported a so-called readability feature, and software like RightWriter and Grammatik existed to measure readability. Wouldn't it be nice to be able to check your copy immediately for readability? To have some way of making sure it is aimed at the intended audience? A completely portable yardstick for measuring reading ease?

The 'Fog Index'
Wait a minute! There is just such a formula: Robert Gunning's largely forgotten "Fog Index." It's an easy-to-remember way of determining readability. In 1944, Gunning, a 36-year-old Ohio editor, quit his job and started a consulting business still not listed in the government's index of occupations. The specialty of Robert Gunning Associates was counseling in clear writing — showing businesses how they could improve the readability of their communications.

Gunning's clients included large corporations like the Standard Oil Co. and General Motors, United Press International, and newspapers such as the Louisville Courier-Journal, Hartford Courant, Washington Star, and Wall Street Journal, whose legendary editor Bernard Kilgore became a disciple.

Gunning preached what most writers had long known — that certain factors played a part in readability: first and foremost, average sentence length in words, with the proportion of simple sentences, strong verb forms, familiar words, abstract words, long words and personal references all playing strong supporting roles.

Until that time, readability measurement had been the exclusive province of educators. But their formulas were complicated and required the laborious counting of certain not easily discerned factors. Many systems — even the highly touted yardsticks of readability guru Rudolph Flesch — employed four-decimal-place multipliers that were difficult to remember and gave a false sense of scientific accuracy.

The two key elements
Gunning discovered that only two qualities were critical to determining readability:

- The average number of words in sentences, and
- The percentage of "hard" words that might cause a reader to stumble.

In his 1952 book *The Technique of Clear Writing*, he described how to apply his innovative "Fog Index," which is ideal for any kind of copy. It's simple to calculate and easy to carry in your head.

1. Count the number of words in successive sentences.
In a long piece, take several 100-word samples distributed evenly throughout. (Stop the sentence count with the sentence that ends nearest each 100-word total.) Divide the total number of words in each sample by the number of sentences. This yields the average sentence length of the copy.

2. Count the number of words of three syllables or more per 100 words.
Don't count proper names, word combinations of short words (i.e., bookkeeper, manpower, etc.) or three-syllable plural or past-tense verb forms as a result of adding -ed or -es (i.e., created or trespasses). This figure is the percentage of "hard" words in the copy.

3. Add these two numbers and multiply the result by 0.4.
This yields the Fog Index, which correlates exactly with school grade reading levels as determined by the McCall-Crabbs: Standard Test Lessons in Reading. Thus, if your copy is addressed to a hypothetical audience with a fifth-grade educational level, the Fog Index of the tested copy should be no higher than 5.

The following table compares the Fog Index with reading levels by grade.

Fog Index Reading Level By Grade
17 College graduate
16 College senior
15 College junior
14 College sophomore
13 College freshman

—DANGERLINE—
12 High school senior
11 High school junior

— EASY READING BELOW THIS LINE —
10 High school sophomore
9 High school freshman
8 8th grade
7 7th grade
6 6th grade
5 5th grade

Two words of caution: A "sentence" in Gunning's terms is not always the distance between a capital letter and a period, which makes it ideal for the punchy writing of direct mail copy.

Units of thought (marked off by semicolons, colons, dashes or ellipsis points) are treated as sentences and so are independent clauses. An independent clause (sometimes called a main clause) is a group of words that make a complete statement, no matter what punctuation comes before or after. Such a clause can stand as a regular sentence, beginning with a capital letter and ending with a period. Or several independent clauses may be separated by semicolons or commas.

(For example, J.N. Hook's parody of Julius Caesar in his *Guide to Good Writing* contains three independent clauses: "She came, I saw, she conquered.")

What is a "word" sometimes causes trouble, too. In applying the Fog Index, we may define a word as anything with white space on either side of it.

The number 13

If your copy tests 13 or more, you are beyond Gunning's danger line of reading difficulty, and your readers are likely to find what you have written to be heavy going.

After measuring the readability of magazines, Gunning discovered a correlation between a magazine's circulation and his Fog Index. Magazines with the highest mass appeal had the lowest average sentence length and the lowest percentage of difficult words.

Gunning also applied his formula to books and found a direct relationship between a low Fog Index and popularity. Still in print, Margaret Mitchell's best-selling *Gone with the Wind* has a 6th-grade reading level. *Peyton Place* also scores a 6.

Mickey Spillane's hard-boiled novels come in at 5, as do the works of Harold Robbins. J.D. Salinger, John Cheever and Truman Capote all average a Fog Index of 7, not markedly lower than Somerset Maugham, Sinclair Lewis or Ernest Hemingway.

Harper Lee's prize-winning novel *To Kill a Mockingbird* has a Fog Index of 5, which must account for its astonishing continuing sales in the millions and its presence on nearly every school reading list.

Heavy slogging

Applying his formula, Gunning gave English poet John Milton a Fog Index of 26. This was 11 points higher than Lincoln's Gettysburg Address, which came in at 15.

Gunning believed that 16 to 20 words was a good average word count for sentences in newspaper articles.

The benefits of a low Fog Index

A low Fog Index for copy you have written is merely an assurance that the piece can be easily read by the widest audience — that readers of it will be induced to move along from one sentence to the next without stumbling and without excessive demands on their attention.

The Fog Index cannot make you or anyone a great writer. Rather it is a measure of complexity in writing — for determining whether a piece of copy is geared to its intended audience.

The Fog Index is a measuring tool, but only for use after you have written, not as a pattern before you write.

"Good writing must be alive," Gunning advised. "Don't kill it with a system."

About Robert Scott
Bob Scott and I met when we were book club directors at Macmillan in the late 1960s. After leaving Macmillan, Bob became publisher at Stoeger Publishing Co. At that time, it was the publishing arm of a gun company whose list had fewer than 10 titles on guns and shooting. In the short space of a couple of years, Bob boosted Stoeger's list to a hundred titles and broadened the areas of interest to include fishing, camping, pets, the outdoors and the environment. The Stoeger crown jewel was the annual Shooter's Bible.

Scott is the author of *Office at Home* (Scribner's, 1985), one of the first books to anticipate the working-from-home revolution. For 18 years, Bob was a pro bono instructor in the Writer's Digest School, teaching correspondence courses in basic and advanced nonfiction writing and conducting a workshop in book-proposal writing and book marketing. For a number of years Bob was the copy editor for my wife Peggy's and my newsletter, *WHO'S MAILING WHAT!*, where this essay on Gunning's Fog Index first appeared.

A jack-of-all-trades and master of most of them, Bob Scott is still going strong at the age of 95 as an occasional ghost publishing consultant and literary agent. He's also a working journalist, writing feature articles on local history for a Westchester weekly newspaper, *The Westchester Guardian*. His blog, *Postscripts*, is described as "an online large print magazine offering a pastiche of articles on current affairs, history, technics, opinion, advice, humor and trivia" and includes a regular department, "The Writing Clinic." The blog's address is www.notorc.blogspot.com.

....

Takeaways to Consider

• Users of Robert Gunning's Fog Index should recognize two things: First, reading ease isn't only the ease of understanding words, phrases and sentences. There's also the problem of how sentences relate to one another in a paragraph and how the paragraphs themselves relate. Any measure of word- or sentence-difficulty certainly correlates with overall reading difficulty, but it's no exaggeration to say that there are writers who use simple words and write short sentences, yet whose copy isn't a pleasure to read.

• The Fog Index really is related to comprehensibility. It's not necessarily about genuine readability — the property of copy that makes a reader want to keep on reading. Making something easier to read doesn't always make it more interesting or more desirable to read. Using shorter sentences and simpler words indeed does yield copy comprehensible to a wider audience, but an increase in comprehensibility will not of itself make for greater readability.

• It's easy enough for writers to raise the comprehensibility of their copy by training themselves to write in short bursts and to choose less complicated words. Writing truly readable copy is quite another matter and less easily learned — you must cultivate an ear for the rhythms of the rich language that is English. Effective copy is not only clear and reads easily, but it also will sound right. In editing your copy (and it's rare copy indeed that cannot be made better with one more revision), you should read not only for sense, but for euphony — the agreeableness of what you've written and its pleasurable effect on the ear (and thus on the eye). In short, try listening to your copy, even going so far as playing it back to yourself on a tape recorder.

• A good writer takes the problem of writing seriously and attempts to marry comprehensibility and readability. It's not easy to develop and maintain the skill of simple writing while at the same time keeping an ear open for the aptness of phrase and sentence. Only then will you succeed at the art that none of us will ever fully master — using the tools and the building blocks in the storehouse of language to create a deceptively simple structure of complex thoughts and emotions to entice readers and move them to action. The paradox is, of course, that if the simplicity is obvious, you've failed.

CHAPTER 21

Masters of Obfuscation

A world of sleazy lawyers in cahoots with marketers

Throughout *WRITE EVERYTHING RIGHT!* you will find a slew of tested, proven rules to make what you write easier for your readers to understand and stay interested. However, in the world of marketing, legions of writers spend their lives creating stuff they hope nobody will read.

Mostly these sleaze-meisters are lawyers.

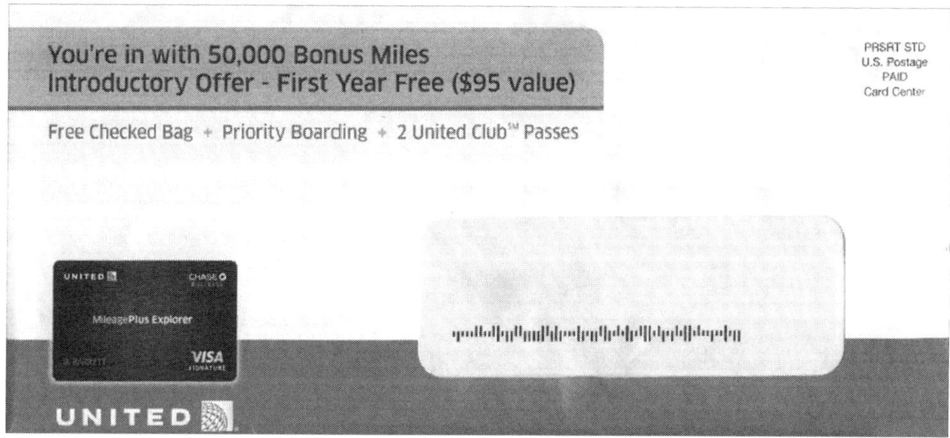

The outer envelope of a joint direct mail promotion from United Airlines and Chase Bank offering a MileagePlus Visa card.

For example, take this direct mail offer for a MileagePlus Visa card from United Airlines and Chase Bank. Stuffed in the envelope was a page full of CYA (cover-your arse) disclaimers, negating the promises mentioned on the envelope.

What's going on is a textbook example of how lawyers and complicit marketers can come up with a way to tell customers they can be screwed with absolutely no recourse. This stuff is typical of the entire financial services industry. The trick: make it so impossibly difficult to comprehend nobody will bother to read the thing.

Most of us receive millions of words a year by these scallywags, who work for manufacturers, marketers, the financial services industry, pharmaceutical companies and the like.

United Airlines-Chase Bank
Mileage Plus Explorer Visa

Purposely Unreadable Disclaimers

Column: 7-point gray sans serif type 190 characters wide

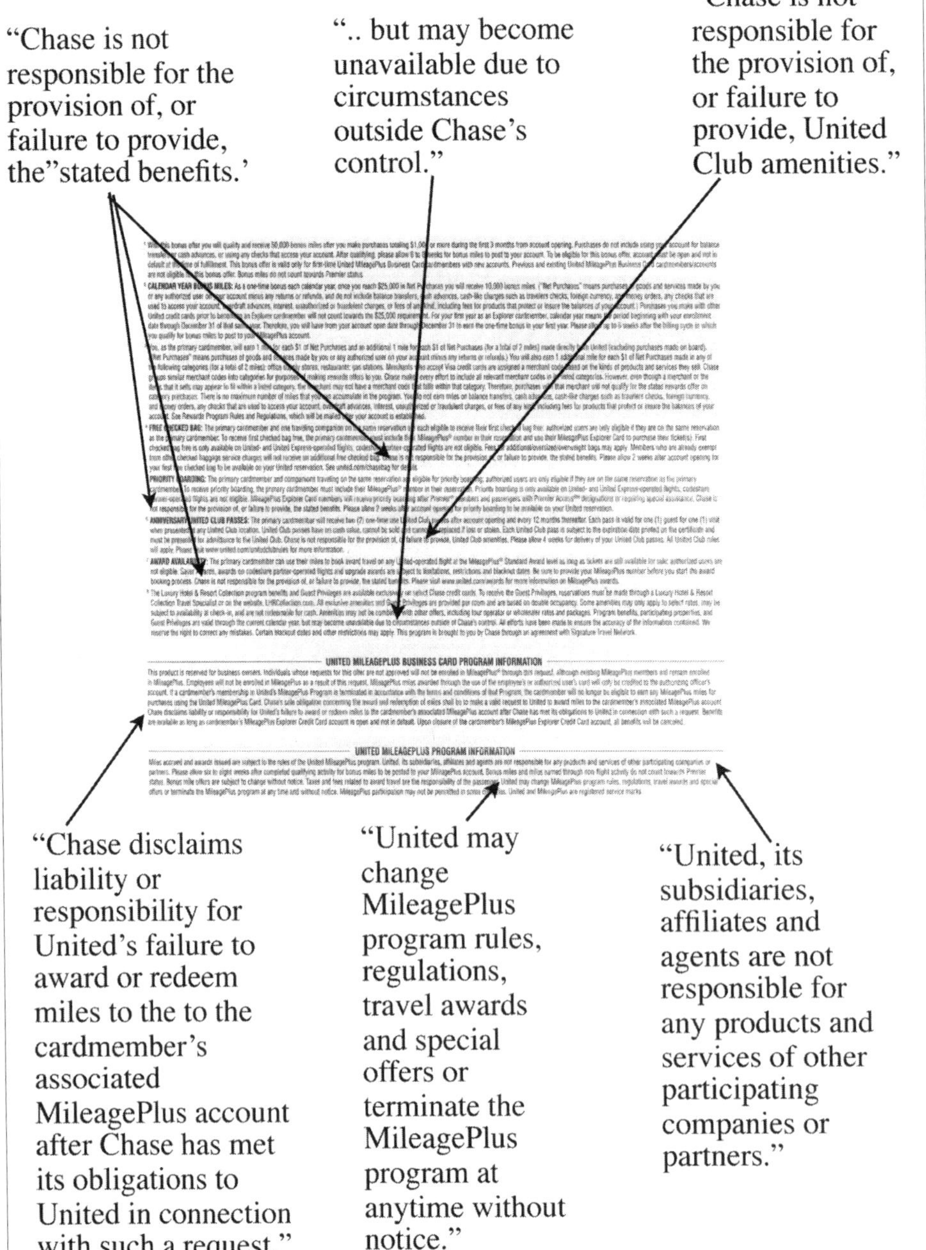

"Chase is not responsible for the provision of, or failure to provide, the"stated benefits.'
".. but may become unavailable due to circumstances outside Chase's control."
"Chase is not responsible for the provision of, or failure to provide, United Club amenities."
UNITED MILEAGEPLUS BUSINESS CARD PROGRAM INFORMATION
UNITED MILEAGEPLUS PROGRAM INFORMATION
"Chase disclaims liability or responsibility for United's failure to award or redeem miles to the to the cardmember's associated MileagePlus account after Chase has met its obligations to United in connection with such a request."
"United may change MileagePlus program rules, regulations, travel awards and special offers or terminate the MileagePlus program at anytime without notice."
"United, its subsidiaries, affiliates and agents are not responsible for any products and services of other participating companies or partners."

If you want to obfuscate, here are the rules to break

• "Column width: 35 to 55 characters is a good target range. Ten or eleven point is generally most readable on a column width of about a third of a page." —*Ed Elliott* (NOTE: The columns in the UAL-Chase disclaimer are 190 characters wide.)

• "Type smaller than 9-point is difficult for most people to read." *—David Ogilvy* (NOTE: The disclaimer copy is 7-point. Maybe smaller.)

• On the computer screen, iPad or smartphone, 9-point type is the equivalent to 7-point type or smaller in print.

• "Avoid gray walls of type." *—David Ogilvy*

• Want to make copy tough to read? Set it in gray sans serif type. The lighter the gray the more impossible to read.

• "Serif type in body copy in print is easier to read than sans serif." *—David Ogilvy*

• Revisit "Why Johnny Can't Read" *(Chapter 16)* to read about the evils of sans serif type in print.

All I could think of when suffering through this series of disclaimers was the day the writer dies after a lifetime of creating crap a maggot would gag on. Imagine being greeted at the pearly gates by St. Peter and trying to put a positive spin on a truly squalid career before being introduced to God.

A final note about financial services

The word "services" (as in "financial services") reminds me of a story told by the late Barry Gray, the mellifluous-voiced fixture on New York talk radio for 50 years.

On a late-night broadcast, Gray did a riff on the boyhood of the great American humorist and trick rope artist Will Rogers and the meaning of the word "service."

When Rogers was 10 years old, he was sitting on the split-rail fence of his family's 400-acre spread located on the shore of Lake Oologah, Okla. He looked up and saw an immense, blue-ribbon-prize bull from the adjoining ranch being led across his property. Its destination was the adjacent ranch where he was scheduled to service a prize heifer.

"Since then, every time I hear the word 'service,'" Rogers said years later, "I know somebody is going to get screwed."

Takeaways to Consider

• A legion of writers spend their lives creating stuff they hope nobody will read.

• Mostly these sleaze-meisters are lawyers who work for manufacturers, marketers, financial services companies, pharmaceutical companies and the like.

• If you want to be a world-class obfuscator, know the rules of communication in print and then break them.

CHAPTER 22

Your Résumé and Chartres Cathedral

Welcome to the 800-year-old craft of creating your résumé mailing

Chartres, France, June 15, 1194 — Lightning struck, kindled a huge fire and Chartres Cathedral burned to the ground. The only elements intact were the façade, west towers and the crypt.

For the town and community of Chartres this was a catastrophe. The very symbol of the city was in ruins. Worse, lost for all time was one of Christianity's holiest relics — the robe believed to have been worn by Mary when she gave birth to Jesus Christ.

The Bishop of Chartres, Renaud de Mouçon, wanted to start rebuilding immediately. But the townspeople, devastated by the huge loss, had no stomach for such an undertaking. Mary's robe was not only holy, but also had the mystical aura of being the city's amulet — or good luck charm. It kept everybody safe. To the residents of Chartres, rebuilding was a non-starter.

A couple of days after the fire, Bishop de Mouçon was at the smoking ruins delivering a passionate plea for rebuilding to a small collection of villagers. Suddenly a procession of monks, nuns and priests appeared, slowly marching up through the smoke from the crypt bearing the reliquary with Mary's robe intact. It was saved!

To Renaud de Mouçon and the God-fearing folk of Chartres this was a sign from the Almighty the cathedral must be rebuilt. The bishop launched a furious letter-writing campaign to French nobility and rich people all over Europe. In addition, he cut a deal with Richard the Lion Hearted (with whom France was at war) enabling him to send fundraising mailings into England.

The rich noble families of France and England responded with cash and gifts. So did the many guilds of workers, the equivalent of unions back then — shoemakers, wheelwrights, bankers, vintners, coopers, furriers, bankers, etc.

Chartres was rebuilt bigger and better than before.

As an eternal "thank you," the donors' portraits and coats of arms were included in the magnificent stained glass windows of the new Chartres, where you can see them today. This was the very first instance of direct mail marketing, unless one of the Dead Sea scrolls turns out to be a sales letter.

800-plus years of testing for success

Over the following 800 years a vast canon of direct mail know-how has been built up — the art, science and arithmetic of intimate, one-to-one communications.

- In the 16th century, the Venetians sold books via direct mail offerings.

- The British in the 17th century sent catalogs throughout the empire selling seeds, fine China and books.

- Benjamin Franklin used direct mail to sell his library in the 18th century. A sidebar: it was Franklin who created the very first mail order guarantee: "Those persons who live remote, by sending their orders and money to said B. Franklin, may depend on the same justice as if present."

- Finally, in the late 19th century Sears and Montgomery Ward put the direct mail marketing show on the road. Their massive catalogs went to every corner of America. Even the most distant frontier families could have the equivalent of a fully stocked general store on their shelves and access to the merchandise.

How the 800-year-old technique was used in 1980

In the mid-1970s, we lived next door to a couple who regularly watched the Rev. Robert Schuller's *Hour of Power*. This Sunday morning televangelism program was broadcast in all 50 states. Rev. Schuller had an Edifice Complex and contracted for the Crystal Cathedral — a soaring architectural masterpiece designed by Philip Johnson and John Burgee. To raise money, Schuller's organization used on-air solicitations and sent out direct mailings to his massive list of contributors. The offer: buy a window for (as I recall) $15.

The Crystal Cathedral, Garden Grove, Calif.

One day with great pride, my neighbor showed me a handsome inscribed Plexiglas memento. It was a "thank you" from Dr. Schuller's organization for the gift of a window for the Crystal Cathedral.

When the Crystal Cathedral was dedicated in 1980, each of the 10,664 windows, the struts supporting the windows and the 2,800 seats were all inscribed with the names of donors.

Imagine! The very same fundraising technique used to rebuild Chartres worked like gangbusters 800 years later!

Direct marketing: the business of changing behavior over distance

If a ransom note results in the promise of a $2 million payment in return for freeing the hostage, the kidnapper (or the kidnapper's copywriter) changed behavior.

If your direct mail package — or e-mail résumé — to a recruiter results in your being contacted for an interview, you have changed behavior.

If you hear nothing back, nothing is changed. Your effort is a failure.

Welcome to direct marketing!

Takeaways to Consider

• Direct mail/direct marketing is a discipline going back more than 800 years.

• No other advertising medium can claim 800+ years of testing what works and what does not.

• The object of your résumé mailing — or your e-mailed résumé — is to change behavior and persuade a recruiter to respond with an invitation to an interview.

• If you do not hear back, your attempt to sell yourself is a failure.

CHAPTER 23

Your Résumé: "Can You Add Value?"

Never send a résumé by itself. Send a sales team!
"It's still really hard to find that candidate for that one critical position. The average engineer now isn't just an engineer, but must also have a business understanding and language skills." *—Christoffer Ellehuus, Managing Director, Corporate Executive Board*

Tom Friedman on getting a job
It is best summed up by the mantra from the Harvard education expert Tony Wagner that the world doesn't care anymore what you know; all it cares "is what you can do with what you know."

And since jobs are evolving so quickly, with so many new tools, a bachelor's degree is no longer considered an adequate proxy by employers for your ability to do a particular job — and, therefore, be hired.

So, more employers are designing their own tests to measure applicants' skills. And they increasingly don't care how those skills were acquired: home schooling, an online university, a massive open online course, or Yale.

They just want to know one thing: Can you add value? *—Tom Friedman, The New York Times*

....

Face it.

Your résumé mailings to prospective employers may be the most important documents you will ever create. If you do get the interview and land the job, you will be on a learning curve and career trajectory. It could determine what happens for the rest of your life.

The odds suck
According to Chris Ellehuus, in all fields when a job is listed, an average of 118 applications are submitted. In terms of odds, your chances of getting a job against 118 applicants are less than 1 percent — 0.0085 percent to be exact.

To be invited to an interview, your pitch to a recruiter — whether snail mail or e-mail — must break through the clutter.

Your résumé has a 30-second life span
Ryan Guina is founder of cashmoneylife.com and author of *Creating the Ultimate Resume — 34 Epic Tips*. He reveals how the 50 to 150 résumés per job opening are dealt with in three rounds.

- **Round 1:** Guina spends 30 to 60 seconds on each résumé. "The mass-marketed résumés and obvious skills-to-job mismatches" are summarily eliminated. The applicant who sends in an all-purpose, one-size-fits all résumé with no reference to the specifics of the job is dead on arrival.

- **Round 2:** The surviving 40 [percent] to 50 percent are scanned to see how well the candidates matched the job requirements. The rating process begins.

- **Round 3**: The highest-rated résumés from Round 2 are sent on to a colleague for a second opinion. Then the top five are called in for interviews.

Malcolm Decker on the direct mail package
I have known Malcolm Decker for close to 40 years. He is the consummate direct marketer, copywriter and designer.

A long time ago, I asked him to jot down his thoughts on creating a direct mail package. His short essay is a classic and directly relates to what a job candidate must send to a recruiter.

Below are the lede paragraphs of Decker's commentary on direct mail and the three essential elements: the envelope (or the subject line of an e-mail message), a letter and a circular or brochure.

Mal Decker on the "sales team"
The direct mail package — especially a full-dress package — is a sales team:

- First the envelope knocks on the door to see if anyone's home.

- Then the letter — the main salesman — takes over. Once the envelope is opened, the letter is the most important member of the team. It sells soft or it sells hard. It spins yarns or it spouts facts. It's long (but never long-winded) or it's pithy. However it comes on, it's loaded with customer benefits … Customer Benefits … CUSTOMER BENEFITS.

- Next the demonstrator — the folder or brochure — goes to work. Like the letter, it can stand on its own. But it's most effective when it demonstrates in graphics what the letter can only say in words. It should convince the reader in images that everything the letter said is true.

With a résumé mailing, the résumé itself is the demonstrator. It demonstrates *you.*

The letter is key
Several years ago, I sat next to a high-powered Wall Street recruiter and we got talking about résumé submissions. I asked her whether or not it mattered if a candidate included a cover letter with the résumé.

"Put it this way," she retorted. "If there's no cover letter, I don't look at the résumé."

This is why Mal Decker calls the direct mail package "a sales team" and why the letter is the main salesman.

Your résumé mailing must change behavior
Changing behavior means persuading the recruiter to pull you out of the big pile and move you to the select group of "A" candidates.

When creating direct mail you start with the envelope — the carrier of your message. *(See Chapter 24 on how to create an envelope.)*

Once the envelope is opened — or the e-mail clicked on — you have arrived at the inner sanctum of the reader. You will never get any closer until you are face-to-face.

I was in Hong Kong with Stan Rapp, legendary founder of the Rapp & Collins Agency and co-author of *M*axi-Marketing: The New Direction in Advertising, Promotion and Marketing Strategy. It was there he came up with the perfect definition of direct marketing: "intimate advertising."

You are among the "in crowd"
Your message arrives in a mailbox or e-mail in-box in select company. To be sure you're in competition with junk mail and spam. But also among the snail mail or e-mail are memos, business proposals, job offers, stock tips and invitations — the entire gamut of deeply personal and often emotional correspondence.

Here you are as one writer given the opportunity to persuade one reader to do something. In the case of a résumé mailing, you are delivering a pitch to get yourself hired.

What arrives on the recruiter's desk must damn well be interesting. If stuffed with platitudes and corporate-speak, your chances of a response are deader than Kelsey's nuts.

The envelope — or e-mail — has been opened. Now what?
These are the elements you have to work with:

- Letter
- Circular/brochure/résumé

Three kinds of copy
In school, our English teachers taught us the three points of view or "persons" in prose:

- First person ("I," "me," "we" or "us")
- Second person ("you" — singular or plural)
- Third person ("he," "she," "they" or "it")

One of my early mentors was Walter Weintz (pronounced "wents"), former circulation director of *Reader's Digest* and later, proprietor of a direct marketing agency he named for himself. Walter explained it with much more simplicity — as "you" copy, "me" copy and "it" copy.

- **"You" copy** is the most important in direct marketing. It is found in the letter where the writer is talking intimately to "you," the reader. This is where the writer can get emotional about "you" — your fears, your wants, your loves, your wishes, your salvation, your need for a person to "add value."

- **"It" copy** is in the circular or brochure where "it" — the product or service being sold — is described and pictured. When applying for a job, the résumé is the "it" copy. In this case the "it" is you — the candidate — your employment history, contact information, etc.

• **"Me" copy** turns up in two places:
—It can show up in your letter. Example: "Here's what I will do for you and your company."
—If you use testimonials from others — such as those in Francine's résumé *(See Chapter 25)* — you'll get "I" and "me" copy. Example: "I've known Louise for seven years and she reported to me from 2010-2012."

Which element will the prospect look at first?
Seattle direct marketer Bob Hacker has pointed out people process information two ways:

• **Rationally and analytically.** Left-brainers. These are folks who want to know the nitty-gritty specifics and data about the candidate. They will reach for the résumé first.

• **Irrationally and emotionally.** Right-brain people — who rely primarily on the emotional and irrational approach — will read the letter first. This tells the recruiter what to look for in the accompanying résumé and why you are the perfect fit for the position being offered.

You are flying blind
As the writer/designer (and job applicant), you have no clue whether a left- or right-brain person will open your envelope.

You do know the right-brainer — the emotional/irrational person — will go for the letter first in hopes of getting to know you personally.

The left-brain reader will go for the résumé in order to scan your job history to see the possibility of a mesh.

Make it easy. Use different type styles
If all the pieces in your mailing are printed in the same typeface, the difference between the résumé and the letter is not immediately obvious.

For this reason, direct mail professionals use different fonts.

Your résumé
Your résumé/circular/brochure is your mass communication. Like a newspaper or magazine, it goes to everybody. My suggestion: use serif font (e.g., Times, Times New Roman, etc.) on snail mail versions. Use sans serif (e.g. Verdana, Helvetica) on your e-mail efforts.

The letter
This may seem corny, but I prefer old-fashioned Courier type. It has warmth and a personal feel to it, as though the writer pounded each individual letter out on an old office Remington.

Obviously the reader knows your submission was written on a computer. But as the great freelancer Bill Jayme said, "In the marketplace, as in theater, there is indeed a factor at work called 'the willing suspension of disbelief.'"

The point is you have made an easy choice for your right-brain vs. left-brain readers. It's obvious which is the letter and which the résumé. It may be a small thing, but people appreciate not having their time wasted.

How to fold the elements
Again, make it easy for your reader.

Fold your letter and brochure with the type facing out, so it's immediately obvious which piece is which. I suggest you not staple the letter to the résumé. These are two separate documents. Let the recruiter do the stapling or paper clipping.

Most direct mail practitioners stuff the envelope with the top of the letter — your logo and date — facing out under the flap. When people receive an envelope in the mail, they generally expect a letter. And using this fold, the letter is the first thing your prospect sees after slitting the envelope.

Takeaways to Consider

- Direct mail is "intimate advertising."

- All résumés look pretty much alike.

- The way to make yours stand out is with a letter or short note pointing out how your experience in the résumé directly relates to the position to be filled.

- When selling something by direct mail — product, service or yourself — you have several elements to work with: envelope, résumé/circular and letter.

- Everybody is either right-brain or left-brain, which means you have no way of knowing which element in your mailing the addressee will reach for first.

CHAPTER 24

Your Résumé: Importance of the Envelope

The envelope and subject line
In direct mail, think of the envelope as the messenger to put your communiqué into the hands of your reader.

If the messenger is untidy, unfriendly or appears irrelevant, it will get as far as the wastebasket.

Same thing with e-mail. When a message arrives in your in-box, it is guaranteed to change your behavior. It forces you to do one of two things:

- Open and read it

— or —

- Delete it

Either way, the sender has made you change your behavior.

An afterthought?
A writer can spend hours sweating over an e-mail message — working to achieve perfection. When it's finally ready, many writers crank out any old subject line and click *Send.*

Trouble is this subject line is in direct competition with hundreds of others in the digital inbox. Worse, if the subject line is not carefully crafted, it hits a spam filter and is not seen by the reader for days or perhaps never seen at all.

In short, never let your subject line be an afterthought.

Dr. Siegfried Vogele's 5 truths about advertising mail envelopes
One of the grand characters of direct marketing — and a consummate professional — was the late "Rocket" Ray Jutkins. For Ray, pure happiness was hopping aboard his Harley-Davidson and tearing across the American West, his white beard blowing the wind. Many years ago he alerted my readers to Dr. Siegfried Vogele, author of the *Handbook of Direct Mail: The Dialogue Method of Direct Written Sales Communication.*

Here is Dr. Vogele on the subject of envelopes:

1. **People first look at their name.** To see if it is correctly spelled. If the initials and title are right, it is for them!

2. **The second thing people look at is the teaser copy.** Especially the teaser copy closest to their name. And then teaser copy elsewhere on the envelope.

3. The third thing people do is look at who sent them this piece of mail. What person, company or organization sent me this piece of advertising mail? This shows how important the upper left area of the envelope — the "corner-card" — of your ad mail envelope is.

4. Next what postage and how it is applied. Most often live stamps get the most attention... and meter mail gets the least attention.

5. And the fifth thing people do is turn your envelope over. Three out of four people who touch your ad mail envelope will turn it over before opening.

What does all this say? It says the following needs to be answered on your envelope:

• Is this ad mail package for me?
• What is it all about?
• And, who is it from?

'Rocket Ray' Jutkins on the four actions people will take when they receive mail

1. They open it immediately. It's important. It's interesting. Something about it gets their attention immediately and they open it at once.

2. Or, they put it in the stack to read nights and weekends. It's interesting, but it's not important. It can wait.

3. They route it to somebody else. They circulate it to another. They pass it on. It's not for them — it's for someone else. And this happens both at home as well as in the office.

4. They round file it. They toss it ... trash it. The wastebasket. The bin. They throw it away.

Note: What's most interesting is the decision to take one of these four actions — read it, stack it, route it or toss it — takes place in just two or three seconds per piece of mail. This says, "You better be good ... and it better be interesting!"

"All direct mail is opened over the waste basket." —*Leah Pierce, freelancer*

Should replies to a recruiter be sent via snail mail or e-mail?

Do what the job announcement says. If e-mail is requested, send e-mail. If a street address is given, use snail mail.

Being an old junk mail hand, I prefer print. E-mail can be inadvertently deleted or end up in a spam file. A physical snail mail envelope must be dealt with by hand. It is either opened or thrown out.

The envelope

"The envelope has two purposes and two purposes only," said freelancer Herschell

Gordon Lewis. "One: to get itself opened. Two: to keep the contents from spilling into the street."

What does the envelope look like? Will it stand out from a crowded mailbox or office inbox?

If sending e-mail, will your subject line pop out from all the spam, scams and promotional junk in the reader's digital in-box?

How important is the envelope — or e-mail subject line — anyway?

My envelope epiphany …

Many years ago I got a request from a lawyer to be an expert witness on behalf of a major publisher of health and fitness books and magazines. The client was facing a nasty lawsuit.

For the test mailing of a diet book, the art director came up with a revolting photograph — a montage of four self-portraits of a stark-naked elderly man in various stages of weight loss from gross fat and revolting to simply revolting. The photographer-model was paid a royalty for x-many usages.

The fact I was grossed out mattered not. The test mailing was a door buster, and the publisher went back to press and mailed out millions. He was about to rake in millions when the photographer-model surfaced and claimed the publisher had not paid him royalties for the massive rollout.

Oops

It was inadvertent, said the publisher. (I believed him; these are scrupulously honest people.) The guy sued the client for theft of copyright. He wanted all the money spent on the mailings (including postage), all the revenue generated from the mailing (including list rental income), all revenues from book sales and a stiff penalty to boot.

The lawyers came to me as a supposed guru in the world of junk mail.

The challenge

The lawyers' instructions to me: assign a percentage of importance to each element of this direct mail package:

- outside envelope
- letter
- circular/brochure
- extra inserts
- reply mechanism

It was their theory I would assign maybe 20 percent of the importance to the brochure. Since this guy's naked photos took up 1/20th or 5 percent of the brochure and they could offer paying 5 percent of 20 percent or 1 percent of the cost of the mailing as the penalty plus the royalties due.

My client and the naked, fat, old photographer-model reached a settlement before they went to court, but I was paid for the analysis. It was a fascinating challenge.

Assigning importance to each element of a mailing is not easy, because everything shifts dramatically depending on when you do the analysis.

The all-important envelope (or e-mail subject line)
In thinking through the makeup of the mailing, I had an epiphany. Quite simply, when it arrives, the outside envelope represents 100 percent of the effort.

If the envelope is trashed without being opened (or immediately deleted from the digital inbox) the entire mailing — 100 percent — is lost.

Thus at the point of arrival, the envelope (or e-mail subject line) is 100 percent of the mailing. Once opened, the value of the envelope drops to 0 percent as the other elements take over.

The same is true for the headline on an advertisement, the title of a book, whitepaper or special report — and the subject line of a memo or e-mail message.

If this element is not compelling, the chances of you turning a prospect into a reader are slim to none. As freelancer Malcolm Decker wrote, "Your envelope stands between you and orders."

What should your envelope look like?
When mailing into the business arena, no rule exists on who opens the envelope. It may be the addressee. It may be an assistant. It may be an envelope-slitting machine in the mailroom, so all envelopes are delivered open.

Two piles of mail
"Remember people sort their mail into two piles — the A pile and the B pile," wrote the late copywriter Gary Halbert. "Your goal is to get your envelope into the A pile."

The "A" pile is the important stuff to deal with first. Everything relegated to the "B" pile can wait.

Envelope quality
Let's say a high-quality ivory or linen envelope arrives with an address label affixed to the front and a return-address label pasted in the upper left corner.

It won't make the A pile. It looks tacky. The sender would be perceived as a slob.

To get a mailing into the A pile, Halbert insisted you must never use a window envelope or a stick-on label. Instead, the name and address should be computer-printed or typewriter-typed on the front of a plain, closed-face (no-window) envelope.

For example, a live postage stamp seems more personal than metered postage (indicia), which indicates a stack of envelopes went through a high-speed machine. And a printed indicia screams junk mail.

What's more, many direct mail experts not only use a "live" postage stamp on their mailings, but also make sure the stamps are affixed ever so slightly atilt, so they look hand-applied.

"Anything to make the mailing look like a human hand touched it," said the great Canadian designer Ted Kikoler, "may well increase response."

Gary Halbert believed the only proper copy for the cornercard — the upper left corner — is the name (or company name) of the sender and the return address.

I believe it's okay to sign your name small in the upper left corner above the return address to let the addressee know it passed through the hands of the person who sent it.

Should envelope copy be used?

With direct mail advertising, a teaser on the envelope is pretty much de rigueur — accepted practice. The exception: when the copywriter wants it to look like a First Class business or personal letter.

For example, in 1974 freelance writer Martin Conroy wrote the famous "Two Young Men ..." letter for *The Wall Street Journal*. It was the most successful advertisement in the history of the world. The mailing ran virtually unchanged for more than 30 years and brought in more than $1 billion in subscription revenue. *(See the full story and read the letter in Chapter 40.)*

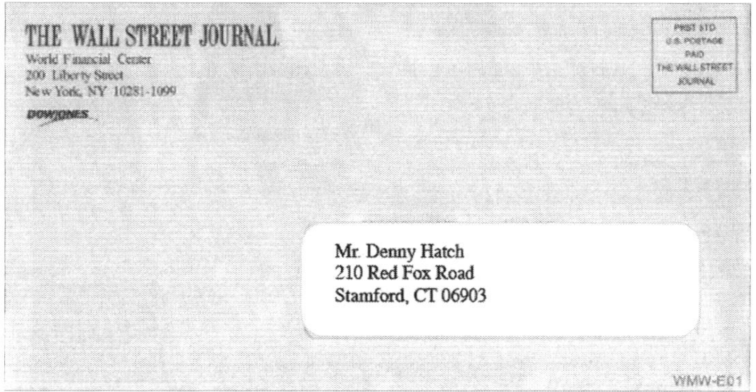

Martin Conroy determined no teaser copy was necessary. The cornercard with *The Wall Street Journal* logo in large type and address was sufficient to get it opened. A teaser might cheapen the look — junk it up.

The 100 percent open rate

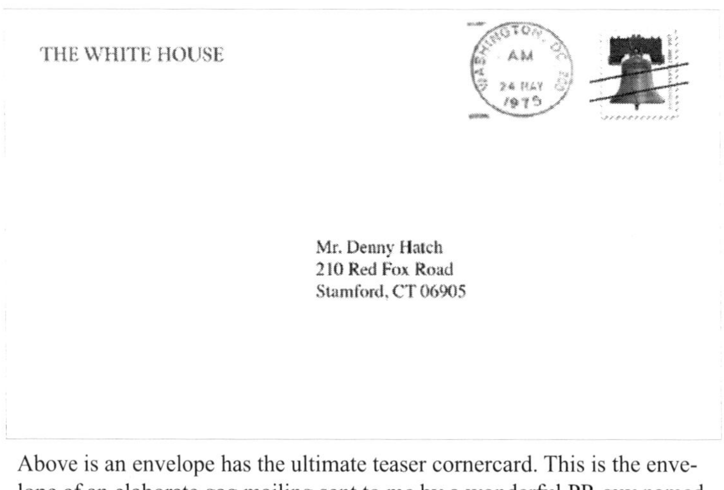

Above is an envelope has the ultimate teaser cornercard. This is the envelope of an elaborate gag mailing sent to me by a wonderful PR guy named Tom Baskind — then of CBS Publications. You bet we opened it!

I was told at the time stationery with the royal blue cornercard and letterhead was easy to obtain. It is in White House bedrooms for guests to use as well as for the president's staff. If an envelope with an apple-green cornercard showed up in the mailbox, it was from the President.

Bill Jayme loved creating intriguing envelopes to stop people in their tracks. Here's one for *Esquire*:

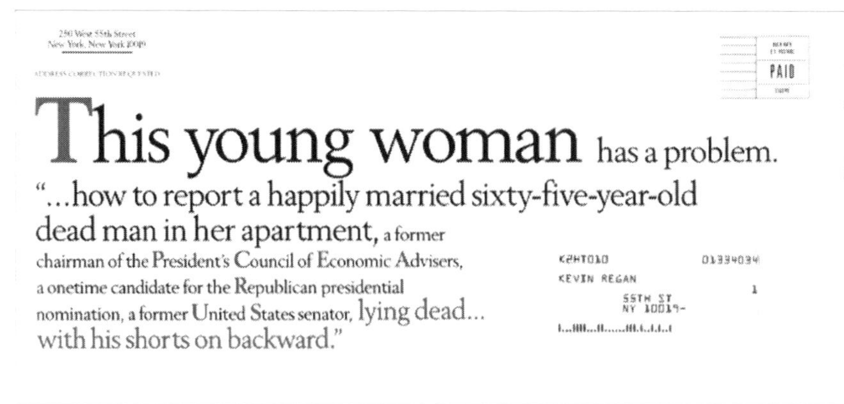

The envelope copy (in case the copy in the reproduction is not clear):

> This young woman has a problem.
> "... how to report a happily married sixty-five-year-old
> dead man in her apartment, a former
> chairman of the **P**resident's **C**ouncil of **E**conomic **A**dvisors,
> a onetime candidate for the **R**epublican presidential
> nomination, a former **U**nited **S**tates senator, lying dead ...
> with his shorts on backward."

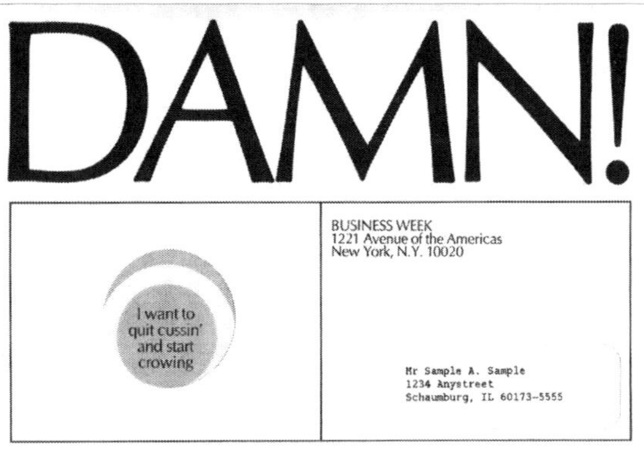

This *Business Week* subscription offer by Jayme-Ratalahti was out in the mail. On a golf course, a guy yelled over to *Business Week* CEO Harold McGraw, "Hey, Harold! I got a junk mailing from you with profanity on the envelope!" McGraw-the-chicken-hearted ordered it quashed, even though it was bringing in a slew of new subscribers.

Junk mail: an aside

Bill Jayme, by the way, loved the term "junk mail" and used it frequently at a time when prissy purists in the direct marketing industry would throw hissy fits when anyone used the "J" word.

"Everybody loves junk," Jayme countered.

> After all, Wall Street loves junk bonds. Automobile collectors love junkyards where they pick up parts. Antique collectors love junk shops. Who among us doesn't love to take a bunch of junk fiction along on vacation? And what's a Chinese fisherman without his j--k? Of course, Heikki and I create upscale junk mail. We spell it junque.

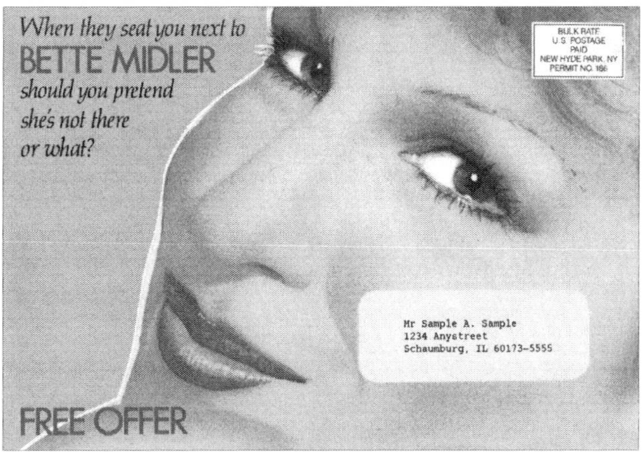

Another favorite of mine by Jayme-Ratalahti

Mel Martin's fascinations

The late Mel Martin was the world's slowest copywriter. He could spend two weeks on the teaser of an envelope. Yet his painstakingly crafted teasers — he dubbed them "fascinations" — were responsible for turning Marty Edelston's tedious Boardroom publications into a $150 million annual business. Mel Martin's teasers made you want to open the envelope.

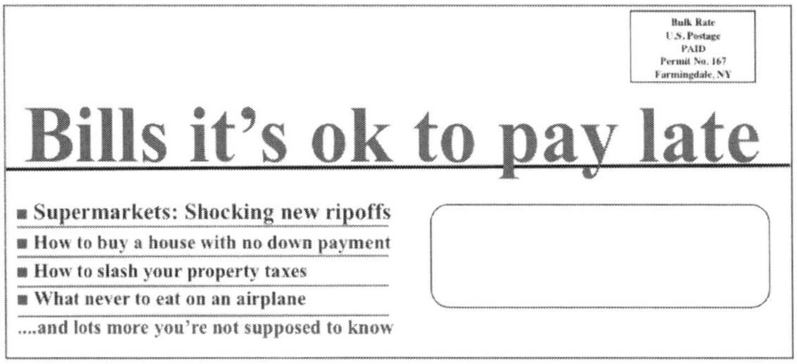

Bulk Rate
U.S. Postage
PAID
Permit No. 167
Farmingdale, NY

Bills it's ok to pay late

- **Supermarkets: Shocking new ripoffs**
- **How to buy a house with no down payment**
- **How to slash your property taxes**
- **What never to eat on an airplane**

....and lots more you're not supposed to know

Envelope copy on a résumé mailing
Obviously you can't do this kind of spectacular graphic design on the envelope of your résumé mailing. But you can make it stand out from the crowd — make it relevant.

For example, it might be a good idea to reference the job offer. This helps to guarantee it will get into the right hands. Example:

Candidate for Job #2031M — Résumé Enclosed

— or —

Candidate for Chief Marketing Officer — Résumé Enclosed

Can a résumé be sent in a 9" x 12" envelope?
Sure. It will stand out from the pile of #10 business envelopes and will certainly be noticed. In addition, since it will be mailed flat (not folded), it should be easier to handle on the other end. To justify this added expense, it's probably a good idea to print the résumé on handsome paper with your cover letter on equally high-quality stock and a letterhead. The possible reaction: this candidate is a quality person and takes pride in any work submitted.

If both the résumé and cover letter are printed on ordinary white copy paper and sent in an oversized envelope, it might look tacky.

What about using FedEx, UPS or USPS Priority Service?
These services are expensive and will get noticed.

But to send a résumé by itself would look peculiar. However, a personal cover letter with the rationale for spending this big money could be a game changer.

The possible message: I wanted to make sure you received the enclosed résumé, because I feel the opening you have described and my experience are a perfect match. I would relish the opportunity to be able to do for you what I did for the last guy ... blah, blah, blah.

Takeaways to Consider

• The envelope has two purposes and two purposes only. "One: to get itself opened. Two: to keep the contents from spilling into the street." *—Herschell Gordon Lewis*

• Your carrier envelope — or the subject line of your e-mail — accounts for 100 percent of the success of failure of your message reaching the intended reader.

• Spend time working on your envelope and your e-mail subject line. These two elements stand between you and a response.

• Keep a stack of envelopes plucked from actual mail deliveries — from First Class business and personal mail as well as junk mail. Before settling on an envelope, print out a dummy of what you intend to use and insert it into your pile of samples. When you come to it, does it pop? If it does not stand out, do surgery.

• Same thing with important e-mail. Send a test to yourself. Does your subject line pop out from all the others in your in-box — spam, headlines, offers, personal notes and press releases? If not, go back to the drawing board.

• Six envelope hot spots by Kansas City freelancer Pat Friesen — what people look at first:

1. Cornercard/return address in upper left
2. Addressing (Window? Label? Computer? Handwritten?)
3. Postage (Live stamp? Metered? Printed?)
4. Teaser copy
5. Back envelope flap
6. Back teaser copy

CHAPTER 25

Your Résumé and Francine's Résumé

Posting your résumé on the Internet
You've posted your résumé online. What kind of response can you expect? Here's a story out of my archive:

> **More Jobs Being Found Online, But That Doesn't Mean It's Easy**
> One of the first things Brooke Christiansen did as college graduation neared last spring was post her résumé on three of the largest Internet job boards: monster.com, careerbuilder.com and hotjobs.com. For the most part, she said, it was an exercise in frustration. *—Barbara Whitaker, The New York Times*

I did not see Brooke Christiansen's résumé, but I know why the response was a big ho-hum at best.

It was all about Brooke.

"Your prospect doesn't give a damn about you, your company or your product," writes marketing guru Bob Hacker. "All that matters is 'what's in it for me?'"

"Always listen to W-I-I-FM," is the rule to remember.

With your résumé and letter, you must prove you have researched the position being offered and convince the recruiter why you are the ideal candidate for the job.

This is not about you. It's about what you can do for the recruiter and the company.

Can you add value?

Your résumé in 15 minutes!
I recently went online and entered into Google: "Résumé Templates."

What follows are the top three results. All promised job candidates could have a résumé ready to send out "in minutes."

> Build a Resume in 15 Mins –
> ResumeGenius.com www.resumegenius.com
> Stop Using Examples to Write Your Resume. Use an Online Resume Builder
>
> Free Resume Templates resume template. myperfectresume.com
> Browse 100s of Eye-Catching Resume Templates & Print Them in Minutes!
> Free Perfect Resume Maker - Free Resume Builder - How to Make a Resume
>
> Resume Templates –
> Write a Resume in Minutes www.resumetemplates.com
> Write a resume in minutes as a Microsoft Word or PDF document. Choice of

professional resume templates that get results. Packed full of examples and expert ... Get Started - Contact Us – How To Write A Resume - Learn More

A bare-bones, do-it-yourself, fill-in-the-blanks résumé
Below is a sample of what's available on the Internet. Download it, fill in the spaces between the [square brackets] and print it out.

This is a quick, easy, down-'n'-dirty solution for a candidate to get basic information into the hands of a recruiter.

As promised on the Internet, it can be created and posted on the Internet (or printed and snail-mailed) in 15 minutes.

[Insert Name Here]
[Address]
[Phone] • [Email]

OBJECTIVE

[Briefly describe your career goal.]

EXPERIENCE

[Job Title / Position] – *[Company Name]* **[Dates]**
[Describe job / technologies used]
[Achievement or responsibility]
[Achievement or responsibility]
[Achievement or responsibility]
[Achievement or responsibility]

[Job Title / Position] – *[Company Name]* **[Dates]**
[Describe job / technologies used]
[Achievement or responsibility]
[Achievement or responsibility]
[Achievement or responsibility]
[Achievement or responsibility]

[Job Title / Position] – *[Company Name]* **[Dates]**
[Describe job / technologies used]
[Achievement or responsibility]
[Achievement or responsibility]
[Achievement or responsibility]
[Achievement or responsibility]

[Job Title / Position] – *[Company Name]* **[Dates]**
[Describe job / technologies used]
[Achievement or responsibility]
[Achievement or responsibility]
[Achievement or responsibility]
[Achievement or responsibility]

EDUCATION

[School attended] - *[Degree obtained]* **[Dates]**
[Achievements or other points of interest]
[Achievements or other points of interest]
[Achievements or other points of interest]

REFERENCES

References available upon request.

It is preposterous to think a job can be secured using a document on which you spent 15 minutes.

The exception: if you are as much a legend in your industry as Bruce Springsteen or Beyoncé are in theirs.

A bizarre, maverick literary style
The résumé is entirely about an individual person. Yet nowhere are "you" or "me" copy ever used.

"I," "me," "we," "us," "our" or "you" never appear in a résumé.

The writer is completely depersonalized.

For example, in applying for a job, the candidate never says in the résumé, "This is what I will bring to your organization."

Nor does a résumé say, "Working at ABC Company, I was able to fulfill my passion for team leadership. Together — working 14 hours a day — this is what my amazing group of dedicated associates accomplished."

Instead, an applicant and a prior career are both reduced to blah, bland, boring platitudinous prose devoid of excitement, enthusiasm and energy. A list of positions and chores accomplished.

Check out the two sample résumés that follow
Imagine yourself as a recruiter — or owner of a business — receiving a pile of 75 to 150 résumés looking like these below.

This first résumé is for an entry-level candidate, much like Brooke Christensen above, who got out of college and posted her résumé online with zero results. From career-advice.monster.com:

Lane Peters

55 Foster St. | Sometown, MA 02453
Home: (555) 555-5555 | Email: lp@somedomain.com | LinkedIn URL

Entry-Level Biochemist

- Recent life science graduate with academic credentials reinforced by internship experience at a respected biochemistry R&D firm.
- Passion for enhancing global human health by contributing to cellular research, disease prevention and diagnostic improvements.
- Able to leverage quantitative strengths to solve technical problems, advance scientific breakthroughs and support innovative assay development.

Professional Experience

ABC Company, Sometown, MA
Biochemist Intern, 2/12 to 5/12
Completed 12-week internship working alongside senior scientists. Assisted in research and development efforts for clinical diagnostics products aiding in the treatment of diabetes. ***Selected Achievements:***

- Gained wet lab experience and knowledge of biochemical and cell-based assays research supporting diagnostic solutions in diabetes treatment.
- Cultured cells, performed laboratory calculations, prepared solutions/dilutions and completed pre-imaging cell staining.
- Participated in cell counting, cell sorting, biomarker detection and protein engineering using state-of-the-art flow cytometry technology.
- Maintained cleanliness, order and organization of laboratory.

DEF Company, Sometown, MA
Membership Sales, 9/08 to 12/11 (seasonal)
Worked throughout college to help finance education. Employed by fitness facility to assist in front-desk operations and sell memberships and fitness-related products. ***Selected Achievements:***

- Met or exceeded membership sales quota by up to 150% every month of tenure.
- Helped coordinate promotions, including bodybuilder appearances, open houses and holiday parties.

Education

ABC University, Sometown, MA
Bachelor of Science in Life Science, Concentration in Biochemistry *(with high distinction),* 5/12
Research Thesis: *Early Signs of Mitochondrial Dysfunction in Parkinson's Disease*

Memberships

- American Society for Biochemistry and Molecular Biology
- American Chemical Society

The second résumé, from careerplaybook.com, is for a seasoned professional looking for a CEO position. What follows are three pages of dry, robotic prose without so much as a smidgen of emotion, color or excitement. Imagine having to plow through 100 such résumés — 300 pages of bland, boring verbiage — from which to choose someone to run a company. In short, these are incomplete portraits of people.

GARRETT R. JACOBSON
275 Northwestern Place
New York City, NY 10001

Email: garrijacobson@email.com
Phone: (212) 123-4567
Cellular: (212) 123-3333

SENIOR EXECUTIVE SUMMARY

President / CEO

Innovative and results-driven leader focused on achieving exceptional results in highly competitive environments that deman continuous improvement. Experienced in driving product, process and customer service improvements while building partnerships with key business decision-makers. Consistenly increased production, reduced operating costs and improved product quality by utilizing World Class Manfacutring concepts (lean manufacturing, six sigma, theory of constraints, etc.) to optimize / rationalized processes and supply chain networks. Areas of expertise in:

- Process Optimization
- Cost Reduction
- Customer Relations
- Productivity Improvement
- Operational & Strategic Planning
- International Operations
- Project Management
- Turnaround Situations
- Budgeting / Forecasting
- Supply Chain Management

Known for building and motivating cross-functional teams that exceed corporate expectations. New product launches in 2004 already account for 40% of current sales and expected to grow to over 50% by year end and drive expansion into new distribution channels.

PROFESSIONAL EXPERIENCE

ABC COMPANY, New York, NY 1982 to present
President / Chief Executive Officer (1994 – present)
Led the company in a turnaround effort that took the company from near bankruptcy and declining sales to stability, followed by rapid sales growth (30% sales growth or $50 million). Developed a 3-year strategy and plan, supporting EBITDA growth of $10 million annualized.

- Transitioned company transformation from a family-owned business to a merger and acquisition of three businesses into one, followed by a management buyout in combination with an investment banker group.
- Drove the operational planning and successful execution for doubling product line manufacturing capacity to exploit market growth opportunities.
- Achieved two-site turnarounds within two years, bringing operational metrics to a baseline standard (saving over $2 million), while maintaining and improving permanent priorities of safety, quality, service, appearance and people.
- Reduced inventories by over 60% or $11,000,000, while improving fill rates by 35-40% and reducing operational lead times in half.
- Developed a logistic partnership with a top-five customer, which reduced total freight costs to that customer by 50% or $500,000 in annualized savings.
- Led a core team of logistics, operational, purchasing and engineering employees who delivered 2-5% in continuous improvement cost savings programs for three consecutive years.

ABC COMPANY, New York, NY
Senior Vice President, Product Supply (1988 - 1994)
Promoted to VP Product Supply in 2002, responsible for a 475 person team which managed a $140 million dollar budged, including supply chain functions of a two-site, five distribution center network, all inclusive from product design, procurement, and planning through quality and operations to customer delivery. Key accomplishments included:

- Presented, gained approval from the Board of Directors and executed capital expenditures plans of $4 million per year with an average ROI of 2 years.
- Developed an effective blend of a best practice, teamwork-based culture, combined with the execution of organization goals, strategies and measures, which supported the turnaround of the company from near-bankruptcy to a stable, rapidly growing business.
- Created a cohesive Product Supply leadership team and provided one-on-one coaching, capitalizing on each person's strengths to deliver high customer satisfaction and quality levels at the lowest total delivered cost.
- Developed communicated and educated Product Supply leaders and employees on the key profit drivers and tide performance, rewards and recognition to those results. This resulted in cost saving of $2.5 million to $7 million in cost savings per year, with plans for up to $16 million ove the next 2 years.
- Led a core team of engineering/ research and development and marketing employees, who redesigned and implemented an upgraded product lineup for our number one product line (60% of sales), which achieved improved customer satisfaction, superior product performance vs. competition and reduced product cost between 5-10% with a quick turnaround of less than a year.
- Partnered with TPS (Toyota Production System) experts to implement the Toyota Production System at PaperPak, which is resulting in improved supply chain effiiciences, fillrates and lead times to customers.

ABC COMPANY, New York, NY
Director, Supply Chain Management (1984 - 1988)
Promoted to Director, Supply Chain Management in 2001, after successfully completing a Project Support Manager role, focused on establishing a company-wide project priority and tracking process to support the transition of the business from a small, family-owned company to a double-the-size company, combing thre separate businesses and cultures into one. Key accomplishments were:

- Managed 60 person team of planning, transportation and logistics employees who optimized the supply chain, resulting in a lower cost structure while doubling inventory turns, which contributed to a successful company turnaround (cash flow sustainability with EBITDA improvement of $9 million with declining sales).
- Led the implementation of a Vendor Managed Inventory (VMI) program with our #1 customer, taking over the management of their inventory while improving freight costs and fill rates, a significant factor in ABC receiving the Supplier of the Year award three times.
- Enable ABE to tak one order, send one shipment and send one invoice to customers, which was critical to regaining customer confidence, increasing business potential, and improving Companies operational efficiencies and cost structure.

GARRETT R. JACOBSON (212) 123-4567 Résumé — Page 3

ABC COMPANY, New York NY
Supply Chain Planning Manager (1982 - 1984)
Promoted and laterally transitions to several supply chain management positions, ranging from inventory Manager to Logistics Manager to Planning Manager. Key accomplishments were:

- Optimized production plans and schedules, which resulted in improved manufacturing efficiencies and customer service levels.

- Developed system implementations of planning, location sensitivity, physical inventories, forecasting and vendor managed inventory, transportation planning and warehousing – on time, on budget and on target.

- Directed an inventory task force to implement tactical solutions that improved inventory accuracy and efficient levels by 30% to 98% location accuracy.

- Streamlined order consolidation challenges and led a warehouse process improvement project, eliminating redundancies and improving traffic flow and warehouse productivity by 20%.

- Oversaw training programs and provided training on supply chain management, MPS/ MRP, project management and systems topics.

XYZ INC, New York, NY
Production and Raw material Planner (1980 - 1982) 1978-1982
Led production planning and raw material planning for the plant. Implemented the plan process monitoring system and production reporting system. Key accomplishments were:

- Performed inventory and sales analysis, such as inventory obsolescence, lost sales trends, and usage trends.
- Led the TQM (total quality management) implementation for the plat as a Cost of Quality Sponsor. Reduced office staff turnover by 50% per year.
- Created a cohesive Product Supply leadership team and provided one-on-one coaching, capitalizing or each person's strengths to deliver high customer satisfaction and quality levels at the lowest total delivered cost.

XYZ INC, New York, NY
Production Planning Supervisor, Western Region (1978 - 1980)
Planned production for six western region manufacturing plants. Key accomplishments were:

- Supervised distribution replenishment of product to western region sales branches.
- Managed up to $35,000,000 in inventory across manufacturing sites and distribution centers.
- Developed system reporting with IS to more effectively manage distribution and planning functions and performed system administrator responsibilities.

EDUCATION

NEW YORK UNIVERITY, Manhattan, NY
MBA, Concentration in Finance

COLUMBIA UNIVESITY, Manhattan, NY
BA, Concentration in Operations Management

10 boilerplate phrases that kill résumés

Stodgy boilerplate phrases in your résumé today mark you as uncreative and "vocabulary challenged." You can make your résumé more compelling and human sounding by rooting out and replacing the boring corporate-speak phrases that litter it, and replacing them with human language — things that people like you or me would actually say.

Here are the worst 10 boilerplate phrases — the ones to seek out and destroy in your résumé as soon as possible:

• Results-oriented professional
• Cross-functional teams
• More than [x] years of progressively responsible experience
• Superior (or excellent) communication skills
• Strong work ethic
• Met or exceeded expectations
• Proven track record of success
• Works well with all levels of staff
• Team player
• Bottom-line orientation *—Liz Ryan, Human Workplace founder, speaker, writer*

Francine's extraordinary résumé

In 2012, I wrote a column based on a website owner who charged a fee to show job hunters how to self-brand — give themselves their own unique selling propositions (USPs). I thought it was a great idea but poorly executed.

Subscriber Will Ezell and I got into an e-mail exchange on the importance of résumé design and readability. Ezell wrote:

> What gets a résumé read are two things:
>
> • It drastically stands out and looks completely different.
> • Social proof.
>
> You of all people know how voyeuristic Americans are.
>
> My friend Francine couldn't score a gig. So we created a new résumé for her (enclosed herewith).
>
> No cover letter required.
>
> We asked her to re-submit her new résumé to 10 companies that hadn't responded to her "traditional-style" résumé previously.
>
> Eight called her in for an interview, and 6 offered her a position. Like me, Francine's picky, and likes the opportunity to weigh all options, so she didn't have any problem stacking the interviews and accepted every job offer knowing she'd only end up going to one (her choice).
>
> She told me the HR people didn't even look at her qualifications. Every question was about what the people said about her.
>
> Note also that we stacked the deck by putting the testimonials on the right-hand side of the page.
>
> I'm also reminded of Dan Kennedy who once said: "Do you want to maybe

sell something someday, or do you want to sell something today?"

One of the smartest men I've ever known (I attribute our fortune to his teachings) was Jay Abraham. He taught me what a USP was, but I can't imagine 5 million kids coming up with their own USP ... And yes — the subject of USP is way old. —*Will Ezell*

Francine Example

address: 1234 Main Street Clearwater, FL 33763
telephone: 727-123-4562 e-mail: Example@gmail.com

PROFILE

Bilingual and Engaging Speaker
Motivated **Instructor**
Training with Passion
Highly **Adaptable**
Works Best with Others in a Team
National Certification - **Medical Assistant**

SKILLS

- **Organized** and **resourceful** in developing successful work systems.
- Coordinating schedules and times of professional associates and vendors.
- Strong **working knowledge** of standard medical and office **equipment**.
- Develop and deliver **customized training** to match specific patient needs.
- **Mentor and motivate** patients with **goal-oriented programs**.
- Counseling patients while **supporting and encouraging** their growth.
- **Inventory control** and management.
- Accurate **maintenance of electronic and paper records**.
- Develops a climate of enthusiasm, teamwork, and cooperation with integrity.
- **Problem-solving** and **coordinating** with many compounding pharmacies.

EXPERIENCE

Abcdefg Industries	Executive Assistant	1993 - 1998
Regis Hair Styling Salon	Hair Stylist	1998 - 2004
Morton Plant Mease Hospital	Medical Assistant	2005 - 2006
ABC Company, The Abcdef *(all owned by the same doctors)*	Medical Assistant / Patient Coordinator	2006 - Present

- **Developed** individual and team **policies and procedures** for intake of all anti-aging and weight loss patients.
- Overall responsibility for **intake, vitals, and work-up** of anti-aging patients, in a practice specializing in bio-identical hormones, and weight loss.
- Administration of patient records and medications.
- **Weight-loss consulting**.
- Delivered **nutritional & supplements training** to patients
- Maintain frequent **follow-up and accountability** with patients.

EDUCATION and CERTIFICATIONS

Pinellas Park High School	June 1992
Longhorn School of Beauty. Longhorn, PA	January 1998
Central Florida Institute - Clearwater, Florida	May 2005
Certified Personal Fitness Trainer	
Cardio-Pulmonary Resuscitation & AED Certification	
National Certification - Medical Assistant	

What They Say About Francine....

*"Great integrity, awesome **attitude**, constantly working on solutions, intense listener, consummate student, and **total team player** – That's Francine wrapped up in a bundle!"*
Dr. Greg Xxxxxxx

*"I've seen you in some difficult and demanding situations, and you **always maintain a diplomatic and calm disposition** never losing your beautiful smile."* Shawn Xxxxxx

*"Francine, you always bring the sunshine in with you! **Your passion and commitment are amazing!**"* Dr. Brian Xxxxxxx

*"**Your capabilities go far beyond your medical training**, and every patient I talk to says they LOVE you! Thank-you Francine!"*
David Xxxxxxx, M.D.

*"I've never met an employee who **always enthusiastically says YES** until I met Francine. She's possibly **one of the best people** I've ever had the honor to work with."*
Xxxxxx Xxxxx, Title

*"Francine is absolutely **the best employee and team member we've ever had!**"*
Jesica Xxxxxxxxx, Office Manager

*"By far, the **most capable and effective M.A.** I've ever worked with!"* Julie Xxxxxx, Team Leader

*"**I never met a person who loved going to work until I met you.** And now I look forward to being at work with you! You're the best Frannie!"* Brittany Xxxxxxxx

*"**Francine was a total asset** – she truly loves her work, pays **close attention to details**, and inspires her co-workers. **If only we had 100 more Francines!**"*
Joan Xxxxxxxxxxx, R.N.

*"I don't really think my patients come to see me. **They come to see Francine, even when they're feeling great!**"* Dr. Rick Xxxxxxxx

Francine Example 727-123-4562 e-mail: Example@gmail.com

Will Ezell suggested Francine's résumé could go out with no cover letter. Of course I disagree. The next chapter on the "almighty letter" is a guide to telling your complete story — in a positive, compelling way — to a headhunter, recruiter or corporate management.

How many pages?
Will Ezell's résumé design for Francine is a single page. Note that Will designed it so the contact information is printed twice — at the top and bottom of the page.

If your résumé can be kept to one page, it's easier on the recruiter. However, CEO candidate Garrett Jacobson's experience takes up three pages.

Can page 2 be printed on the reverse side of page 1?
Your call. Three pages plus a cover letter is a lot of paper. If the résumé is printed front-and-back, make sure a notation flush right at the bottom of page 1 says,

Please turn page ...

— or —

Please go on to page 2 ...

'50 percent of interviewees lied'
I received a fascinating comment from a reader who shared his hiring practices. If you're looking for a job — and asking for an interview — the following will be worth your while.

> **1. Face-to-face interview with human resources or office manager.** Prior to that interview, we do a social media search, and custom tailor questions based on our research, mostly to catch them in lies. 50 percent of the 1,000+ interviewees we've met with over 10 years lied. We don't confront them when they lie. Also, during that interview, they're in our conference room — no windows. A team member goes out to our parking lot (we own our office building, so it's a dedicated parking lot) and looks in the car. We're looking for 3 things:
>
> **a. Cigarettes/cigars, etc.** We're a non-smoking office and we frankly don't want to smell it on people.
>
> **b. Baby seats?** Those mean 20+ absences/year because mom always calls in sick when the kids are sick. It's unlawful to ask about children.
>
> **c. Is the car trashed,** or is it neat and clean?
>
> A note is passed to the interviewer mid-interview with discovery info from car inspection. Example: "Are you typically neat and organized?" We've discovered that work habits emulate how people keep their cars. We know they're full of crap when they say yes, and their car is trashed.
>
> Also — our interview questions are designed to garner more than one answer for each question, and to institute a dialogue.
>
> **2. Psychological/intellectual/skills testing.**
>
> **3. Final interview with team leader for division we're hiring for.**

We hire 1 in 10 applicants. Most fall out with step 2. Our average tenure/employee is 4-plus years. I'll spend $900 ($100 x 9 prospective hires) for the fallouts, as who knows how much it costs us to train new team members.

A gallery of high-profile résumé bluffers

The Internet makes it relatively easy to discover if a résumé has been buffed up or is rife with untruths.

A database of university graduates and their degrees exists for professional investigators. Being caught in a lie — even one going back many years — can range from an embarrassment to a financial catastrophe. Some folks who erred:

> **Sandra "Sandy" Baldwin** was forced out as president of the U.S. Olympic Committee in 2002. In her curriculum vitae, she had awarded herself a 1967 Ph.D. in literature from Arizona State University and a degree from the Colorado State University.
>
> **Richard Blumenthal,** Connecticut state attorney general, once told a crowd he had served in Vietnam. "There was one problem," wrote Raymond Hernandez in *The New York Times*. "Mr. Blumenthal, a Democrat now running for the United States Senate, never served in Vietnam. He obtained at least five military deferments from 1965 to 1970 and took repeated steps that enabled him to avoid going to war, according to records."
>
> **Marti Buscaglia,** hired as publisher of the *Orange County Register* in 2007, billed herself as a graduate from Lima University, Peru. After admitting she lied on her résumé, she did not get the job.
>
> **"[Professor] Joseph J. Ellis,** the Pulitzer Prize-winning historian who admitted in June he lied to his students and others when he said he had been a combat soldier in Vietnam," wrote Jodi Wilgoren of the New York Times in 2001. "He has been suspended for a year without pay by Mount Holyoke, the women's college in western Massachusetts where he has taught since 1972."
>
> **Marilee Jones,** MIT dean of admissions, was caught claiming she had degrees from Rensselaer Polytechnic Institute, Union College and Albany Medical College. "I misrepresented my academic degrees when I first applied to MIT 28 years ago," she admitted, "and did not have the courage to correct my résumé when I applied for my current job or at any time since." She resigned.
>
> **J. Terrence Lanni,** resigned as chairman and CEO of MGM Mirage in 2008. The MGM website proclaimed he had a master's degree in business administration from the University of Southern California. It was discovered he did not.
>
> **Scott Thompson,** Yahoo CEO, claimed he held a computer science degree from Stonehill College. Not true. In 2012 he was canned after just 130 days on the job.

Takeaways to Consider

• Make sure every statement on your résumé is true.

• Always run your résumé (and all other documents) through a spelling check program.

• The world's knowledge is at your fingertips via the Internet, and it should be easy to research a person. However many people are very difficult to find and contact.

• As one reader wrote: "50 percent of the 1,000-plus interviewees we've met with over 10 years lied."

• Think through carefully whom you list as references.

• Always ask permission to use someone's name and testimonial as a reference. And get permission in writing.

• Do not date testimonials. Even if it's 20 years old, you want it to be evergreen.

• Don't make copies of your résumé in the office copier. If you are suddenly called into a meeting and you leave your original behind, you could be embarrassed.

• Don't use the company e-mail and phone for job hunting. Chances are management is spying on you.

• "Almost 33 percent of 140 North American businesses nationwide report they conduct regular audits of outbound e-mail content." *—Proofpoint Inc., 2004 Study*

• "Your prospect doesn't give a damn about you, your company or your product. All that matters is 'What's in it for me?'" *—Bob Hacker*

• "Always listen to W-I-I-FM," is the rule to remember.

• "Do you want to maybe sell something someday, or do you want to sell something today?" *—Dan Kennedy*

CHAPTER 26

Your Résumé and the Almighty Cover Letter

Cover letters get you in the door, so be sure not to dash them off
Eager to snare a hot job opening, you quickly scribble a cover letter and attach it to your flawless résumé.

Too bad. You probably just blew your chance to be hired. Your hastily written missive missed the mark — and you misspelled the target company's name.

A great cover letter is the golden key to any job search. Yet despite a glut of advice books and websites, an estimated 85 percent of cover letters are so flawed that senders never land an interview, career coaches say. *—Joann S. Lublin, The Wall Street Journal*

....

How to research a company
In the BI era (Before the Internet), research was a nightmare. It required many hours at the library winding through newspapers on reels of microfilm looking for stories and biographies of the players.

Today, you can take advantage of the greatest research miracle of the modern age: Google. You can do in minutes what used to take many hours.

When a person or organization has a job opening of interest to you, run a private Google search on the company and the players. You want history, stories, press releases and bios of the founders and managers. Download them into a word-processing file. Go through all this raw material and create associations in your mind. How does your résumé directly relate to the needs of this prospective employer?

You should find plenty of relevant stuff to talk about in your cover letter.

Don't repeat in the letter what's in your résumé
It turns the letter into more "it" copy and wastes the one opportunity to connect personally with the recruiter. Your cover letter is benefit-oriented "what-I-can-do-for-you-and-your-company" copy.

What's more, if the prospect reads the letter first and then sees the same material in the résumé, the immediate reaction will be, "I've seen this before, so I can move on."

Same thing if the résumé is read first.

Since the résumé — the circular equivalent — goes to everybody, the cover letter can be used as the vehicle to versionalize your communication. It can show how your experience and background relate to — and can directly benefit — the chemical company, software developer or sales organization you're contacting.

Pat Friesen's 12 hot spots of a letter

1. Letterhead/masthead
2. Salutation
3. First sentence — first paragraph
4. "Johnson Box" — billboard above the salutation and letter body
5. Last paragraph
6. Signature
7. Title with signature
8. P.S. and P.P.S.
9. Copy indented from both margins or underlined
10. Copy in bullet form, second color or boldface type
11. Indented subheads
12. Anything added in handwriting

A note on the Johnson Box mentioned above by Pat Friesen

Frank Johnson was a truly lovely guy — the world-class copywriter who put Jim Parton's magnificent American Heritage hardcover magazine on the map and made it a huge success.

Frank told me, yes, he invented the Johnson Box. But he hated to be remembered for it. He was far more proud of the "bedsheet" circulars he created for *American Heritage* and Time-Life Books. These were splashy, full-color brochures — 5-1/2" x 8-1/2" or 8-1/2" x 11"(depending on the size of the envelope). They unfolded to a massive 17" x 22" poster size of blazing full-color graphics dominating everything on the desk or coffee table. They were glorious!

AMERICAN HERITAGE

* * * * * * * * * * * * * * *

The Publisher
of
AMERICAN HERITAGE MAGAZINE
Cordially Invites You to Accept
The Current Issue
as a
FREE GIFT!
No cost. No Risk. No obligation
R.S.V.P.

* * * * * * * * * * * * * * *

Dear Afficiando of American Hisory,

A copy of the current issue of AMERICAN HERITAGE has been reserved in your name as a FREE GIFT - your introduction

The "Johnson Box" is the headline of a letter. Sometimes it is a series asterisks typed in the form of a box with a headline inside. For example, above is how a Frank Johnson circulation letter — with the Johnson Box — might look for *American Heritage*.

Business Week

By agreement, our magazine solicits subscriptions from men and women in middle and upper management positions.

With this letter, the Editors now invite you to join this exclusive and knowing circle...to save yourself or your company $29.50 on your subscription...and to receive free as a welcoming gift one of the most valuable business handbooks that's ever been privately printed.

With our compliments

Dear Colleague:

Hasn't it happened to you in business? It sure used to happen to me.

Let's say you go into a meeting. Everyone present has lots to say -- ideas, opinions, news. Finally you put in your own two cents' worth. You mention something you've just heard ...

> ... only to discover that everybody else has known about it for days. So you find yourself saying "Damn!"

Above is the Johnson Box by Bill Jayme and Heikki Ratalahti for their *Business Week* mailing with DAMN! on the outer envelope.

Generally the Johnson Box is found in direct mail marketing. No rules exist to preclude this technique from being used in a personal letter.

In the case of a résumé mailing, the headline on the actual résumé is the candidate's name — hardly an exciting benefit. The typical letter starts with a salutation: "Dear So-and-So" — also not very visually exciting.

Since headlines are attention-getters, a strong headline here might separate your mailing from the pack. Or not.

Your call.

However, if you go the headline route, make sure it's a grabber! Spend as much time on your headline (or Johnson Box) as you do on your letter.

With the cover letter, you are selling yourself
You probably never thought of yourself as a salesperson. But when applying for a job, it's imperative you let the recruiter know you are absolutely the right person for this position and how you want it more than anything in the world.

If you don't sell yourself, who will?

On letters by freelancer Malcolm Decker

• **The letter is itself is the pen-and-ink embodiment** of a salesperson who is speaking personally and directly to the prospect on a one-to-one basis. It is the most powerful and persuasive selling force in direct marketing, once the product, price and offer are set. The writer creates the salesman, usually from whole cloth, and you must be certain that this sales representative is truly representative of your product or service as well as of your company.

• **The letter is likely to be the only "person"** your market will ever meet — at least on the front end of the sale — don't make him highbrow if your market is lowbrow and vice versa.

Make sure he speaks your prospect's language. If he's a Tiffany salesman, he writes in one style; if he's a grapefruit or pecan farmer or a beef grower, he writes differently ('cause he talks diffrunt). I develop as clear a profile of my prospect as the available research offers and then try to match it up with someone I know and "put him in a chair" across from me. Then I write to him more or less conversationally.

• **The letter MUST be quickly scannable:** that is, a reader should get the gist of the proposition simply by reading the 1) eyebrow or Johnson Box 2) lede paragraph, 3) crossheads, 4) wrap-up and 5) P.S. If not, send it back for surgery, because without a strongly integrated skeleton, the body of the argument will slump.

• **The letter MUST be easy on the eyes,** open, inviting and varying in its texture — with normal margins ... individual paragraphs with line space between... at least one crosshead or subhead per page (two per page for long letters) ... occasional variation in paragraph width ... a quotation, underlined sentence or phrase... numbers or bullets to list benefits ... and/or other bits of "color" to maintain reader interest by promising visual variety. The longer the letter, the more important these devices.

• **How long should a letter be?** The best-known answer to that age-old question is: "As long as it has to be."

That doesn't tell you much, but perhaps it suggests two important criteria: economy and — above all — efficiency.

As a sometime angler, I get a better sense of length by remembering a fishing trip to Maine when we used dry flies with barbless hooks. Unless you kept up the tension all the way to the net, you lost the trout. Try it. You should feel the same sort of tension when you write and when you read a letter. If not... reel in the slack.

Since the direct mail letter is the most highly personal, intimate form of commercial writing:

• **It is NOT** a monolithic corporation addressing a computer-generated market profile; it is not impersonal in tone, form or content.

• **It is NOT** one or more pieces of 8-1/2" x 11" paper with a letterhead on top and a signature on the bottom and the most cherished sales pitch of the VP of Marketing sandwiched in between.

• **It is NOT** set in standard type, is not illustrated with photographs and is not printed in four-color process.

• **It CAN have an "eyebrow"** or "Johnson Box" above the salutation to tease, tantalize or help the reader preview what's coming in the letter.

• **The color, weight, quality and texture** of your letter stock also communicate. Choose them very carefully. They're your verbal clothes.

• **Don't overlook the color, size and vitality of your signature;** they're your salesman's handshake. Even people who aren't graphologists pick up a lot from the way a name is signed. For example, would you hire this guy?

Jacob J. Lew, Secretary of the Treasury

Or this guy?

• **The other signature that can work for you** is your personal letterhead. Use it to tell your prospect what kind person you are: traditional, avant-garde, industrial, financial.

Make the elements in your mailing look different from each other
I urge you not to use the same typeface for both your résumé and cover letter. Since the right-brain person — irrational and emotional — will want to read your letter first, remember the late Dick Benson's advice: "A letter should look and feel like a letter."

How long should your cover letter be?
Mal Decker above suggested it should be as long it needs to be.

However, recruiters are horrendously busy people. If they are going through 100 résumé mailings, they won't let themselves get bogged down reading a four- or six-page letter. My suggestion for your cover letter: one page and no more than two pages.

> **"The top of every page deserves a new lead!" says fundraising copywriter and tax expert Roger Keeling**
> You never know where people will start reading ... it may not be on page 1. And you never entirely know where their eyes will skip to. But the tops of every page are likely candidates. So don't waste this opportunity: start every page with a punchy new sales pitch ... a golden opportunity to grab that customer!

Please Note
The advice below from Don Hauptman and Ted Kikoler was written 25 years ago. In my opinion, this is still relevant. As the legendary John Caples wrote many years ago:

"Times change. People don't."

"Human nature is perpetual," wrote Claude Hopkins in *Scientific Advertising*.

> In most respects it is the same today as in the time of Caesar. So the principles of psychology are fixed and enduring. You will never need to unlearn what you learn about them.

Feel free to disagree — and disregard — these suggestions. However, you may find one or more to be useful (e.g., Hauptman on underlining).

Don Hauptman's checklist
Freelancer, teacher of copywriting and theater aficionado Don Hauptman has plenty to say about the look of a letter:

- **Use a typewriter-style font.** Split tests of typewritten vs. typeset letters appear to yield contradictory results; sometimes typewritten beats typeset, while other tests show no difference.

  Still, it seems wise to continue employing the "old-fashioned" typewriter look. When people open an envelope, they expect to see a letter, with its familiar conventions. The image of a personal, me-to-you message may indeed be an illusion, but it's one that most of us have come to expect. What's more, the typewriter format helps differentiate the letter from other components of the package.

- **Stick with Courier type,** which is available with most of today's software and impact and laser printers; it's closest to the familiar typewriter look.

- **Avoid these circusy tricks.** A serious (and common) typographic error is the use of a dizzying variety of fonts, sizes, etc. After all, people may reason, it's easy, so why not?

- **Indent the first line of each paragraph.** How much of an indent? Four to six characters. The "neat" look of blocked paragraphs (i.e., the left margin flush with subsequent lines) was once fashionable. But tests (and common sense) suggest that paragraph indents make for easier reading.

- **To avoid a gray "wall" of type** that discourages reading, paragraphs shouldn't be more than seven lines. A visual and dramatic break can be provided by an occasional paragraph of one sentence, one line or even one word. (But don't mail a letter that consists of all one-sentence paragraphs — unless it's intended for toddlers.)

- **Use a ragged-right margin.** Again, it's so easy for a computer and printer to execute flush-right (justified) margins that people do it without realizing that it detracts from the letter illusion.

- **Don't break words at the end of a line.** The "word wrap" function of most word-processing programs can be instructed not to hyphenate. Also avoid a dangling "a" or "the" at the end of a line. Keep such articles adjacent to their nouns.

• **Use familiar attention devices.** Even if the bells-and-whistles offered by desktop publishing are eschewed, as I recommend, certain techniques can be used to relieve the "gray" look of a typed letter, and to flag and emphasize key points. For instance:

—**Underscore key words,** sentences and even entire (short!) paragraphs. Always underscore with a continuous rule (i.e., NOT "hatched" or broken between each word). Unfortunately, some fonts and printers create a rule that cuts into the lower edges of letters; use a font that cuts a hairline space above the rule.

—**Bullets, round or square** (always solid), can be inserted via computer.

—**Do NOT use asterisks,** hyphens, periods or the letter "o" as substituted for bullets.

—**Check marks** work nicely, especially for a list of benefits.

—**Subheads/crossheads help break up long copy.** They should be cen tered, capitalized and underscored.

—**Inset paragraphs,** centered (10 or so characters worth of space both left and right), and blocked. Useful for calling attention to important points.

• **Use page breaks to arouse curiosity.** Ideally, every page should break in the middle of such an exciting sentence the reader cannot resist turning the page. ("Harold then discovered that the secret of eternal life is ...")

Realistically, however, it's tough to achieve this goal throughout a long letter. But it's worth making the effort on page one. Adding, "over, please" at the bottom of the first page can't hurt, but I suspect that many readers find it offensive on every page.

• **Use your real signature.** Don't let a computer sign your letters.

• **Always include a P.S. say experts.** It makes a provocative point that kicks the reader back into the letter. Use a "hanging indent" — that means the entire message is positioned to the right of the P. and S.

• **Avoid superlatives** and brag-and-boast language.

• **Wherever possible, incorporate anecdotes,** testimonials, success stories and other believable elements of human interest.

• **Use specifics to add power and credibility.** Use precise, documented figures and facts in advertising. Cite data or opinions from outside, impartial sources. A lot of copy is anemic and ineffective because it's superficial, vague and unspecific. Concrete statements and detail supply the ring of truth. But to find this kind of material, you've often got to dig for it.

• **Be a "creative plagiarist."** You can learn by studying the work of others. But don't imitate; emulate or re-create. When you see an idea you admire, try to identify the principles behind it, then apply those principles in a fresh, original way to your own work.

Advice from the great Canadian copywriter/designer Ted Kikoler

• Don't fall into the desktop publishing trap. If you have a "Mac" (or any other desktop publishing system) don't fall into the trap of making your letters "prettier."

• If you are using a typesetting font (such as Times, or worse, Helvetica) — instead of real typewriter (Courier or Prestige) — you are giving your letters the kiss of death. I can't stress this point enough. A typewriter-written letter will almost always beat one that's typeset.

• It's true that more people in business are now using prettier typefaces than typewriter, but it's not the accepted norm. At least not yet. Wait about five to 10 years. Until then, give your letters a true typewriter look.

2 tips from Harry Walsh

The late Harry Walsh was a big red-headed copywriter who taught gunnery to fighter pilots in World War II. I remember him as a world-class consumer of dry martinis and a splendid luncheon companion. His self-imposed rules for the letter:

The tone of a good direct mail letter is as direct and personal as the writer's skill can make it.

Even though it may go to millions of people, it never orates to a crowd, but rather murmurs into a single ear. It's a message from one letter writer to one letter reader.

Tell a story if possible.

Everybody loves a good story, be it about Peter Rabbit or King Lear. And the direct mail letter, with its unique person-to-person format — is the perfect vehicle for a story. And stories get read. The letter I wrote to launch the Cousteau Society twenty-some years ago has survived hundreds of tests against it. When I last heard, it was still being mailed in some form or other. The original of this direct mail Methuselah started out with this lead: "A friend once told me a curious story I would like to share with you..."

13 tips on creating a cover letter

Slate.com editor Katherine Goldstein has read more than 500 cover letters from applicants looking for an entry-level position at slate.com. Here is her take:

1. Focus on the cover letter.
2. If I hate the cover letter, I won't even look at the résumé.
3. Keep it short.
4. Avoid awkward phrasing and attempts to be overly formal.
5. Do not lede with: "I am sure you are getting many qualified applicants for this job, many of whom are more qualified than I.
6. Show me you read my site [or researched my company].

7. Explain how selecting you will benefit me.
8. I am not interested in anything you did before college.
9. I am not interested in your life journeys.
10. When I read "senior thesis," my eyes glaze over.
11. Your college and GPA aren't as important as you think.
12. I don't really care what classes you've taken, either.
13. Follow the application instructions to a T.

Takeaways to Consider

• "A letter should look and feel like a letter." *—Dick Benson*

• "Cover letters get you in the door, so be sure not to dash them off." *—Joann S. Lublin, The New York Times*

• "A great cover letter is the golden key to any job search. Yet despite a glut of advice books and websites, an estimated 85 percent of cover letters are so flawed that senders never land an interview, career coaches say." *—Joann S. Lublin*

• Do not repeat in the letter what's in your résumé. If the prospect reads the letter first and then sees the same copy in the résumé, the immediate reaction will be, "I've seen this before, so I can go on to the next applicant." Same thing if the résumé is read first.

• You probably never thought of yourself as a salesperson. But when applying for a job, it's imperative you let the recruiter know you are absolutely the right person for this position and how you want it more than anything in the world. If you don't sell yourself, who will?

• Recruiters are horrendously busy people. If they are going through 100 résumé mailings, they won't let themselves get bogged down reading a four- or six-page letter. My suggestion for your cover letter: one page and no more than two pages.

• In a letter, skip a line between paragraphs.

• "Short words. Short sentences. Short paragraphs." *—Andrew S. Byrne*

• Always run your copy through spelling software.

CHAPTER 27

The Raw Power of a Letter

In December 2010, Peggy and I went at separate times to our TD Bank branch on the corner and saw a different officer on the floor.

Our request: kindly tell your computer people we are going to Moscow and please allow us to use our TD debit cards to get rubles from Russian ATMs. Both of them made the calls while we sat there (at different times) and confirmed we would have no problem.

Neither card worked, and we were stuck with no rubles in one of the most financially unpleasant, non-English-speaking countries of the world. Our Moscow trip was a nightmare.

Fast-forward to 2012 when I acquired a consulting client in Paris, France. To facilitate the monthly retainer payment, the client requested direct deposit information for my corporate account.

The same oaf on the floor who screwed up Moscow handed me a cruddy little Xeroxed form with the generic transfer information. I added my checking account number and e-mailed the data to the client along with an invoice for the first month's retainer.

The wire deposit was declined by TD Bank and returned to the sender. The client tried again, this time sending three months' worth of retainer fees. Again, the deposit was declined.

I went into the bank and sat down in front of the same jerk and showed him the e-mail information I had sent to the French. He gave it glance. Our exchange:

> BANKER: These look right. There is nothing we can do. This is their fault.
>
> HATCH: Look, I'm not a banker. I want to find out what happened, so this does not happen again and so I can get my money every month.
>
> BANKER: But this is their fault. You have to ask them.
>
> HATCH: You received the money and returned it. Can't you find out what happened?
>
> BANKER: This is not our fault. You have to go back and ask them.
>
> HATCH: So you won't do anything to help me.
>
> BANKER: This is their fault. Ask them.

I left the bank with a pain in my gut. Would I be unable to work for this client because

TD Bank would not take the money?

Back home I composed a snail-mail letter to Bharat B. Masrani, President and Chief Executive Officer, TD Bank Group in Portland, Maine. It was a formal complaint vs. TD Bank and the turkey who refused to help me. I recounted precisely what happened, including the exchange above. I assembled a fat packet of supporting documents and copied the six TD Bank executive vice presidents listed on the website.

Waiting to send the letter
I then printed out the letter, attached all the exhibit documents and stuck this Post-It note on the upper right of the main letter to CEO Masrani. The text:

TO: TD Bank
DATE: 09/05/12

If I do not hear back
from you by 3:00 PM
5 September 2012,
this letter will go out to
the 7 TD Bank officials
listed.

Thank you.

TO: TD Bank
DATE: 09/05-12

If I do not hear back
from you by 3:00 PM
5 September 2012,
this letter will to out to
the 7 TD Bank officials
listed.

Thank you.

/s/ DH

I marched over to the bank at 11:00 a.m. The guy in question was with a customer, so I handed the letter to another officer who was playing with a customer's dog. This is the guy I always see outside the bank sneaking a cigarette. I pointed to the villain of the piece who caused me the misery and asked that my letter be handed to him. The doggie man nodded and I left.

This was fortuitous. Another officer saw the letter, and soon it would be the gossip of the branch.

Within a half hour the branch manager called me from far out of town where she was on holiday and asked: "Did Mr. [NAME] call the bank's wire service department while you were sitting there?"

"He didn't call anybody."

"That's not right," she said. "I'll speak to him. Meanwhile, I'll be back in three days and will follow up on this and get you your money."

She did.

I never had to send the letter.

"Of all the formats used in direct mail," wrote the late catalog guru Dick Hodgson, "none has more power to generate action than the letter."

Snail mail. Not e-mail.

What's more, just the threat of a letter can be as effective as actually sending a letter.

Takeaways to Consider

• "Of all the formats used in direct mail, none has more power to generate action than the letter." *—Dick Hodgson*

• Snail mail. Not e-mail.

• If a letter or document is important, do not use e-mail. It can get lost in the ether or in spam filters. It can be overlooked in a full in-box.

• If really important, send it Certified, Priority or Federal Express. When one of these babies arrives, it gets noticed.

CHAPTER 28

The E-mail Conundrum — Receiving and Sending It

Be suspicious of every e-mail you receive
Every couple of weeks I receive an e-letter in my Yahoo mailbox from someone I recognize. Yet when I open it, the entire message consists of a hyperlink. No greeting. No cover note. Just a link to something. If this happens to you, do not click on the hyperlink!

Same thing if the hyperlink is preceded by a strange message — something this person would never say to you.

A good chance exists a scammer has hijacked the e-mail account.

If you click on the hyperlink, all will seem benign. You'll get an innocuous sales message of some sort. But most likely your computer will be infected with some kind of evil malware and you will find yourself swimming in electronic waters filled with sharks and alligators.

A good chance exists you will be "spoofed" by scammers sending out evil messages using your e-mail address as the originator of scams.

What I do
With a strange e-mail from someone I know shows up, I click on "Forward" and send the following message:

> [Name], I think your computer has been hacked.

I do not click on "Reply," because I don't know whether my response is programed go back to the hacker.

I am almost always correct when this happens and my acquaintance sends a thank-you note and gives me a new e-mail address.

Important!
It is dangerous to go through your e-mail inbox if you are tired and not mentally at the top of your game. The reason: "Dealing with e-mail requires a person's highest cognitive functions!" said Dela Quist, CEO of Alchemy Worx, UK.

When e-mail arrives, it raises myriad questions:

- Should I open it or delete it?
- Do I know the sender?
- If I delete without reading could I get fired?
- Does the message have an offer that could advance my career or make me rich beyond the dreams of avarice?
- If I open this message, could it contain malware? This means my computer will be hacked, my privacy violated and my bank account looted.

Stressed by data overload? Declare e-mail bankruptcy
This was the headline of a 2007 Mike Musgrove story in *The Washington Post*. Musgrove wrote:

> Last month, venture capitalist Fred Wilson drew a lot of attention on the Internet when he declared a 21st century kind of bankruptcy. In a posting on his blog about technology, Wilson announced he was giving up on responding to all the e-mail piled up in his inbox.
>
> "I am so far behind on e-mail that I am declaring bankruptcy," he wrote. "If you've sent me an e-mail (and you aren't my wife, partner, or colleague), you might want to send it again. I am starting over."
>
> College professors have done the same thing, and a Silicon Valley chief executive followed Wilson's example the next day. Last September, the recording artist Moby sent an e-mail to all the contacts in his inbox announcing that he was taking a break from e-mail for the rest of the year.

Somewhere in my vast archive (I'm darned if I can find it) is a struggling entrepreneur's horror story. He discovered a weeks-old e-mail in his spam folder with a serious offer to buy his company for a very good price. The story had a happy ending and the company was sold. But here's proof of Dela Quist's admonishment about the importance of being at the top of your game when dealing with e-mail.

In short, dealing with e-mail and spam is a bitch. But one can't be too careful.

All e-mail looks alike
A snail-mail envelope can come in various sizes and can be made of junky newsprint all the way up to elegant linen and vellum papers.

The appearance, the feel, the type style, the stamp (affixed, metered or printed) and the teaser — they all say something about the sender and the message inside.

All e-mail looks alike when it arrives on the computer, tablet or smartphone. To get your prospect's attention, you have just two elements to work with: "From" line and "Subject" line.

'From' line
Generally, the From line is what the reader looks at first.

When the name of the person or organization is recognizable and generates positive feelings, the chances of the e-mail getting opened are exponentially better.

However, when the "from" line is International Monetary Fund, Mrs. Violet or FBI Director James Comey — where no relationship exists — the strong odor of a scam is in the air.

Your subject line is more important than your message
When writing to an absolute stranger, *your subject line is everything.*

With e-mail, you are a mouse click away from oblivion. Any subject line not relevant, not intriguing or just plain odd is destined for the "delete" key.

If your e-mail is opened, the subject line was 100 percent successful. If deleted without being opened, the subject line was a 100 percent failure.

Do not spend hours creating e-mail and then toss off a subject line as an afterthought. Many copywriters spend as much time (or longer) on the subject line as the message.

How long should a subject line be?
In the years when e-mail was always sent and received on desktop devices, most experts agreed the subject line should be 40 characters or less.

You have 40 characters including spaces.

The sentence just above this one is exactly 40 characters (including the period at the end.)

This is not a lot of characters to grab a reader's attention with a message so compelling it will be eagerly opened.

The mobile device revolution
Some eye-opening statistics in 2013:

- 79 percent of smartphone owners and 72 percent of tablet owners use their devices for e-mail.
- 47 percent of all e-mails are opened on mobile devices — smartphones or tablets.
- 32 percent of e-mails are opened on desktop computers.

On the screen width of a pocket-size smart phone, here are the parameters:

• From Line:	25 Characters
• Subject Line	35 Characters
• Pre-Header	85 Characters

The "pre-header" is made up of the first few words of the message. These appear following the subject line in the mobile device in-box.

Responsive Design — one size does NOT fit all
In the world of e-mail marketing — where illustrations and blocks of copy are used — "responsive design" is the current coin of the realm. This means the message automatically formats itself to look wonderful no matter whether it is opened on a smartphone, tablet or desktop device.

Put another way, a complex design meant for the big desktop can get very screwed up on a wee smartphone. *The BlueHornet Report* on digital marketing found "75 percent of consumers say a poorly designed e-mail negatively affects their perception of a brand."

For this reason, e-mail designers start with the smartphone layout, working up to the tablet and ending with the desktop.

Click vs. Tap
In the old days of pure desktop e-mail, no problem existed when you sent one or more hyperlinks. You simply clicked on the link to open it.

On the touch screen of mobile devices, the cursor and "click to open" are not part of the deal. Instead of clicking, the user taps the link with a finger. Let's say you want to send these three links:

http://online.wsj.com/home-page
http://www.huffingtonpost.com
http://online.wsj.com/home-page

A fat finger could not tap an individual link here. The rule of finger: a link or order button must be at least 44 pixels square or 0.59 inches x 0.59 inches. So the URLs should be separated for ease of tapping.

http://online.wsj.com/home-page

http://www.huffingtonpost.com

http://online.wsj.com/home-page

The cut-off danger
A subject line longer than 40 characters (35 on a small smartphone) is subject to being cut off. My recommendation is to type the subject line you want; at the 35th character separate the rest of the line. Is it a grabber when cut off at 35 characters? If not, go back to the drawing board.

Beware that using a word in a subject line — if split in half — could trigger prudish spam filters. Examples: cocktails, pussyfoot, assignment.

Jill Bastian on 11 potential spam filter triggers
First, always have someone proofread your e-mail! A typo in a benign word can suddenly create a delivery nightmare when it transforms into the hottest new spam word.

If a word in your subject line gets truncated or broken, it could go to a spam folder or, even worse, cause unsubscribes. An example I saw was the phrase "Buttons and Bows" in a long subject line. Because the subject was too long, the word Button was broken in the middle and caused delivery and unsubscribe problems.

In addition, a subject line is not the place to use the short words for texting, like 4U, U or even #1. Sometimes unsavory types want to use known spam words and try to get around delivery issues by breaking them up with spaces or disguising them. Spam filters know these tricks, so C r e d i t, C*r*e*d*i*t or CREDIT can still put your e-mail in a spam folder.

Using all caps for a word or a whole subject line can flag the e-mail as being spam. Plus, all caps in the Internet world means you're yelling, and you don't want to do that to your readers.

And now the list you were looking for — 11 spam triggers:
• Affordable
• Apply Now
• Additional Income/ Extra Income
• Dear Friend
• Free
• Home Based/Work from Home
• Mortgage Rates
• Opportunity
• Remove
• Save $
• Weight Loss —*Jill Bastian, Verticalresponse.com/blog*

Send important e-mails to yourself first as a test
In my opinion, the only way to be sure your e-mail is free of layout bugs is to send it to yourself. Open your own e-mail on a smartphone, tablet and desktop device. If readable on all three, it's good to go. By sending e-mails to yourself, here's what you test:

• You'll see how the subject lines may break.

• When you send e-mail to yourself, you'll see how your subject line compares with others in your in-box. Is your subject line a grabber? If not, go back to the drawing board, rework the copy and send it to yourself again.

• How does the message read? Is it easy to comprehend? Does the eye move? Do you discover any slow patches to be reworked or deleted?

Here's a disastrous e-mail PR pitch
This unreadable document turned up in my in-box from a public relations person I receive releases from all the time. She should know better. This thing breaks all the rules:

• Mouse-type. Maybe 9-point. To my ancient eyes on my laptop, it looks like 7-point or less.

• According to Christian Holst of Baymard Institute, online readability means line widths should be 50 to 75 characters including spaces. In this PR lady's message, the width is more than double this ideal — a whopping 134 characters.

Had she sent this disaster to her own e-mail box as a test, she could have made modifications to make it readable.

For example, to avoid obscenely long line widths, many e-mailers (myself included) eyeball sentence lengths and hit the enter key whenever I've reached 50 or 60 characters.

Takeaways to Consider

• If you receive a strange e-mail message with a hyperlink from someone you know, don't click on the hyperlink. It's likely to be a spam scam or worse.

• Instead forward the e-mail to the sender and suggest the possibility the e-mail account has been hijacked.

• You have two shots at getting your e-mail opened: 1) From line and 2) Subject line.

• When the name of the person or organization is recognizable and generates positive feelings, the chances of the e-mail getting opened are exponentially better.

• If the e-mail is opened, the subject line was 100 percent successful. If deleted without being opened, the subject line was a 100 percent failure.

• Do not spend hours on creating e-mail and then toss off subject line as an afterthought.

• Most experts agree the subject line should be no more than 40 characters including spaces.

• Do not use words in the subject line that could trigger spam filters.

• Beware of using a word in a subject line — if split in half — that could trigger prudish spam filters. Examples: cocktails, pussyfoot, assignment.

• We are all one mouse click from oblivion. When you have important business, I suggest you to use snail mail — USPS Priority, Express or Certified Mail, UPS Next Day Air or Federal Express.

• Send important e-mails to yourself first as a test.

• 79 percent of smartphone owners and 72 percent of tablet owners use their devices for e-mail.

• 47 percent of all e-mails are opened on mobile devices — smartphones or tablets.

• 32 percent of e-mails are opened on desktop computers

CHAPTER 29

Public Relations, Publicity and Press Releases

In my fifteenth summer — more than 60 years ago — I signed on as a lowly apprentice at the Ivoryton, Connecticut, summer playhouse. I spent 12 splendid weeks working like a demon for no money doing whatever they told me to do. I painted scenery, cleaned johns, shoveled garbage, hefted blocks of ice into the air-cooling system, did sound effects and cued actors who were likely to muff lines.

I had to pay tuition (acting lessons) plus room and board. I thought I wanted to be an actor, but quickly discovered 1) I had no talent and 2) hated being out in front of people.

But I had the unmatched excitement of working with a then unknown Bob Fosse, who was spectacular as the star of Rodgers and Hart's *Pal Joey*. Others I worked with included Joan Bennett, Eve Arden, Lawrence Tibbett, Marlon Brando, Cedric Hardwicke and Viveca Lindfors, to name a few.

The season was coming to an end when it was suddenly announced an extra week would be added to the schedule. Judy Holliday — who won the Academy Award in March for Garson Kanin's *Born Yesterday* — had just been signed to appear in Elmer Rice's *Dream Girl* with Richard Derr.

Evelyn, my first mentor
The theater publicist was a big, faded, hard-drinking, heavy-smoking blonde named Evelyn Lawson. She had once danced in the Ziegfeld Follies and was a product of the 1930s and 1940s — an age epitomized by Walter Winchell, the Stork Club and *Casablanca*.

Evelyn had spent the summer working and drinking and wanted to go home. She was tired, she said, and needed help. I volunteered. During the week Evelyn taught me the basics of publicity and public relations.

About public relations (PR) and publicity
"PR is letting people in on what you are doing," Evelyn told me on the first day. We were sitting in her little, smoke-filled office in the back of the rehearsal barn.

"Editors are basically lazy. Give them a story they can use, and running it is easier than going to the trouble of writing something themselves."

"How do you know what they can use?" I asked.

"You've got to know their publications... know who they are talking to... and then give them a story of interest to their readers and in the style of the publication."

My first press release
Under Evelyn's guidance, I wrote a 3-page, double-spaced release announcing *Dream Girl* for the local papers. Using an old Remington office typewriter, I two-fingered it on

purple stencils. Every typo required stopping to paint the error with purple stencil goo and retyping the word.

The next step was to lay the stencil on the inky drum of the mimeograph machine and crank it out by hand onto paper. This was followed by collating, stapling and folding the three pages. The release was inserted in #10 envelopes with the headline facing out (so it was the first thing the addressee saw).

The second operation was typing the labels and affixing them to the envelopes, which I licked — along with postage stamps — and took them to the post office.

Wonder of wonders! *The Middletown Press* ran my release verbatim!

It was the first time I had seen anything I had written in print. It was thrilling! Neither Evelyn nor my parents nor I could believe it. It ran because Evelyn taught me the rules and I followed them.

Best of all, *Dream Girl* played to sold-out houses.

I became hooked on writing.

Press releases in the pre-Internet era

For my press release to be printed, someone at the newspaper had to retype my words, which were then formed into lead type set in trays. The type was inked and the paper printed. Afterward, the type was melted down and reused for another story and another and another.

When I was in the army in the late 1950s — serving overseas on Governor's Island in New York Harbor — I wrote press releases for the First Army Public Information Organization. The only difference was the Army mimeograph machine was electrified. Otherwise it was the same process I had learned under Evelyn Lawson.

During my first job after the army, I wrote press releases on upcoming books for Prentice Hall in New Jersey. The highest compliment I could receive — the ultimate success — was when a book critic signed my release and called it his review.

This happened more than once, and it was thrilling.

I had gamed the system.

Press releases in the digital age

Today, press releases arrive by snail mail and/or e-mail. They can go in an envelope with a paper label and crooked stamp in the corner just like the old days.

As e-mail, they come directly into a computer. Sentences and entire paragraphs can be lifted, reworked and shaped into an "original" story by the editors receiving them. Or they can be printed as is.

When distributed over the Internet, among the possible bells and whistles you can include: hyperlinks, videos, attachments, photos and documents.

Editors are just as lazy as they always were, and the computer has enabled them to be lazier.

Trust me on this. I am an editor and I am lazy.

The object of a press release
Before writing and posting a press release, decide what you want for a response:

- Publicity
- Investors
- Customers
- Sales
- Inquiries
- Contributors
- Buzz
- Interviews

What a press release is
Bill Stoller, proprietor of publicityinsider.com, defines a press release as:

> ... a pseudo-news story, written in third person, that seeks to demonstrate to an editor or reporter the newsworthiness of a particular person, event, service or product.

A press release is rather like a résumé. It can be sent out on its own by e-mail, fax or snail mail.

- **A release can also be accompanied by a personal cover letter.** If a direct mail package, the press release would be akin to the brochure — the "it" copy, all about the person, event, service or product.

  The cover letter is an emotional, personal, "me-to-you" message pointing out why you are receiving it and how the various features directly affect you, your readers, your customers or the world.

- **A release can be enclosed with an actual product.** A marketer of software could send a sample disc along with a cover letter and a press release. The release never has to be sent out. But it adds credibility — as though it is newsworthy.

  Same thing if the enclosure is an item of merchandise going to a store buyer or a cataloger. The cover letter is the personal message suggesting the item be inventoried and sold along with an irresistible discount schedule. The press release (which never has to be sent to the media) gives off the aura of national importance.

- **A release can be part of a full-dress press kit.** When you want media coverage of an event, a person or a product, put together a press kit. Included would be a press release and cover letter. Other possible additions: photographs, testimonials, reviews, FAQs, a CD and/or a DVD and Q&A with the CEO or inventor.

All these goodies should be enclosed in a handsome 9" X 12" presentation folder. The object is to give the reporter or broadcast writer so much usable background material it is easier to cover this story than scramble around looking for something else. You may find the late Dick Benson's direct mail rule to be valid for press kits: "Adding elements to a mailing package, even though obviously adding cost, is more likely to pay out than cheapening the package."

What a press release looks like

Company Logo
Address

Contact: Sample A. Sample Tel. 555/345-1234 (Rings on my desk) Cell Phone: 555/345-4321 E-mail: samplesample@gnet.com www.companylogo.com/prpitch	FOR IMMEDIATE RELEASE

Your Headline and Subhead Must Be Stoppers

Your first ten words are more important than the next ten thousand

DENVER, Feb. 19, 2013 — Like a news story, use the "inverted pyramid" format. The short lede paragraph describes who, what, where, when and how. This enables the reader to grasp the basics and decide whether or not to continue.

Subsequent paragraphs fill in details, from the most important down to the least important.

When an inverted pyramid story goes out over the wires or Internet, editors can pick up as much or as little as they want, depending on the space available. Even if all but the first two paragraphs are lopped off, readers still get the guts of the story.

The above technique is a viable concept for press releases, news stories, memos, whitepapers, reports, PowerPoint presentations and virtually any other nonfiction writing you create.

....

A press release should followthe rules of nonfiction writing
- Powerful, interruptive headline and subhead.
- Short words. Short sentences. Short paragraphs.
- Skip a line between paragraphs.
- Crossheads to break up monotony.
- No gray walls of type.

• Newsworthy, or at least the appearance of newsworthiness.
• Try to include one or more quotes from outsiders.
• Line width no more than 75 characters including spaces.

Razzle-dazzle releases over the Internet

The press release has come a long way from the old days where I cut a stencil, hand-cranked a mimeograph machine, typed labels and licked envelopes.

A number of distribution services are available, enabling you to reach tens of thousands of prospects with your message. Among them: prweb.com, prnewswire.com, webwire.com, businesswire.com and others.

If you opt for the PRWeb Premium Service, here are examples of your options:

Format

Your interactive, Web-optimized news release can include:
• Keyword links to your website to boost search engine rankings.
• Ability to embed images that show your business, your merchandise, etc.
• Ability to add video to your releases.
• Personalized RSS feed within your release, so your readers can subscribe to news about you.

Distribution

• Major search engines — Google, Yahoo, Bing, etc.
• Major online news sites like Yahoo News.
• Premium news outlets such as *USA Today, NY Times, Washington Post* and more through the Associated Press.
• More than 250,000 PRWeb news subscribers and 30,000+ journalists and bloggers.

Targeted distribution

• Choose 10 industries and 5 regions you want to reach.
• Permanent hosting on prweb.com.
• Link to your actual website within the release.
• File attachments: add documents, photos, presentations, whatever helps you tell your story.
• "ShareThis" makes it easy for readers to send your news to others through blogs, Facebook, Twitter, Technorati, Digg, LinkedIn, etc.
• Custom URLs for better search engine result. *—PR Web Premium Service*

Why all your communications must be world-class

Looking back more than 60 years — my hand-typed press release for the Ivoryton Playhouse went to 13 publications. The idea of reaching 250,000 readers in an instant is staggering to me today.

Blogger Jeremy Porter of journalistics.com heard from a reporter at a small local paper who received 80 press releases in one day. In a 10-hour workday, this represents one new press release every seven-and-a-half minutes!

According to Jeremy Porter's blog, PR Newswire and Business Wire regularly send out 1,000 news releases a day (2,000 total). You can add to this mix the output of 43 other release distribution services in the Yahoo directory. Plus completing the e-tsunami are myriad bloggers, media websites and RSS (Rich Site Summary) feeds.

In short, all of us — media, working stiffs, consumers and everybody with Internet access — are up to our eyebrows in e-information.

If you want people to read and heed you, your output must be riveting.

To whom do you send a press release?
The late direct marketing practitioner and teacher Ed Mayer came up with a formula for success in direct marketing: 40 percent lists, 40 percent offer, 20 percent everything else.

Same thing with a press release. If it is industry-specific and goes to the wrong list, it will not be disseminated. An irrelevant message will be trashed.

Sure, you can send it out through one of the distribution services and get coverage and search engine listings. But this is the equivalent of throwing raw eggs against the wall and hoping something sticks.

The secret of direct marketing is careful research — figuring out the right offer to the right person at the right price at the right time.

For direct mail or e-mail to be successful, it is essential to work with an expert on lists — or be one yourself. In PR, know your media:

- Read the publications, websites and blogs.

- Know by name the writers, reporters, columnists, bloggers and experts who write, consult and make presentations at industry conferences.

- Figure out ways to make their jobs easier.

- Contact them personally only when you have something important to promote — something you believe in.

- Do not waste their time with trivia.

- Never forget Elmer "Sizzle" Wheeler: "The first 10 words are more important than the next ten thousand."

- When you get a response to a press release — a request for the special report you promised or to schedule an interview with the corporate officer you quoted — have the information on hand and reply at once.

- Have all fulfillment materials ready to go before release is posted.

One word to guarantee readership: 'Embargoed'
Two great direct marketing gurus — Axel Andersson and Bob Hacker — came up with a list of the seven key copy drivers. These are the emotional hot buttons causing humans to act:

fear — greed — guilt — anger — exclusivity — salvation — flattery

Axel Andersson was a Swede who created the largest home study business in the world — the Axel Andersson Akademie in Hamburg, Germany. He once analyzed 872 American direct mail letters in different business categories and discovered 43 percent were based on flattery.

Presidential flattery and exclusivity

When Barack Obama announced his run for the presidency back in early 2008, I signed up to be in his mailing list (and also Hillary Clinton's). The chutzpah of an unknown African-American former Chicago community organizer (whatever that is) was too juicy to ignore. I now have in my archive more than 2,400 e-communiqués from the Obama campaigns, Democratic officials and from the White House Media Affairs Office.

Every so often the White House makes me feel like a real insider by sending me a press release with a single word guaranteed to make me pay attention. A sampling of the subject lines:

> **EMBARGOED: Remarks of President Barack Obama's Address to the Nation on the End of Combat Operations in Iraq — As Prepared for Delivery**
> EMBARGOED UNTIL DELIVERY Aug. 31
>
> **EMBARGOED Fact Sheet: The Six-Month Anniversary of the Affordable Care Act**
> EMBARGOED for 6:00 AM EDT on Wednesday, Sept. 22
>
> **EMBARGOED: Background on the President's Recovery Act Announcement Tomorrow**
> EMBARGOED for 12:01 AM EDT Friday

What 'embargoed' means

You are a trusted insider and important to us. We don't want you to be caught by surprise, so we are alerting you in advance of the rest of the media — and the country. But you may not use this news until the date and time specified.

This is exclusivity and flattery.

How to employ this technique

I would use the embargoed press release only for special occasions — not routine announcements (e.g., appointment of a new marketing manager or vice president).

Instead, save it for the launch of a new product or service or corporate acquisition. Send this embargoed press release out with a personal cover letter to your private contact list — people with their own followings. They can help you get the word out:

- Media people who could write about it or get you TV coverage.
- Potential investors.
- Major retailers that could carry it in their stores or catalogs.
- Your in-house file of customers, friends and prospects.

If the list is not huge, consider sending this effort two ways — e-mail and snail mail — both scheduled to arrive on the same day.

The snail-mail package
If affordable, send a 9"x12" envelope so all the elements lie flat. It will stand out from other mail. If you have the budget, send it via Federal Express, Priority Mail or UPS so the recipient knows you mean business. The elements:

- **The embargoed press release:** Under the title in large boldface type insert the following:

  EMBARGOED UNTIL [DATE AND TIME]

- **The cover letter:** This is personalized, warm and enthusiastic. Include a backstory and details to whet the appetite of the recipient. Offer to send a sample or arrange for a private demonstration. Make the key players available for private interviews before the news hits, so these special folks can enjoy a sense of exclusivity.

- **Other elements:** photographs, testimonials — anything to help make your pitch come alive.

What to send by e-mail
Be wary of including attachments with your e-mails to strangers. Images can be automatically blocked or the entire effort can end up in the spam file and never be seen.

Instead, send the cover letter as e-mail, followed by the embargoed press release in the body of the e-mail.

Your e-mail — and press release — should have a killer subject line and short, powerful copy. Include a hyperlink that invites the reader to a special landing page. Once the prospect is in your territory, you are in control.

Takeaways to Consider

- "PR is letting people in on what you are doing." *—Evelyn Lawson*

- "Editors are basically lazy. Give them a story they can use, and running it is easier than going to the trouble of writing something themselves." *—Evelyn Lawson*

- "You've got to know their publications... know who they are talking to ... and then give them a story of interest to their readers and in the style of the publication." *—Evelyn Lawson*

- According to Jeremy Porter's blog, journalistics.com, PR Newswire and Business Wire regularly send out 1,000 news releases a day (2,000 total). You can add to this mix the output of 43 other release distribution services in the Yahoo directory. Plus completing the e-tsunami are myriad bloggers, media websites and RSS (Rich Site Summary) feeds.

• In short, all of us — media, working stiffs, consumers and everyone with Internet access — are drowning in e-information.

• If you want people to read and heed you, your output must be riveting.

• A magic word to increase interest: EMBARGOED.

• Before writing and posting a press release, decide what you want for a response:
—Publicity
—Investors
—Customers
—Inquiries
—Contributors
—Buzz
—Interviews

• "A press release is a pseudo-news story, written in third person, that seeks to demonstrate to an editor or reporter the newsworthiness of a particular person, event, service or product." —*Bill Stoller*

• A press release should follow the rules of nonfiction writing:
—Powerful, interruptive headline and subhead.
—Inverted pyramid format.
—Short words. Short sentences. Short paragraphs.
—Skip a line between paragraphs.
—Crossheads to break up monotony.
—No gray walls of type.
—Newsworthy, or at least the appearance of newsworthiness.
—Try to include one or more quotes from outsiders.

• In PR, know your media:
—Read the publications, websites and blogs.
—Know by name the writers, reporters, columnists, bloggers and experts who write, consult and make presentations at industry conferences.
—Figure out ways to make their jobs easier.
—Contact them personally only when you have something important to promote — something you believe in.
—Do not waste their time with trivia.
—Never forget Elmer "Sizzle" Wheeler: "The first 10 words are more im portant than the next ten thousand."
—When you get a response to a press release — a request for the special report you promised or to schedule an interview with the corporate officer you quoted — have the information on hand and reply at once.
—Have all fulfillment materials ready to go before your release is posted.

• Responses to inquiries or replies must be immediate. If you or your staff is engaged in other pursuits — on the phone or in a meeting — leave a voice mail that promises instant attention. And then live up to the promise.

• Users of e-commerce expect instant gratification.

• The hyperlink in the cover letter and in the press release should not take the reader to your all-purpose home page. Instead, create a separate landing page that refers directly to the release and create a Web experience around it.

• Make yourself immediately available in myriad ways: e-mail, phone, etc.

CHAPTER 30

The Secret of a PR Blitzkrieg Campaign

Use it to launch a book, a product, a service, yourself — anything at all
MacRae Ross was a client many years ago and a great guy. He taught me a lot. Everybody who knew him loved him. Mac was smart, bubbling with energy, a devout rugby player, great conversationalist and party animal. I heard he married a lady named Marji and became a father. But he was in the Washington, D.C. area while Peggy and I were living in Connecticut. We lost touch. I was deeply saddened to hear Mac had died of pancreatic cancer in 2006. He was so very young. In the July 16, 1998, issue of *Fast Company*, Lisa Chatterton wrote:

> MacRae Ross, for example, a marketing consultant at Ross & Co. in McLean, Virginia, says that over the past nine years, he's told more than 5,000 companies to "Fish where the fish are."
>
> "It communicates a simple but powerful idea," he explains. "To sell what you're selling, you have to be talking to the right crowd."

This theme was picked up and pounded home at a Publishing Business Conference & Expo in Manhattan. The presenter was President and Publisher of Regnery Publishing, Marji Ross, who is every bit as articulate and savvy as her late husband.

Marji Ross
How savvy is Marji Ross? Half the books she publishes reach *The New York Times* Best-Seller List. No other publisher comes close to her percentage.

If you are going to launch a book, a product or a service, commit to memory the Marji Ross formula of Blitzkrieg PR, which she shared with at the Publishing Business Conference in New York.

Then go and do thou likewise.

About Regnery Publishing Inc.
The company founded in 1947 by Henry Regnery has become the beating heart of book publishing in the U.S. for the Conservative movement. It has a take-no-prisoners attitude and a string of *New York Times* best-sellers to die for. Among its blue-ribbon roster of authors past and present: William F. Buckley Jr., Newt Gingrich, Laura Ingraham, Mark Fuhrman, Pat Buchanan, Ann Coulter, G. Gordon Liddy and Oliver North.

Regnery has always thrived on controversy. And hype. It has grabbed headlines and sometimes changed history. A prime example: *Unfit For Command: Swift Boat Veterans Speak Out Against John Kerry* very likely cost John Kerry the presidency in 2004.

What are the secrets of launching a best-seller? And how can you make these PR and publicity techniques work for you when launching a non-book product or service?

Pick the right book, product or service in the first place
Regnery publishes relatively few titles, so it can concentrate on marketing each product with great precision and care. Before a book is accepted for publication, it must get over many hurdles and satisfy a lot of different criteria:

- Breaks news.
- Unique, fun, shocking, appalling.
- Relevant.
- Controversial: creates buzz, anger, discussion, debate, controversy.
- If it is not entertaining, you will have a tough sell.

The author interview
Before a book is accepted, the author is invited to a meeting to sell the editorial and marketing people on the project. The author must be:

- Passionate.
- A crusader.
- On a mission.
- Revealing something new.
- Impressive to everybody sitting around the table.

The first question: "Who will this book be for? Who will buy it?"

It is the kiss of death when an author replies, "This book is for everybody."

"No book is for everyone," Marji Ross will snap. "In the words of Mac Ross, 'Fish where the fish are.'"

It is imperative to know precisely whom the book is for. Knowing your reader affects every facet of the product: cover, chapter headings, the type and the voice, as well as where and how to publicize it.

Make sure it's a book and not a magazine article
Marji Ross described a book about a soldier who lost a leg in Iraq. He was given a prosthetic limb and, after much rehab, was judged fit to return to the battlefield and lead his old unit. This was inspiring stuff and got a huge spread in *People* magazine. Since *People* gave readers the whole story, they had no need to spend $25 for the book and didn't.

Involve everyone at the outset
In most publishing houses, the editor works with the author. When the book is ready for production, it is then passed on to the designers. Thereafter it goes to the marketing, publicity and sales departments to work their alchemy.

At Regnery, the entire team is involved from the moment a title is accepted for publication.

Go dark
The project and the author are kept under wraps for a month before launch:

- No advance publicity.
- Get advance copies into the hands of influencers, but embargo all discussion until the publication date.

Publicizing a book (or getting buyers excited about a product or service) when it is not yet on sale and is unavailable is a waste. (The exception: live music, theater and movies. Advance tickets must be sold or theaters will open empty.)

The USP (unique selling proposition)
Regnery does not publish books. Its authors make news.

A Regnery press release never-oh-never has a headline saying, "So-and-so wrote a book." Instead it tells people this is news and here is how you get it. The book is incidental to the author and news being made.

Marketing: the wholesale phase
In the case of launching a book, everything leading up to the publication date is the early phase of the campaign.

The pub date is D-Day — the surprise assault on the world.

Plan your campaign as meticulously as General Dwight Eisenhower and the commanders who planned Overlord, the invasion of Normandy, June 6, 1944.

Sampling
During this wholesale phase, advance copies of the new title must be put into the hands of the right reviewers, bloggers and influencers, giving them time to read and reflect on it. However, reviews and discussion by print and online journalists must be embargoed until publication date.

Each review copy should be accompanied by an embargoed press release and, if possible, a personal cover letter.

Author appearances must be booked, e-mail addresses assembled and readied for the big e-blasts.

As with D-Day, the Pub Date is the commencement of the action — the retail phase. The public is bombarded from every possible direction with news, publicity and sales pitches for the product. This is the Blitzkrieg.

Collecting e-mail addresses
Regnery has the e-mail addresses of roughly 800,000 conservative readers. Does the author have a list? If so, it should be added to the Regnery pot, with duplications eliminated. If you do not have a list of relevant e-mail recipients, assemble one. It should be ready for an e-mail blast the day of publication (or launch of the new product or service).

The murder board: prepping the author
The author is the main salesperson. With the exception of talk-show hosts such as Laura Ingraham and Pat Buchanan — or a practiced politician such as Newt Gingrich — authors must be coached before they make media appearances.

Bring them into the office and expose them to a murder board — a hard-nosed panel charged with giving the author a hard time with tough, nasty questions. A grilling by the murder board will keep authors from stumbling and flubbing answers when live on the air.

Impress on the author to never neglect the core audience. It is tempting to try and convert the uninitiated, but the core audience is where the sales are. It's easy to walk away from your base, said Marji Ross, and not sell to them. But an author must talk to the base — "fish where the fish are."

Pub date

By the publication date, printed books must be in bookstores where they can be physically pawed over by customers.

In addition, at 12:01 on Pub Date morning, the order mechanism goes live on the Internet retailers — amazon.com, barnesandnoble.com, powells.com and the other online sellers.

Books need to be in the online bookstores' warehouses and ready to ship. It is a catastrophe to allow a book to go out of inventory in the middle of a selling bonanza and become unavailable when customers want it.

And it must be available for sale in the various e-book formats.

Retail: the one-week Blitzkrieg assault

The object is to get as much action, publicity, buzz and sales as possible the first week the title is available. This convergence of action and pressure will get it on the best-seller list the very first week:

- Regnery authors do 10 to 15 talk-show interviews every day of Blitzkrieg week.

- These are not five minutes on a Saturday morning satellite show. Shoot for 15 to 20 minutes or more on every relevant radio show in the country.

- Book the author on cable news shows: Fox, PBS, CNN and MSNBC, as well as local TV news shows.

- Plus the ABC, CBS, NBC morning shows.

- Also shoot for Leno, Letterman, Bill Maher, Ellen DeGeneres and *The View.*

- If the Pub Date is Monday, unleash the 800,000 e-mail blast on Monday with crackling prose and breaking news peppered throughout with hyperlinks to amazon.com and barnesandnoble.com. Not hyperlinks to these booksellers' home pages, but directly to the title itself.

- Continuously read results.

- Pay attention to the blogosphere. This is a major information and discussion community. It can create buzz and viral marketing.

Takeaway Points to Consider

• "Fish where the fish are." *—Mac Ross*

• "It communicates a simple but powerful idea — to sell what you're selling, you have to be talking to the right crowd." *—Mac Ross*

• Plan your PR/publicity campaign with precision.

• Involve your entire staff at the outset. Don't spring the job on the team late in the game.

• Separate your efforts into a wholesale and retail phase.

• Consider the Blitzkrieg approach — storming the marketplace from every possible direction during a narrow period of time — rather than leaking information over weeks and months.

• If you decide on a Blitzkrieg, go dark the prior month.

• Get relevant materials into the hands of influencers, but embargo all coverage until the launch date.

• Make your spokesperson battle-ready using the murder board technique.

• Assemble e-mail addresses and sort them by relevancy.

• Do not ignore the blogosphere. This is the prime source of viral marketing.

• Remember the late Ed Mayer's formula for direct mail success: 40 percent lists, 40 percent offer and 20 percent everything else. This holds for PR and publicity as well as direct marketing. A sample sent to the wrong influencer is a dead loss.

CHAPTER 31

When You're Asked for a Review

Here's the lede of a review that had me salivating to order the book:

> **The Great Train Robbery**
> As the civil war entered its second year in 1862, it was still possible to imagine that the war would be short and relatively bloodless. But nothing that the Union or the Confederacy had accomplished during the previous year had resulted in a decisive advantage, and so soldiers and civilians on both sides began proposing imaginative schemes aimed at ending the war in a single brilliant stroke.
>
> Russell S. Bonds's masterly *Stealing the General* captures those early days by recounting one such scheme: a Union plot to steal a railroad locomotive deep in the South and race north, leaving destruction in its wake. The theft of the engine called the General — together with the frantic chase that ensued — is one of the most fascinating stories of the Civil War. Mr. Bonds's compelling narrative and convincing analysis give the episode its due at last. *—J. Tracy Power, The Wall Street Journal*

I adore trains. I love rip-snorting tales of high adventure and hijinks. When I read these first two paragraphs — a screaming rave — I decided then and there to order the book.

If only the reviewer had folded his tent and gone home ...
Had the reviewer stopped after the second paragraph, *Stealing the General* would have been in my Kindle 60 seconds later. Alas, the reviewer committed one of the Three Deadly Sins of book reviewing. He talked me out of buying the book.

The good news: I saved $29.95 plus tax.

The bad news: Richard de Wyngaert — proprietor of Headhouse Books, a stylish little emporium two blocks from my house — was screwed out of the sale, as were the author and the publisher. And I was screwed out of a delicious reading experience.

How newspapers deal with book reviews is symptomatic of why their circulation is off, why advertising is down, and why they're becoming vestigial.

It's an object lesson in how businesspeople must communicate or become vestigial themselves. Here are the Three Deadly Sins committed by reviewers — of books, movies, TV, theater and everything else:

Sin No. 1: Give too much information
J. Tracy Power, who reviewed *Stealing the General* for *The Wall Street Journal*, is a minor southern literary figure. He is the author of *Lee's Miserables* and a historian at the South Carolina Department of Archives and History.

To prove he had read the entire book, this reviewer summarized the plot in excruciating detail. The result was *The Wall Street Journal*'s own *CliffsNotes* edition in 1,510 words. By the end of his "review," I knew the entire story — beginning, middle and end, including the fate of the perpetrators. (Eight were hanged, eight escaped and made their way back north, and six remained in prison for the duration of the war.)

Test me on my knowledge of the book and the professor would give me an A+, guaranteed!

Why would a reader buy this book after knowing everything in the book and being robbed of any and all suspense?

In my opinion, this is not a review by a legitimate critic. J. Tracy Power swiped author Russell S. Bonds's research and created a feature article for *The Wall Street Journal*. This was naked theft.

Sin No. 2: Covering two or three books on the same subject in the same review
This is a favorite stunt of book editors. They hand off three new titles on Islam to a reviewer, who compares them to one another and leaves the reader totally confused about which to buy. The good news: the incompetent book editor got three reviews for the price of one. The bad news: three authors, three publishers and a slew of booksellers got screwed out of sales.

Sin No. 3: Showing off
Many insecure editors feel compelled to allow their insecure reviewers to bore the hell out of readers. These critics spend three or more paragraphs describing all the author's prior books before getting to the new one. The purpose of this tiresome exercise is not so much to impart information, but rather to show off the smarts and credentials of a reviewer while making the reader feel stupid.

This is true also of theater and film reviewers. Examples:

> ***Kinky Boots***
> Inspired by the little-seen 2005 movie of the same title, *Kinky Boots* is assembled from plot parts that have shown up all too frequently during the past decades in shows that were also based on films. Like *The Full Monty* (choreographed by Mr. Mitchell) and *Billy Elliot the Musical*, it is set in a hard-times British factory town, where jobs are in jeopardy and spirits need lifting. Like *La Cage aux Folles* and *Priscilla Queen of the Desert* it presents drag queens as the show's official spirit lifters. *—Ben Brantley, The New York Times*
>
> ***Spies of Warsaw***
> There is no such thing as a good old-fashioned spy story. The best, especially the novels of John le Carré, focus on the cracks in the system, double agents like Kim Philby who did more damage from within than the enemy could manage on the other side. Some look into the margins of history, digging out improbable subplots, like *Operation Mincemeat*, a book about the disinformation campaign British intelligence created to mislead Hitler about the invasion of Sicily. The FX television series *The Americans* looks at cold war espionage from the Soviet point of view: the heroes are two K.G.B. agents living undercover in Reagan's America. *—Alesandra Stanley, The New York Times*

Lee Daniels' The Butler
"Nobody who has seen *Shadowboxer*, *Precious* or, heaven knows, *Paperboy*, would mistake Lee Daniels for a realist." *—A.O. Scott's lede, The New York Times*

A retrospective hoot
Occasionally, a critic will pull this stunt off with flair and fun. Here's the lede by Giles Coren in his *Times of London* review of the delicious 2006 remake of Ian Fleming's *Casino Royale:*

> BY HECK, DANIEL CRAIG looks nice in his pants. I haven't fancied a Bond so much since David Niven. It's mostly the fact that he has a proper chest. Connery's you couldn't see for the rogue pubes on northward manoeuvres, Roger Moore's was so slack that his nipples were lower than his waistband (though I'll grant you the waist on those trousers was high) and Pierce Brosnan had that old-man-sucky-tummy-puff-yer-chest-out thing going on, so that he appeared to have an actual embonpoint. But Daniel, with those hoddy's shoulders and the square-cut trunks … yum, yum.

Orson Welles nailed it
From *My Lunches with Orson* by Peter Biskind:

> Graham Greene was a movie critic for about six years. His reviews were not very good. They were neither witty, nor amusing, nor original. They were just intelligent, plain, ordinary reviews. If you're going to be an interesting critic, you have got to have a little zing. It's all right to be wrong, but you've to be interesting. We're all in the same business. We're entertaining the public. —*Orson Welles to Henry Jaglom*

Why the current book review system is a train wreck
When my first novel, *Cedarhurst Alley*, was published in 1969, the total number of new titles being brought out by all publishers was 15,000 a year. As a result, my little marshmallow fluff of a comedy received some nice reviews including an okay one in *Time* magazine.

Today more than 200,000 new titles are being published annually — more than 4,000 a week!

Or maybe it's 400,000 new titles a year. The statisticians seem to be at odds over the total number.

A recent Sunday *New York Times Book Review* — operating on a 1950s publishing model — covered just 19 new adult titles. The cover story was a thumb-sucker by Jim Windolf on Stephen King's literary output. Stephen King? Is the publication of his new chiller really worth a 2,339-word retrospective when 3,999 other new books last week were crying for attention?

The worst show-off reviewer: Joyce Carol Oates
Here's a sampling from *The New York Times* — a review by Joyce Carol Oates. Her lede paragraph is made up of three sentences, the first two being an unreadable 63 and

62 words, respectively. She discusses the works of 12 other authors before getting to the review at hand:

> ***American Wife***
> by Curtis Sittenfeld
> Is there a distinctly American experience? *The American*, by Henry James; *An American Tragedy*, by Theodore Dreiser; *The Quiet American*, by Graham Greene; *The Ugly American*, by William Lederer and Eugene Burdick; Philip Roth's *American Pastoral* and Bret Easton Ellis's *American Psycho* — each suggests, in its very title, a mythic dimension in which fictitious characters are intended to represent national types or predilections. Our greatest 19th-century prose writers from Washington Irving, Nathaniel Hawthorne and Herman Melville through Henry James and Mark Twain took it for granted that "American" is an identity fraught with ambiguity, as in those allegorical parables by Hawthorne in which "good" and "evil" are mysteriously conjoined; to be an "American" is to be a kind of pilgrim, an archetypal seeker after truth. Though destined to be thwarted, even defeated, the pilgrim is our deepest and purest American self.
>
> The young heroines of Curtis Sittenfeld's previous novels *Prep* and *The Man of my Dreams* like the more mature protagonist of Sittenfeld's third and most ambitious novel, *American Wife*, are sister-variants of the American outsider ...
> *—Joyce Carol Oates, The New York Times*

Were the *Times'* editors serving their readers, authors and publishers? Hell no. If they were doing their jobs, they would bring cogent information about as many new books as possible to its pages. Let these windy, self-indulgent critics such as Oates bloviate somewhere else.

Can blogs make up for the paucity of book reviews?

A story in *The New York Times* by Motoko Rich described how newspapers are bailing out of the book review business. Rich suggested bloggers would take up the slack. Mentioned in the story were several blogs. I visited them and downloaded some of the ledes:

> ***The Lighthouse: An Adam Dalgliesh Mystery***
> by P.D. James
> To be honest, a whodunit is not my cup of tea. One is thrust into the guessing game very early on, the detective always gets his culprit, and this person is the least likely suspect. As a genre, the detective novel is conventional and predictable and does not often make for a good reading experience. *—curledup.com*

> ***Boomsday***
> by Christopher Buckley
> One thing I hate: any book that reads as if it's based on an "idea" — you know, those plots that occur to you on your way to work in the morning. Usually, they seem great on the surface, but any attempt to build an entire book on one reveals just how empty the idea actually is. As in, "Why hasn't anyone written a book about a time traveling serial killer?" or "What if a blind man was cured but didn't like what he saw when the bandages were removed?" Novels like this clog bookstore shelves, often sell well, and are usually terrible. *—bookslut.com*

> **Be Brave**
> Thanks to the part-time paying gig, I didn't get the chance to finish up the first set of reviews I wanted to share today. I blame the broken promise on the fact that I had to spend an evening proofreading text full of Chinese characters, typeface not people. Let's just say I'm still hungover, so here's a little something from Roberto Bolaño's "Advice on the Art of Writing Short Stories." — *Syntax of Things ("One person's crap is another person's blog")*

Blogs clearly are not the answer to providing readers with the information they want.

My solution: the 55-word book review
I wanted to see a good movie — one that rated three or four stars. I opened the *Philadelphia Inquirer*, and in under a minute, I homed in on the following:

> ***The Hoax ***1/2*** Richard Gere stars in this smart, witty tale based on a stranger-than-fiction yarn that really, truly occurred: Clifford Irving's legendary 1971 scam in which he convinced a publisher to pay him almost $1 million for the exclusive, authorized biography of billionaire recluse Howard Hughes. 1 hr. 56 R (profanity, adult themes) —*S.R.*

Steven Rea had boiled down his full-length review to just 44 words, telling me everything I needed to know to make a buying decision. The $9 admission and 2-1/2 hours of my time were well spent.

In a 2007 issue of *Business Common Sense* I wrote, "The Book Business: An Industry of Whiners," I proposed an online (for-profit) book review service: quickiebookreviews.com. It would feature short reviews (55 words of actual review text) and one to four stars — just like movie reviews. Here's a sampling of what I had in mind:

> *******In FED We Trust: Ben Bernanke's War on the Great Panic*** by David Wessel. A superb primer on the Fed — lender of last resort — its inner workings and the machinations of the cast of characters that dealt with the current crisis, headed by Ben Bernanke, whose in-depth research of the Great Depression enabled mostly right decisions to be made. Must reading for history buffs, news junkies and, yes, economists. Crown Business, 336pp, ISBN-13: 978-0307459688, $26.99 hardcover. —*DH*
>
> *******Churchill*** by Paul Johnson. A wonderful, short biography with a brilliant analysis of the 10 reasons why Winston Churchill was the man who saved Britain, Europe and very likely western civilization. It also captures Churchill's rollicking wit, extraordinary command of language, ability to prioritize and an incredible constitution that enabled him to work 16-hour days for weeks on end. Viking Adult, 192pp, ISBN-13: 978-0670021055, $24.95, hardcover. —*DH*
>
> *******The Looming Tower: Al Qaeda and the Road to 9/11*** by Lawrence Wright. A riveting masterpiece that explores the twisted mind-set of the jihadists, their pathological hatred of the West and their bleak lives. Among the players and their stories: the founding Islamic scholar, Sayyid Qutb, Ayman

al-Zawahiri plus Osama bin Laden and the evolution of al-Qaeda. Especially upsetting: the failure of American intelligence and its sad-sack bureaucracy. Vintage, 576pp, ISBN-13: 978-1400030842, $15.95, paperback. *—DH*

****Empires of the Sea: The Siege of Malta, the Battle of Lepanto, and the Contest for the Center of the World*** by Roger Crowley. The 16th century struggle between Christianity and Islam with the best descriptions of sea and land battles you will ever read — guaranteed! Plus magnificent portraits of the players — Barbarossa, Charles V, Pius V, Suleiman the Magnificent and Jean Parisot de la Valette and the Knights of Malta. Grim, brutal, brilliant, diamond-hard prose. Not for timid readers. Random House, 368pp, ISBN-13: 978-1400066247, $30, hardcover. *—DH*

****Moon River and Me: A Memoir*** by Andy Williams. I saw a lot of Andy Williams when I was an NBC page on the old Steve Allen Tonight Show. This lovely guy has written a delicious show biz insider's remembrance punctuated by laugh-out-loud stories and tempered by two horrific murders that touched him — Robert Kennedy and skier Spider Savitch, accidentally shot by Williams' ex-wife, Claudine Longet. Viking Adult, 320pp, ISBN-13: 978-0670021178, $25.95, hardcover. *—DH*

*** The Way of the World: A Story of Truth and Hope in an Age of Extremism*** by Ron Suskind. Wildly overwritten and under-edited with vast chunks that can be skipped. But the guts — excruciating details of the administration's dealing with intel and the CIA's forged letter about Mohammed Atta being trained in Iraq — are worth the price. The most chilling line: after learning no WMD existed, President Bush said, "F**k it, we're going in." Harper, 432 pp, ISBN: 978-0061430626, $27.95, hardcover. *—DH*

***** Guerilla P.R. 2.0: How You Can Wage An Effective Publicity Campaign without Going Broke*** by Michael Levine. The art, science, chutzpah and insider secrets of doing high-octane, low-cost PR and publicity using 21st century media and technology. The stories of Jean-Claude Baker, Candy Lightner, Roger Ailes and Dick Rutan are worth the price. The sample press releases and "Tips & Traps" are invaluable. Read it. Then go, and do thou likewise. Collins, 2008, 368 pp, ISBN-978-0-06-143852-3, $14.95, trade paperback. *—DH*

***** Troublesome Young Men: The Rebels Who Brought Churchill to Power and Helped Save England*** by Lynne Olson. The gripping story of 30 members of Parliament that engineered the political coup that ousted do-nothing Prime Minister Neville Chamberlain in 1940. The chapter titled "In the Name of God, Go!" is so thrilling that it's worth the price of the book. As relevant today as any current book on the Iraq War. A stunner. Farrar Straus Giroux, 436pp, ISBN-13: 978-0374179540, $27.50. *—DH*

****Devil May Care: The New James Bond Novel*** by Sebastian Faulks writing as Ian Fleming. Pure, nail-biting, page-turning fun filled with girls, gadgets, gore and a deliciously evil, deformed villain. The backdrop is the narcotics trade with extreme action taking place in London, Paris, Teheran, Stalingrad and the grim deserts in between. Bond is older, but is he wiser? Uh-uh. But, hey, this is Bond at his best. Doubleday, 2008, 285 pp, ISBN-978-0-385-52428-5, $24.95. —*DH*

*******The Forger's Spell: A True Story of Vermeer, Nazis, and the Greatest Art Hoax of the Twentieth Century*** by Edward Dolnick. A page-turner centered on greed, revenge and intrigue, plus a brief history of art and a fascinating course in Forgery 101. The dumbest amateur art enthusiast could see at a glance that Van Meegeren's forgeries could not possibly be authentic Vermeers. Yet the experts and leading museums in Holland were conned. Brilliantly written and illustrated. HarperCollins 2008, 349pp., ISBN-13: 978-0060825416, $26.95, hardcover. —*DH*

Takeaways to Consider

• When asked for a critique or a review, remember it's not about you.

• The reader wants to know about the thing itself — the book, movie, employee, business model, whitepaper, PowerPoint lecture or whatever.

• If you can bring relevant information from past experiences, do so — quickly and tersely and then get back to it.

• Many critics love to show off. They are determined to prove to the reader how much smarter they are than the writer (and the reader).

• Are you giving useful background and/or actionable information, or are you showing off how much you know?

• "Remember that your readers are as smart as you are." —*Jim Rutz, Freelance copywriter*

CHAPTER 32

Don't Hide Your Emotions

"When emotion and reason come into conflict, emotion wins every time." *—John J. Flieder*

This is the unlikely tale of two women unwittingly bound together.

Marissa Mayer has the warmth and sensitivity of a rhinoceros.

Kara Swisher is a loving, fearless, articulate and dead honest journalist.

These women have very different writing styles.

In over her head
When Marissa Mayer, Yahoo's new CEO, decreed employees could no longer work from home, a storm of controversy rippled through the high-tech industry and made news nationwide.

It was a PR catastrophe. It should have been avoided.

"Always try to convert a disadvantage into an advantage," Grolier Enterprises Chairman Elsworth Howell told me on my first day of work.

The great direct marketing guru Lester Wunderman said it a little differently: "Always try to turn a marketing disaster into a marketing opportunity."

This was all about direct marketing. It was a botched attempt to sell 14,000 Yahoo employees worldwide on why face-to-face interaction is more important than promises made to employees hired to work from home.

Yahoo's new wunderkind CEO
Marissa Mayer was employee No. 20 at Google. A specialist in artificial intelligence, she was running Google's Maps and Street View products when tapped to become CEO of Yahoo.

At age 37, Mayer arrived at Yahoo in July 2012 — the fifth CEO in as many years. She was very pregnant, had an estimated net worth of $300 million and had negotiated a $71 million compensation package.

Marissa Mayer had every reason to be ticked
Yahoo has been a problem child for years. February 2012 saw a drastic shake-up in leadership and the board of directors. Four months later, 2,000 employees were fired. A huge data breech in August resulted in the hacking theft of 400,000 passwords.

When Mayer arrived as the new CEO at Yahoo, she found an anemic corporate culture.

Morale was in the tank. From Claire Cain Miller and Nicole Perlroth's account in *The New York Times:*

> Parking lots and entire floors of cubicles were nearly empty because some employees were working as little as possible and leaving early. Then there were the 200 or so people who had work-at-home arrangements. Although they collected Yahoo paychecks, some did little work for the company and a few had even begun their own start-ups on the side.

So a memo went out to Yahoo employees stating work-at-home arrangements would no longer be tolerated as of June 2013. Employees who were promised work-at-home privileges had to come to the Yahoo offices.

Corporate and industry reaction was like a turd in the punchbowl
First off, if the *Times* story was correct — and only 200 employees had telecommuting arrangements. They and their managers could have been contacted individually and handled in a humane, friendly way.

Dealing with those office workers who were arriving late and leaving early should be left to their managers, department heads and VPs.

The executive nursery
Shortly after the memo arrived, it was revealed Marissa Mayer had personally paid for the building of a fully equipped nursery adjoining her office so she could bring the new baby to work. In the words of Leslie Larson and Hayley Peterson in *The Daily Mail*:

> Many employees are upset because they don't have the money or clout to build their own nurseries at work. And many assume Mayer has a whole team of people, from nannies to cooks and cleaners, helping her raise her son - after all, she does have a $5 million penthouse atop the Four Seasons hotel in San Francisco in addition to her $5.2 million 5-bedroom home in Palo Alto.

As blogger Kara Swisher wrote for *The Wall Street Journal* in allthingsd.com:

> "I wonder what would happen if my wife brought our kids and nanny to work and set 'em up in the cube next door?" joked a husband of another employee who will be losing her work-from-home privileges.

What follows is the leaked, ham-handed memo Marissa Mayer ordered sent to employees and signed by her new vice president of human resources, Jackie Rees:

> **YAHOO! PROPRIETARY AND CONFIDENTIAL INFORMATION — DO NOT FORWARD**
>
> Yahoos,
>
> Over the past few months, we have introduced a number of great benefits and tools to make us more productive, efficient and fun. With the introduction of initiatives like FYI, Goals and PB&J, we want everyone to participate in our culture and contribute to the positive momentum. From Sunnyvale to Santa

Monica, Bangalore to Beijing — I think we can all feel the energy and buzz in our offices.

To become the absolute best place to work, communication and collaboration will be important, so we need to be working side-by-side. That is why it is critical that we are all present in our offices. Some of the best decisions and insights come from hallway and cafeteria discussions, meeting new people, and impromptu team meetings. Speed and quality are often sacrificed when we work from home. We need to be one Yahoo, and that starts with physically being together.

Beginning in June, we're asking all employees with work-from-home arrangements to work in Yahoo offices. If this impacts you, your management has already been in touch with next steps. And, for the rest of us who occasionally have to stay home for the cable guy, please use your best judgment in the spirit of collaboration. Being a Yahoo isn't just about your day-to-day job, it is about the interactions and experiences that are only possible in our offices.

Thanks to all of you, we've already made remarkable progress as a company — and the best is yet to come.

Jackie

....

Bypassing the chain of command

In World War II, Eisenhower never would have ignored Generals Bradley and Patton and the entire command structure with a nuts-'n'-bolts order to troops of the First and Third Armies.

This would tell G.I.'s their superiors — from platoon leaders all the way up to corps and army commanders — were castrated and did not own their jobs.

Okay, prior to the Battle of Trafalgar, signal pennants went up the mast on Admiral Nelson's flagship, *Victory*: "England expects every man to do his duty."

And for sure, Ike addressed his troops (and the world) on June 6, 1944. But this was noble stuff designed to make the wings of the eagle flutter:

> Soldiers, Sailors and Airmen of the Allied Expeditionary Force! You are about to embark upon a great crusade, toward which we have striven these many months. The eyes of the world are upon you. The hopes and prayers of liberty loving people everywhere march with you. In company with our brave Allies and brothers in arms on other fronts, you will bring about the destruction of the German war machine, the elimination of Nazi tyranny over the oppressed peoples of Europe, and security for ourselves in a free world.
>
> Your task will not be an easy one. Your enemy is well trained, well equipped and battle hardened, he will fight savagely.
>
> But this is the year 1944! Much has happened since the Nazi triumphs of

> 1940-41. The United Nations have inflicted upon the Germans great defeats, in open battle, man to man. Our air offensive has seriously reduced their strength in the air and their capacity to wage war on the ground. Our home fronts have given us an overwhelming superiority in weapons and munitions of war, and placed at our disposal great reserves of trained fighting men. The tide has turned! The free men of the world are marching together to victory!
>
> I have full confidence in your courage, devotion to duty and skill in battle. We will accept nothing less than full victory!
>
> Good Luck! And let us all beseech the blessings of Almighty God upon this great and noble undertaking. *—Gen. Dwight D. Eisenhower*

Bypassing emotion
When announcing a sea change in corporate culture designed to turn lives and careers upside-down, a me-to-you, passionate, personal selling job must be carefully crafted. It should come directly from the warm and loving heart of the new CEO. Marissa Mayer is now captain of the ship, who cares deeply for every member of the crew right down to the cabin boy and the scullery.

The key copy drivers — emotional hot buttons to use guaranteeing a positive response:

- **Fear.** "In 2012, Yahoo managers had to tell 2,000 of our associates they were no longer needed and would be fired. I will do everything in my power to not let this happen again. I need your help ..."

- **Greed.** "Yahoo must increase revenue and profitability. Your input is desperately needed to grow the company. I cannot do it alone ..."

- **Guilt.** "I am the fifth CEO in five years. Only you can make it possible for none of us to go through the uncertainty of a possible sixth ..."

Where is the 'I'?
"The most important word in direct copy is not 'you' — as many of the textbooks would have it — but 'I,'" freelancer Richard Armstrong wrote to me.

> What makes a letter seem 'personal' is not seeing your own name printed dozens of times across the page, or even being battered to death with a never ending attack of 'you's.' It is, rather, the sense that one gets of being in the presence of the writer… that a real person sat down and wrote you a real letter.

Instead, what Yahoo employees got was a lecture from the cold, impersonal "we," who dislocated their shoulders patting themselves on the back for their innovative wizardry.

Cowardice or stupidity?
Marissa Mayer did not issue the order and sign it. Rather she foisted responsibility off on her new human resources director and hatchet woman, Jackie Rees, forcing her to be the bad cop for sending it out.

Eisenhower — the classiest of American commanders — would have been a fool to send out his exhortation to victory over the signature of his dour chief of staff, Lt. Gen. Walter Bedell Smith. This was Ike's show and Ike's responsibility. What's more, "Bee-tle" Smith was despised throughout the Army.

A slap in the face

The Yahoo memo out of HR was a stinging no-confidence vote to all Yahoo employees, from Sunnyvale to Santa Monica, Bangalore to Beijing — VPs, managers and worker bees.

The Kara Swisher connection

A number of years ago at a Direct Marketing [Association] conference in San Francisco, I heard a speech by *Wall Street Journal* technology reporter Kara Swisher. I was impressed. She was articulate, persuasive and held the attention of a large audience.

As a sometime novelist, I am always on the lookout for unusual names for fictional characters. Kara and Swisher are wonderful names. I remembered them.

In researching this sad story, I kept bumping into Kara Swisher. Now writing for *The Wall Street Journal* blog, allthingsd.com, she is the media's leading expert on all things Yahoo. Her in-depth coverage of Yahoo — dozens of posts and columns on the company and its management — is widely quoted all over the world.

When I wanted to see Yahoo's confidential no-work-at-home memo, I found it in Kara Swisher's blog. In addition, she produces a torrent of stories on other companies and people — all superbly researched and elegantly written.

Ethics statement

On every Swisher landing page, next to her picture is a link: "ethics statement."

Why would a reporter need an ethics statement? What's going on with this renowned corporate reporter at the world's leading business and financial publication?

I clicked on her ethics statement and suddenly found myself smack in the middle of the most powerful, highly charged 1,506-word manifesto I have ever encountered in 77 years.

Swisher was facing a major challenge. She had to prove her journalistic cred to her *Wall Street Journal*'s management and colleagues as well as her readers, competitors and the individuals she would be covering.

Otherwise she would be forced to give it all up for love. Swisher let it all hang out — personal life, career, finances and business philosophy. Anyone who reads this piece will be deeply moved.

Let me say I have zero interest in people's personal lives or gender preferences. I care about competence. What follows is Swisher's lede — the first three paragraphs of an extraordinary document:

> Here is a statement of my ethics and coverage policies. It is more than most of you want to know, but, in the age of suspicion of the media, I am laying it all out.

> Let's begin with a critical piece of information every reader of this site needs to know about me: My spouse, Megan Smith, has been an executive at search giant Google since 2003, where she is vice president of new business development. More recently, she also added the job of general manager of the company's philanthropic arm, Google.org. (Yes, Megan works too much, but so do I.)
>
> Obviously, a substantial amount of her income from Google is in shares and options, some of which she has sold and some of which she still holds. Megan makes all her own decisions related to these shares and options, and I do not own or have future rights to own or control any of them. In addition, Megan still holds a number of shares and options (none of which I own, have future rights to own or control) in PlanetOut, where she served as CEO before she moved to Google. *—Kara Swisher, allthingsd.com*

What has this to do with Marissa Mayer? Everything!
Marissa Mayer allowed her HR director to sign off on a bunch of rah-rah, yuppie hooey. If she had exhibited a scintilla of the courage and class of Kara Swisher, she might have won over her Yahoo crew.

She could have been seen as the beleaguered, beloved young mom doing everything possible to right the good ship at Yahoo.

Instead Marissa Mayer and Jackie Rees — who damn well should have known better — blew it. They showed themselves to have zero sensitivity.

This is why Kara Swisher is an authentic hero to businesspeople everywhere and Marissa Mayer isn't.

Takeaways to Consider

• "When emotion and reason come into conflict, emotion wins every time." —*John J. Flieder*

• "We" do not write a letter, and "we" do not sign it.

• "The most important word in direct copy is not "you" — as many of the textbooks would have it — but "I" ... It is, rather, the sense that one gets of being in the presence of the writer ... that a real person sat down and wrote you a real letter." *—Richard Armstrong*

• "Be sure the right person signs the letter. Some time ago, two investors' newsletters — *Advance Planning Letter and Investors World Intelligent Report* — sent out long (12- and 16-page) highly technical promotional letters filled with forecasts with recommendations. The former was signed by Bobbie Bunch, Assistant to the Publisher; the latter was signed by Joan Pendergraft, Executive Assistant to Sid Pulitzer. Obviously neither wrote the letter, so believability is out the window." —*Malcolm Decker*

• Think long and hard before you bypass your command structure, and tell the world none of the people who work for you own their jobs.

• The way to run a company is to let people own their jobs. If they screw up, deal with them accordingly.

• For example, in World War II, scores of generals and colonels were fired for incompetence, including five corps commanders and 16 generals who commanded divisions.

• "[Army Chief of Staff Gen. George C.] Marshall saw relief as a natural part of generalship. Firing, like hiring, was simply one of the basic tasks of senior managers. It was inevitable when selecting human beings for extraordinarily complex and difficult jobs that some percentage would fail." *—Thomas E. Ricks, The Generals: American Military Command from World War II to Today*

• "Two rules and two rules only exist in marketing: Rule No. 1: Test everything. Rule No. 2: See Rule No. 1." *—Malcolm Decker*

• Let's say you created a document labeled: *PROPRIETARY AND CONFIDENTIAL INFORMATION — DO NOT FORWARD.* In this era of WikiLeaks, expect a disgruntled employee will put it in the hands of the media.

• Before you distribute it, have your defenses in place. Otherwise you could be on the wrong end of a PR crisis.

• "There are two speeds in modern P.R. — fast and dead." *—Michael Levine, Guerilla P.R. 2.0*

CHAPTER 33

Books: It's So Easy to Be Published These Days

Books in pre-Internet times

In the old days before the Internet, if a writer wanted to get a books published the choices were:

- **Find a book publisher** or a magazine to print your material.

- **Find an agent,** who, in turn, will find a book publisher or a magazine for you.

- **Start a your own magazine or newsletter,** as Peggy and I did in 1984 with *WHO'S MAILING WHAT!*

- **Pay top dollar to a "vanity" press to publish your book.** This was a financial killer. An author who could not find a publisher could bring the manuscript to a vanity publisher and pay to have the book printed. The costs: $2 to $5 for each hardcover book. Minimum print order: 2,500 copies or $5,000 to $12,500 out of pocket. Additional expenses: editing, book design, jacket design plus hefty fees for publicity, pubic relations and advertising.

Vanity publishers and the double-screwing of authors

After an investment of $10,000 to $25,000 or more, a total of maybe 200 copies would have been shipped. One hundred were wasted on book reviewers.

Why wasted? Vanity books were never reviewed in the mainstream media.

Forty books went to friends and relatives for Christmas and 40 were kept in the basement. With luck 20 books were actually sold in the marketplace.

The end result: 2,300 books remained on a pallet in the warehouse.

The ransom note

Six months later the publisher would write you a letter offering to sell you the remaining books for $3 each. Otherwise, they would be disposed of, because they are taking up too much room in the warehouse.

It made no never mind you paid to have the books published and they were your property. Under this patently dishonest scheme, the publisher was making you pay for them twice.

Many naïve authors could not stand the idea of their precious books being turned into landfill and ponied up another $5,000 to buy back their books. In addition, they had to pay for them to be trucked to their garages — where they gathered dust while the family car rusted in the driveway.

Vanity publishers, who double-charged authors, were not nice folks.

Book critics and vanity authors
For decades it was virtually impossible to get a self-published book reviewed in the mainstream media. The stated reason: if not good enough to be picked up by a leading publishing house, a vanity title didn't deserve to be reviewed.

What's more, a major source of income for book critics was selling their many hundreds of review copies a year to secondhand bookstores. As a thank-you to major publishers for sending every new book published, critics reviewed only those books and let vanity authors twist in the wind.

In the digital world, publishing your book is a walk in the park
Authors wanting their books published in print can use a system called Print on Demand (POD). Instead of a warehouse with 2,500 books sitting on a pallet, your book is warehoused in a computer.

When a copy is ordered, the computer tells the book machine to print a copy — crisp white pages bound in a handsome cover — and sent to the customer. No minimum print order required. Under the POD scheme, everybody can make money on the printing of a single copy.

It's bloody brilliant!

On the Internet you'll find a number self-publishers who will pitch their wares and guide you through the process — Amazon's CreateSpace and Lulu among them.

Author's editorial expenses
Unless you are eagle-eyed and know the English language cold, hire a freelance copy editor to tidy up your prose. Otherwise embarrassing typos will follow you to the grave and beyond.

Your cost for getting your book into a Print on Demand system and available for sale: a few hundred bucks.

Or, go the e-book route
I had a novel languishing in my computer for 10 years. Figuring it had film possibilities, I decided to explore bringing it out with Amazon in the Kindle e-book format.

I hired a freelance copy editor to clean up typos and sticky syntax. Another $99 was spent with a guy who took my Word file and translated it into Kindle language.

Kindle offers a slew of do-it-yourself cover designs, but I chose to design my own. One day I uploaded the text and cover design to Kindle, and it was for sale the next day, complete with its own ISBN (book ID number) and landing page on Amazon.

My cost: zero. Zip. Nada.

Okay, no movie sale. But it's out there and available.

Once your book is published, you are completely on your own
While it's relatively cheap and easy to publish a book, it will disappear into oblivion

unless publicity and PR are generated. Friends and family will buy it — and that may be perfectly okay.

But selling books outside your immediate circle takes work — and investment in PR and publicity. If you're not an expert, I urge you to hire a professional.

5 reasons why writers should love Kindle

1. You may have some editorial and design expenses as well as minor costs of translating your word-processing file into the Kindle format. Otherwise publishing is free. And you'll get your own landing page on amazon.com.

2. Tell Amazon/Kindle what you want the selling price to be.

3. Instead of the lousy 10 percent — 12.5 percent — 15 percent royalty you'd get from a print publisher, Kindle authors get up to a whopping 70 percent of net sales.

4. Sell a bunch of books, and the royalty payment is instantaneous. (As opposed to the old days when royalty checks were issued semi-annually.)

5. With print titles, 40 percent of royalty payments are withheld in anticipation of probable returns. Kindle returns are seldom to none.

16 reasons why I love my Kindle

1. Physical ease of handling is terrific — with conditions such as trigger fingers and carpal tunnel.

2. The ability to carry hundreds of titles in my jacket pocket when traveling.

3. Price is often $9.99 per title — sometimes more, but often much less.

4. The vast Kindle library contains 1 million+ new titles and classics. Many titles are available from free to peanuts (e.g., *The Complete works of Mark Twain*, $1; *King James Bible*, 99 cents; and *Mr. Midshipman Easy*, free).

5. The built-in wireless system puts new titles in my Kindle within 60 seconds from virtually any locale in the country. (Ahhh, instant gratification!)

6. We live in a 16-foot wide row house in Center City Philadelphia — with minimal storage room. I no longer have to lug finished books as a contribution to the Book Trader or leave the damn things on the front stoop with a sign saying, "FREE!"

7. A wee jolt of electricity leaves a far smaller carbon footprint than paper, printing, binding, shipping and reshipping returns followed by sending them to a landfill.

8. I love seeing a book one page at a time. No more do I endure the deep depression of realizing how little progress I've made in an 800-page behemoth laying on the coffee table. No more discomfort holding the monster in my arthritic hands.

9. Two commentators can be discussing a book on TV. I can order a free sample of the text — or the book itself — in 60 seconds. I'm reading it while the talking heads are still talking about it.

10. I can make the type larger or smaller to fit my eye comfort.

11. *The Wall Street Journal* technology guru Walter Mossberg liked Kindle. He wrote, "I did find that the screen was good enough to make me forget I wasn't reading the book on paper."

12. The white background of the screen with black type means you can use Kindle outdoors in sunlight — unlike backlighted screens, which go dark in bright sunlight.

13. The printing system is fascinating. Turn the page and you are expending a tiny spritz of power to rearrange black specks into letters, words and sentences. No electricity is used while you are reading — only when the page is being turned. Hence long battery life — 10 hours or so.

14. The built-in dictionary enables me to look up words on the fly. Trust me. A lot of authors love to show off with big words.

15. If my library of titles becomes overwhelming, I can send books back to Amazon. They will be stored in the "cloud." I can retrieve them any time.

16. When I order a title for my Kindle, it is also available on all Kindles using the same Amazon account — wife, children, etc.

10 reasons publishers should love Kindle (and all e-books)

1. Logistical ease — no paper, printing, binding, shipping.

2. Ecologically sound. No dead trees. No carbon footprint.

3. No returns — normally 40 percent of all books produced are sent back to the publisher and "remaindered" (sold for a buck or two with no royalties for the author). Or trashed in a landfill.

4. Immediate payment — no marginal bookstore owner jerking around the accounting department with the first great lie of mankind: "The check is in the mail."

5. Once sold to a Kindle user, the book is captive in that Kindle account and cannot be resold, given away or read by someone else unless the Kindle itself is relinquished (fat chance!).

6. Selling a minuscule electrical surge means virtually no cost of goods sold. Everything is pure gross profit.

7. The online store is open for business 24/7 to shoppers from anywhere in the world (even on Christmas).

8. Titles are never out of print or out of stock.

9. The timeline from manuscript to finished product can be a fraction of its printed cousin — which means faster return on investment.

10. An e-book can be updated and a new edition published in minutes.

Takeaways to Consider

• Kindle is a spectacular traveling companion.
—You can archive up to 3,500 titles in your purse or pocket.
—You can adjust the type size for your ocular comfort.

• Beware: photographs, artwork and maps are lousy on Kindle.

• Kindle works using tiny black flecks rearranged to form words. This requires a wee jolt of battery power. However, once the page is "turned," no electricity is required. This is different from tablets, smartphones and backlighted readers requiring perpetual battery power.

• Kindle can run 10 hours on a single battery charge.

• Kindle does gobble up battery power when connected by phone line to Amazon or the Internet.

• The traditional print book-publishing model is the world's most efficient system for turning trees into landfill.

• Because Kindle text is printed on a whitepaper-like surface, it can be read in bright sunlight (e.g., at the beach).

• For writers, Kindle is a glorious vehicle to self-publish.

CHAPTER 34

Speeches: Write and Deliver Them With Power

Direct Marketing Days New York
I attended Direct Marketing Days New York (DMDNY) for 50 years.

In its great days the conference was held at the Hilton Hotel & Towers on Sixth Avenue. The booths on the exhibit floors seemed jammed together and the aisles narrow so you continually bumped into people and were forced make eye contact. The speakers had all rehearsed their presentations down to a gnat's eyebrow. The seminar rooms were mostly small, which meant a standing-room only crowd. The electricity in the air was palpable.

But the owners of the conference became greedy and wanted it bigger. It moved to perhaps the dreariest venue in America — the Javits Center on the far West Side of Manhattan. The place is grotesquely out of the way. Hundreds of are forced to wait for taxis in a line that can stretch half the length of a football field. No decent restaurant is anywhere nearby. Architecturally it has all the charm of a correctional facility.

Instead of an intimate, high-energy gathering, it became a listless, sparsely attended affair with wide aisles, little eye contact and exhibitors spending much of the time talking to one another.

Purchased by the Direct Marketing Association, Direct Marketing Days New York went out of business.

What killed the conference: PowerPoint
When covering a convention for my newsletter and magazine, I would drop in on many sessions, wait for a pithy, information-rich quote delivered with relish and eliciting gasps of astonishment from a surprised audience.

Then I would move on to the next session. The result, stories filled with hot quotes. They not only titillated the reader but also generated interest in the presenters and their services.

With the coming of the laptop and PowerPoint, my quest for pithy, punchy quotes went up in smoke.

A typical PowerPoint presentation
Picture this: when a new speaker with a laptop gets to the podium, here's the sequence:

- A long pause occurs as the big screen goes blank.

- Then on the big screen is the boot-up pattern of the speaker's laptop.

- After fussing around with the cursor, the speaker clicks on an icon.

- What follows: a series of slides, bulleted points, charts and graphs in mouse-type. Not even those seated in the first row are able to read what's on-screen.

• The speaker — with eyes glued to the screen — reads the mouse-type in a halting monotone with zero eye contact and zero enthusiasm.

"Power corrupts," said professor Edward Tufte. "PowerPoint corrupts absolutely."

The 10-20-30 Rule for PowerPoint users
This is easy to remember. When using PowerPoint:

- No more than **10** slides.
- No longer than **20** minutes.
- No type on the screen smaller than **30**-point.

'Word cloud' nuttiness
Every now and again a PowerPoint presenter will put up on screen a "word cloud."

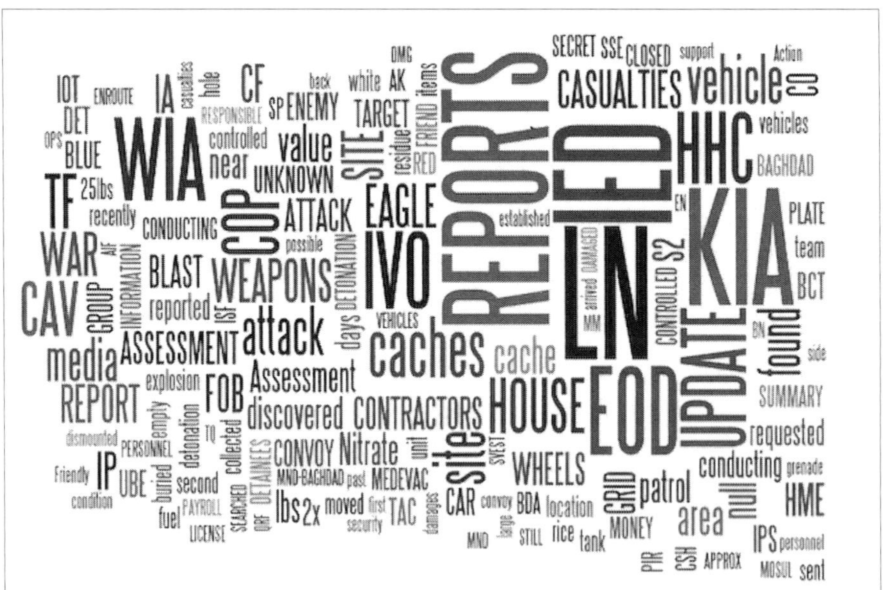

To techies, it's brilliant and fascinating. To me, it is confusing and a gross distraction. I am not alone. "Word clouds are bad data journalism," wrote Steve Myers:

> *New York Times* developer Jacob Harris explains why "every time I see a word cloud presented as insight, I die a little inside." The reason: Word clouds don't live up to the best practices of data journalism. "At The New York Times, we strongly believe that visualization is reporting, with many of the same elements that would make a traditional story effective: a narrative that pares away extraneous information to find a story in the data; context to help the reader understand the basics of the subject; interviewing the data to find its flaws and be sure of our conclusions." Simply counting the frequency of words and arranging them artistically doesn't help the reader understand the information, Harris writes. A word cloud of the Iraq war logs, for instance, merely tells readers that the war involves a lot of [sic] IEDs and explosions, "which is likely news to nobody." *—Steve Meyers, poynter.org*

Enter Harvey ("Mr. Make Things Happen") Mackay!
Harvey Mackay is founder of the $100 million MackayMitchell Envelope Company headquartered in Minneapolis.

A syndicated columnist and inspirational speaker, his four *New York Times* best-sellers have sold millions of copies, been translated into 35 languages and distributed in 80 countries. His titles include *Swim With the Sharks Without Being Eaten Alive* and *Beware the Naked Man Who Offers You His Shirt.*

One of the greatest keynoters
Born in 1932, Mackay is a spectacular keynote speaker. He bounds up to the podium, shakes hands with his introducer and promptly strides to the front of the stage where he flashes a dazzling Joe Biden smile. He wears an elegantly tailored blue suit accented by a bright red tie and matching red pocket square. Mackay has a square jaw and a rugged, tan face beneath a full head of beautifully trimmed white hair.

No PowerPoint here.

On the two giant screens on either side of the stage is Harvey Mackay live and three times larger than life. He spends 50 minutes regaling his audience with anecdotes, bon mots, business philosophy and an endless string of ideas on how to differentiate yourself from rest of the herd. A few of the highlights:

- The Mackay Envelope Company mission statement is very simple — just five words. "TO BE IN BUSINESS FOREVER."

- If you find something you love to do, you'll never work a day in your life.

- Mackay Envelope people love their work so much they say "TGIM!" (Thank God It's Monday!)

- Once asked how many salespeople Mackay Envelope has, Mackay replied he had 600. "Six hundred salespeople!" the person exclaimed. "I cannot believe that. How many total employees do you have?" Mackay replied, "600."

• A goal is a dream with a deadline.

If you ever get a chance to hear Harvey Mackay, run — do not walk — to his presentation. He is a star with star looks, star charisma and star power. The only power he lacks is PowerPoint.

A sampling of Harvey Mackay's checklist for speakers

• Studies show that people remember more and laugh more in brightness. Turn the lights up full blast, unless you are showing slides. Then, dim the screen area but light up the audience. Now, you can still have excellent eye contact with your audience.

• If you are addressing a breakfast, lunch, or dinner audience, ask your introducer to request politely that the people with their backs to the stage turn their chairs forward so they don't have to crane their necks.

• Request that the photographer not take pictures during the first 10-15 minutes of your speech. You want no distractions while you are in the process of feeling out the microphone, adjusting to the lights, and getting the pulse of the audience.

• Never, never, never end your program with a question and answer session. You cannot control the agenda or the quality of the questions and the fireworks of your topic can end with a fizzle.

• Start the Q&A five minutes before the end of your talk. Then transition from one of your answers to a real climax.

• Most people are shy about asking the first question; therefore, you may get stymied by an awkward silence. Break the ice by stating that problem and then saying ... "Okay, we'll start with the second question!"

• Always request that an engineer be in the room during your entire talk in case of microphone problems.

• Never, never mispronounce a proper name. If you're not sure, check with the sponsor. Then double-check.

• Whether it's ten minutes, or ten hours, do not go over your allotted time. This puts additional pressure on all concerned. Remember: Agreements prevent disagreements. Have a perfect understanding of your time frame and what is expected of you.

• Station someone in the back of the room whose sole job is to put out fires for you. Let them search for extra chairs, adjust the lights, quell outside noise, welcome late arrivals, and catch slamming doors, so you don't have to think about it.

• If you don't have a smashing "opener" and "closer," go back to the drawing board. And, don't step up to the microphone until you do. *—From "Harvey Mackay's 35 to Stay Alive," www.harveymackay.com*

Study the great speakers and steal smart
I don't perform before live audiences anymore. I have become more of a write guy than a talk guy. But watching great speakers at work is a hobby of mine. I am less interested in what they say than their delivery and how they connect with an audience.

Hot vs. cool medium
Marshall McLuhan (1911-1980), co-author of *The Medium Is the Massage*, was once called the "Oracle of the Electronic Age."

To McLuhan, radio was a "hot" medium and television was "cool." Knowing when to be hot and when to be cool is the mark of a great communicator.

Adolf Hitler, for example, was pre-television. He came to power through radio and public address systems. It has been suggested if TV had been widely extant in the 1930s, Der Führer's shouting, fist pumping and grotesque facial expressions would have been too hot for the tiny screen in the viewer's living room. He would very likely have been dismissed as a clown akin to Charlie Chaplin's manic little tramp.

The magic of John F. Kennedy
The best TV politician in my lifetime was John F. Kennedy. He was a sickly rich kid with a strange New England accent and minimal political experience — who used television with stunning effect to win the presidency.

Kennedy instinctively knew how to talk to people — be it a crowd of 50,000, 50 or five.

• When addressing a mass audience in an arena — or at the Capitol for his inaugural address — Kennedy was hot. He would talk with great forcefulness, always addressing his remarks and sound level to the folks farthest away. At the same time, he would be watching the reactions of his listeners in the first few rows to see how he was being received. If they had rapt expressions, he would know that he was scoring. When he saw them fidgeting, looking around or glancing at their watches, it was time to shift gears.

• In smaller groups, he was cooler as he reined in the oratory, exuded charm and continually made eye contact with as many people as possible. As a result, everyone felt special.

• It was television that won the presidency for Kennedy. He saw the camera as a person and focused all of his intellect and magnetism on the little red light. He spoke quietly, intimately and looked directly at the camera.

JFK vs. HHH
In the 1960 Democratic primary, Kennedy's most serious opponent was Minnesota Senator Hubert H. Humphrey, one of the great orators of his generation. But Humphrey had two major flaws in his delivery:

• He was incredibly long-winded, incapable of giving a short, succinct answer to a question.

• Humphrey did not understand television. He orated at the camera as though it were a room full of people. As one writer pointed out, a television appearance by Kennedy was like having him as a charming, urbane guest in your living room. Hubert Humphrey's TV persona, on the other hand, would be a guy coming into your house and vomiting on the rug.

The helicopter president
John Kennedy also had two secret weapons when it came to communicating with people:

• He always gave the appearance of being completely engaged and focused on the audience — be it one or one thousand. At the same time his mind was always thinking ahead — the next sentence, the next subject, the next appointment after the speech was over.

• Kennedy also had the unique ability to mentally hover over himself. He could dispassionately watch his performance and the audience and make adjustments in his presentation. Some critics call this the "helicopter effect."

In 1967 — four years after the assassination of John F. Kennedy in Dallas — the American realist artist Jamie Wyeth painted the late president's portrait. Kennedy's face dominates the picture. He is looking directly at the viewer with his left eye while the right eye is looking over the viewer's shoulder. It's as though he was seeing some distant scene in his mind's eye. When Jacqueline Kennedy saw the picture for the first time she reportedly was stunned. Wyeth had caught Kennedy's essence.

Kennedy vs. Nixon: the first debate
In the general election, Senator Kennedy faced Vice President Richard Nixon in four live black-and-white television debates. In the first debate, Nixon wore a gray suit, which turned him into a shapeless blob against a gray background. Kennedy wore a crisp blue suit and looked very much in charge.

The director, Don Hewitt (later of *60 Minutes* fame), called the camera shots for drama, focusing frequently on the candidate listening as well as on the candidate talking. Kennedy looked sharp and attentive while Nixon sweated, mopped his face with a handkerchief, and was shifty-eyed and nervous.

The radio audience gave the first debate to Nixon. On the other hand, the television viewers knew it was Kennedy all the way. Many observers believe the first debate (plus Democratic vote-getting shenanigans in Chicago and Texas) cost Nixon the presidency.

This Presidential Debate Changed History
Sen. John F. Kennedy vs. Vice President Richard M. Nixon
September 26, 1960. WBBM studio, Chicago, Illinois

The greatest communicators: televangelists
My advice to all public speakers is to go around the dials and study the highest rated religious preachers past and present. Among them:

> Bishop Fulton J. Sheen — the young Billy Graham —
> Jimmy Swaggart — Mike Murdock — Bishop T.D. Jakes —
> Joyce Meyer — Joel Osteen

It matters not whether you agree or disagree with the content of their messages. What's important is to home in on their performances — how they connect with the audience, drawing listeners and viewers into their worlds.

To me, these are among the most fascinating people on television.

America's dreariest, most uninspiring speakers
In my opinion: Senators Harry Reid and Mitch McConnell.

A perpetual irritation in Philadelphia
Whenever a civic issue came up in my Philadelphia neighborhood directly affecting my life, I would attend a neighborhood meeting to learn more about it. The subject could be the construction of a massive casino complex 20 blocks from my house or a reassessment plan to triple my real estate taxes.

I stopped going to these meetings because the head of the local organization and main speaker would constantly say "UMMMMMM."

Not a quiet, low-key "um."

Rather, it was with lips pressed and a loud "UMMMMM," with the sound projecting from the mask and out the nose like an opera singer humming.

"And … UMMMMM … if you will talk to Barb Whosits, she'll … UMMMMM … get you a copy of the report."

I started hearing only the "UMMMMM" and nothing else.

Not just local yokels
The British use the term "newsreaders" to describe TV anchors. While they appear to be looking directly at you and speaking conversationally, they are — in fact — reading from a script unrolling in front of them.

Some newspeople are good ad libbers. Examples of flawless extemporaneous speakers: Brian Williams, Chris Wallace, Chris Hayes, Brian Lamb, Rachel Maddow, Bill O'Reilly and Bret Baier.

One night, NBC Pentagon correspondent Jim Miklaszewski delivered a polished analysis of the Iraq situation, which he obviously read off a Teleprompter. Anchor Brian Williams then asked follow-up questions and "Mik" started punctuating his answers with "uh." Just about every sentence began with "uh" and frequently "uh" popped into mid-sentence as well. Miklaszewski may be a first-rate newsman, but he's a second-rate performer.

Another serial "uh" user is CNN's Wolf Blitzer.

If Jay Leno's delivery were this poor, he'd be driving a bus rather than a classic car from his multimillion-dollar collection.

Takeaways to Consider

• "Power corrupts. PowerPoint corrupts absolutely." —*Edward Tufte*

• The 10-20-30 Rule for PowerPoint users
— No more than 10 slides.
—No longer than 20 minutes.
—No type on the screen smaller than 30-point.

• In short, audiences come to see and hear YOU, not to ooh and ah over your art director's unreadable PowerPoint slides.

• Remember, PowerPoint was never used by the great communicators of our time — Winston Churchill, Huey Long, John F. Kennedy, Ronald Reagan, Bill Clinton, George W. Bush, Billy Graham, Bishop Fulton J. Sheen, Bishop T.D. Jakes and Jimmy Swaggart.

• "When writing copy, pause every paragraph or so and read it aloud. Do you keep stumbling over certain words or phrases? If so, rewrite. Does it flow smoothly and easily? If not, rewrite." —*Jack Maxson*

• Have the text in front of you — printed in very big type. The analogy is of an orchestra conductor who knows the music so well he keeps the score in front of him for occasional reference.

• President Obama almost always uses two invisible glass Teleprompters to his right and left, so he can maintain eye contact with his audience. He also has a loose-leaf notebook containing the text. If the Teleprompter conks out, he has backup.

• Rather than the loose-leaf notebook, professional speechmakers and presenters more likely have the speech printed in large type as a loose manuscript on the podium. Instead of turning the pages, which is obvious to the audience, they unobtrusively slide the finished pages to one side while maintaining eye contact with the audience.

• Dwight Eisenhower used 3" x 5" cards with large type containing the main point he wanted to make.

• Actor Peter Turgeon once told me of a long alcoholic evening spent with the great actor John Carradine. Carradine pointed out young and inexperienced stage actors — who start losing the interest of the audience — try to compensate by talking louder. Seasoned performers know otherwise. When an audience starts to get restless, savvy actors begin to speak softer and softer, forcing the audience to lean forward in order to hear. Once attention has been regained, volume can be gradually increased.

• Do you have any speech patterns of which you're unaware that inadvertently drive your listeners crazy?

• If you have a good friend (or a not-so-good friend) that unknowingly uses a dumb word or phrase constantly, should you quietly and privately point it out? Your call, not mine.

CHAPTER 35

Words and Phrases That Irritate People

No. 1 offender: "LIKE"
When my wife, Peggy, and I moved to Philly to take over the management of *Target Marketing* magazine, editorial meetings came with the territory. We had a bunch of young editors who said "like" a lot.

Not an occasional "like," but rather two and three of them per sentence.

Finally, in desperation, I brought a little sterling silver bell to the office and placed it in front of me on the conference table. I then handed everybody at the table two dozen pennies. "This is the 'Like Bell,'" I announced during a meeting. "Any time I hear the word, 'like,' I'll ring the bell."

"If I ring the bell when someone says 'like,'" I added, "the perpetrator must put a penny in the pot on the table. At the end of the meeting, the person with the most pennies remaining wins the pot."

The session started out with a lot of bell ringing. The habit was broken fairly quickly. "Like" is — for me — one of the most offensive words in the English language.

For example, when I walk down Philadelphia's raffish South Street crawling with teenagers, they smoke cigarettes and loudly use the word "like" — like it might like go out of like style. They like yammer to each other or like into a like cell phone. I want to slash my wrists.

Other words and phrases I wish people would avoid
• ackshully — amazing — Amurkin
Newt Gingrich is one of the most fascinating men in Washington. Yet when referencing this nation, he talks about "Amurka" and "Amurkin." This pronunciation instantly transforms him from an articulate, political philosopher and historian into a red-neck, Georgia hayseed.

Saying "Amurkin" requires a sour pout, a downturn of the mouth. Franklin D. Roosevelt always said "A-merry-kin" — with the accent on "merry" — and it always came out with a happy smile. Roosevelt's infectious optimism got us through the Depression and World War II.

Incidentally, Gingrich might be persuaded to change his pronunciation if he knew the dictionary definition of "merkin" (pronounced "mûrkn"). Merkin is a "17th century term for a pubic wig, worn for nude stage appearances by women after shaving their privates to eliminate lice."

• as it were — if you will — per se — as we speak
Fillers and useless.

• awesome
This is one of the most misused words in English — especially among kids. "Ooooh, that's an awesome car!" or "This pie is awesome!" In my opinion, four things are awesome:

- The Grand Canyon.
- Men walking on the moon.
- Google's ability to bring me all the world's knowledge in a nanosecond.
- GPS systems.

• brilliant!
The Brits use this the way Americans use "awesome!"

• chum — dude — pal
Gratuitous appellations used with an implicit sneer.

• I mean — incredible — y'know — kind of — sort of
I'm guilty of "I mean" and "y'know."

In a guest column that appeared in *Business Common Sense*, titled "Developing and Delivering High-Impact Sales Presentations," Ray Butkus emphasized the need for everyone to rehearse before delivering a speech. It's also a good idea to tape yourself and play back to make sure you're not using such irritating words as "like," "ya know" and "sort of."

• Lemme astcha question
Chris Matthews, the ebullient host of MSNBC's Hardball, prefaces every question to a guest with, "Lemme astcha question."

• Okay?
Some speakers use this in conversation and in presentations. They say "Okay" at the start of a sentence and ask "Okay?" at the end as if to make sure everybody "got it."

• Once again, ladies and gentlemen ...
This is a line used by people with so much time to fill they repeat themselves. On a cruise through the Baltic, the shore manager used this line two dozen times and more in every talk.

• on the same page — unreal — Ya know what I'm sayin'?
Enough already!

• Well ...
This word is used constantly by interviewees on television. I would estimate 90 percent of all answers to questions begin with, "Well ..."

• **Wow** or **Oh, wow ...**
To me an irritating and inane phrase is: "I mean it was like wow."

• Same thing with **"cool"**
I know a woman here in Philly who says, "cool" in every third sentence.

• Your call is important to us ...
The ultimate oxymoron in the world of recorded phone jail. The real meaning of the recorded voice saying, "Your call is important to us" is: "It's happy hour here in Mumbai, and you are a big fat pain in the ass."

The Plain English Campaign
When the 25th anniversary was celebrated by the Plain English Campaign ("Fighting for crystal-clear communication since 1979"), it surveyed 5,000 supporters in 70 countries. They voted on the most irritating phrase in the language. The results:

1. **At the end of the day**
2. **At this moment in time**
3. The constant use of **like** as if it were a form of punctuation
4. **With all due respect**

From the Plain English press release of Mar. 23, 2004:

> Spokesman John Lister said overused phrases were a barrier to communication. When readers or listeners come across these tired expressions, they start tuning out and completely miss the message — assuming there is one! Using these terms in daily business is about as professional as wearing a novelty tie or having a wacky ringtone on your phone.
>
> **Other nominations from the Plain English survey:**
> 24/7 — absolutely — address the issue — around (in place of "about") — awesome — ballpark figure — basically — basis ("on a weekly basis" in place of "weekly" and so on) — bear with me — between a rock and a hard place — blue sky (thinking) — boggles the mind — bottom line — crack troops — epicenter (used incorrectly) — glass half full (or half empty) — going forward — I hear what you're saying — in terms of — it's not rocket science — literally — move the goal—posts — ongoing — prioritize — pushing the envelope — singing from the same hymn sheet — the fact of the matter is — thinking outside the box — to be honest/to be honest with you/ to be perfectly honest — touch base — up to (in place of "about") — value-added (in general use)

The Factiva study
On Aug. 15, 2006, mediabistro.com released a study titled: "At The End Of The Day, Study In Hot Pursuit of Popular Press Clichés Reveals Low-Hanging Fruit."

From the study:

> Citing a whopping 10,000 news sources, including *The Wall Street Journal,* Reuters and the Associated Press, an analysis by Factiva of clichés used by the press, by far the most commonly used is "at the end of the day."
>
> "In the black" and "in the red" follow at No. 2 and 3, respectively. While lazy, we're not quite sure how "concerned residents" qualifies as a cliché, but at the end of the day, you have to think outside the box.

> The other 17 clichés most used in the American business press (in descending order for frequency):
>
> level playing field — time and again — about face — wealth of experience — split second — time is running out — outpouring of support — think outside the box — last—ditch effort — time after time — concerned residents — unsung heroes — low hanging fruit — clean bill of health — hot pursuit — up the ante

The B.S. factor
In guest article for *Business Common Sense*, Seton Hall management professor Ray Butkus suggested:

> Platitudes like "cutting edge technology" or "state of the art infrastructure" are nearly worthless, so don't waste your time by including them in your presentation.

What Butkus has suggested is — to coin a phrase — the tip of the iceberg. A truly great website is the Web Economy Bullshit Generator. It not only lists verbs, adjectives and nouns to be avoided in speech and writing, but also allows you to see them in combination with one another.

You can visit the interactive website and enter any word listed. Click on "make bullshit," and the phrase popping up will cause you to giggle and cringe at the same time.

One final thought on B.S.
On Bullshit is a slim volume by Harry G. Frankfurt, emeritus professor of philosophy at Princeton University, published by Princeton University Press.

Frankfurt's meandering exploration of the nature of B.S. is written in the dense, turgid and undisciplined prose typical of academia — boring and utterly unreadable.

But the idea of this title coming from a world-renowned scholar and teacher — and published by the respected Princeton University Press — is hilarious. On Bullshit is a great gift and a wonderful coffee table book to show off your eclectic tastes. In short, *On Bullshit* is itself splendid B.S.

> **A *Business Common Sense* column on verbal irritants generated these fascinating comments:**
> Don't forget these two common ways to slaughter pronunciation: "a whole nother" and "rate" when the speaker means "right." *—Susan Boucher*
>
> How about "agree to disagree." In my book, that is a disagreement. Or lately, it's been "fair enough." One ex-jerk boss used to say it to dismiss your input. It was a short version of agree to disagree. *—Katie*
>
> "Sweet" is bad enough when teenagers say it but when adults say it, it's like chewing tinfoil. *—Phil DaSilva*

"Have a good one." I scream silently whenever I hear it. *—Bill Gohde*

Thoughtful article. I am passing it to our (much) younger staff and hope they learn as much from it as I. You did miss two words/phrases that simply bring up the hairs on the back of my neck. "Guys" as in "you guys" when addressing a group (or even a table of two in a restaurant.) "You people" as in the most accusatory, egotistical sense. Oh, yes, there is a third — "these ones" as in —oh — how about just plain "these." Thank you for the chance to vent. *—Donna Lendvay*

I start screaming when I hear "like" used when "as" is the correct word. "As" seems to be disappearing from our lexicon. *—Sylvia Fogelman*

What about the infamous "irregardless"? *—Kathleen Brackeen*

Denny, nicely done. I'd consider adding the use of the word "great," as in he's a great somethingerother. I think that word has now become so abused it fails to communicate its original intent. I guess everyone is great at something, just not at the things with which we usually connect the term. Thanks. *—Ken Helmers*

Denny, you forgot two of the worst. "Basically" and "I'm sorry." How many times to people actually mean I'm sorry when they say it. Argh, it hurts my head. And basically is just a longer drawn out version of um. Argh. *—Rob*

Thanks for the terrific piece, Denny. Thanks especially for pointing out overuse of the phrase "if you will" — used most memorably by our clueless Vice President, to lend phony gravitas to his clueless pronouncements. I was fortunate to have studied with the man found at this site: sourcetext.com/grammarian. Readers who enjoyed this piece ought to check him out. *—Rich*

As I sat at a management meeting listening to my boss refer to something as a "mute point" my mind would wander away from the discussion, thinking thoughts like, "I hope my cat doesn't think outside the box ... or I'll have a mess to deal with" and "If the rain keeps up, it won't come down...." Great, thought-provoking article-I can't stop thinking about my pet peeves! *—Marian Savage*

Denny — a very good primer for all of us. However, I think we would be a bit more forgiving of those who speak differently from "us" if we had a better understanding of the American dialect. PBS has an insightful program on the subject - http://www.pbs.org/speak/speech/. Not long ago there was talk of legislation to make English the official language of the United States. I guess we should decide which "English" first. *—Mark*

The word "Um" was the only thing that would keep us awake in my 1965 Contemporary Affairs class - we counted the number of times the instructor said it. I can't remember anything else from that class. Too bad I was so distracted. *—Eva Williams*

Another of my non-favorites: "No Problem," as a replacement for "You're Welcome," "Thank You," and other more useful expressions. Thanks for another very informative and instructive article! *—Robb Ruyle*

Thanks for fingering "at the end of the day." William Kristol of the *Weekly Standard* wears this one out every time he talks. And while we're at it, let's not forget "problematic." What's wrong with, instead of saying, "That could be problematic," you say, "That could cause problems." *—Damon Thompson*

I'm shocked that "Nukeyouler" didn't make the list! *—Diane Weaver*

I'm surprised nobody mentioned Toastmasters. A great place to learn how to speak and pause with silence instead of um, ah, duh, etc. They're everywhere. toastmasters.com. And yes, I'm a former member. *—Fred Mason*

At the risk of sounding colloquial, Denny, I must say, "right on!" I nearly gave you a standing ovation right here at my desk when I read this. The crushing laziness that is becoming the norm in everyday conversation (business gab included) breaks my heart. I am, alas, guilty of it as well, to a degree, but I'm at least aware of my foibles and work to correct them. One thing about this installment of BCS saddened me, however: You obviously haven't been eating the right chocolate desserts! *—Margaret*

Dialect and speech patterns are slightly different — and we should be more tolerant of non-professionals, and hold the bar higher for pros. I'm less bothered by a random "like" or "um" than I am with clichés or grammatical errors. I'm also more bothered by professionals (like news anchors and interviewees) who regularly speak and communicate poorly than by people with little or no experience in public speaking, who are behind a cause, and find themselves in front of a camera for the first time. Of course that would be nerve-wracking! *—Kimber Smith*

Dear Denny, While I loved this article, I'm sad that you didn't touch on my least favorite mispronunciation — having to do with a certain category of bomb. Why is it that we've had three presidents (Eisenhower, Johnson, George W. Bush) who couldn't pronounce "nuclear" even though they had the power to launch a nuclear device that could unleash a global firestorm? Every time I hear somebody in the White House say, "Noo-kew-lar" I want to scream, "It's NEW-KLEEE-ARR, you moron!" On the other hand, the governor of California can't even seem to pronounce the name of his state correctly and hardly anybody on the Left Coast seems to mind. Go figure! (Or is that a cliché, too?) *—Peter Hochstein*

Geez Denny, while I hear what you are saying, with all due respect at the end of the day like fer sure you absolutely don't have to be a rocket scientist to recognize that "news" people are actors; NOT journalists — I mean, like literally that is the bottom line and to be honest like it boggles the mind to learn that a man like with your wealth of experience believes otherwise — I mean, like do the math ... *—Carl Street*

Overall (one of those words?) you are right on target (oops I did it again). Um, one problem I see, however, is the fact that many of the phrases that have been highlighted in your article are phrases that attempt to act like photos (you know what I mean, the old "a photo says a thousand words"). Well, I think many writers become too verbose at times trying to create the desired image in the readers' minds. Although maddening to some people, utilizing certain clichés actually do work in conjuring up the desired image in the readers mind. Thank you for writing this article. It is one that needed to be written. *—Pierre Orantes*

If I may add one more to the business lexicon of over used phrases it would be "it is what it is." *—Matt*

Denny, Thanks so much for this much needed foray into the bastardization of my beloved language!! But, "lemme ax" you if it's cold enough to "schnow" in "Philthadelphia" yet, and if you will buy your wife "joollary" for Christmas? Also, I understand some "rilators" are interested in your property. "With that having been said", I will leave saying thank you, Dr. Purcell, for bringing this all to my attention in your 1957 English 101 class. *—Tom Girgash*

I had a journalism teacher who deplored the use of "that" when we should have used "which" or when it wasn't needed at all. After the first red-inked paper, I learned and to this day always review any sentence in which I use "that." Thanks for calling us all to attention. *—Trish Tickle*

I have a voracious appetite for business education, especially as it relates to my own field. So it was with great disappointment that I listened to a recorded interview between an industry leader and a large purchaser of his products. Here was a unique opportunity, to gain perspective from the customer side — and a big customer — but all I could focus on was the interviewer's constant, meaningless response: "wow." The customer, a bright, well-spoken woman, would admit that she had preferred vendors, and they were usually the ones who sent her specially made samples. She would spend six figures with these vendors. "Wow," said the industry pro. If the vendor was particularly helpful and creative, price was never an issue. "Wow," was the response. I felt sorry for the woman; she deserved better than that, as did the audience. *—Mike Spanjar*

Could this be, like, why so much awesome ad copy, like, never sells anything? *—Jim Brown*

Here is another irritating phrase that I frequently hear during meetings: "Let's take that offline." I'd prefer, "Let's discuss that after the meeting." I realize that we are in the computer age. But the thought of human beings as "online" or "offline" bothers me. *—Patrick*

Another irritating source of speech-mangling comes from those who call into talk radio. As a caller, once you are on the air, there is a very brief period in which to make an effective comment that is both compelling to the listeners and interesting enough to the host that he/she might even ask you for a little more. I sometimes find myself shouting at the radio "get to the point already" as the momentum of the conversation begins to drown in too many words. Clichés are one thing. People also tend to just talk too much. The same is true in written material. A good copy writing philosophy is that the less words you use, the more likely someone will read them all. *—Rick Olson*

Denny: You hit both of my hot buttons: "awesome" and "like." When my kids were young, instead of the silver bell I would interject: "Oh, you're 'like' hungry. OK well we'll eat when you are hungry not when you are similar to being hungry." After the 10,000th time they got the point. They are the only kids in their group of friends that do not say "like." Awesome article by the way, I was like floored by it. *—Ray Butkus*

My least favorite expression is "no offense, but ... " It makes me cringe every time I hear it, because I know it will be followed by something offensive! *—Eva Bowie*

This is a good review of the state of the language; good for speakers and writers alike. Another good source for writers to look into is Stephen King's "On Writing." Funny and a very good remedial trip to grammar school. Thank you for posting this article! *—Patrick*

Takeaway to Consider:

• Tape yourself in conversation and see if any of the above comes out of your mouth frequently.

CHAPTER 36

The Art of Being a Superb Interviewer

I believe the greatest interviewer on the scene today is C-SPAN's founder, Brian Lamb. Low key, elegant and erudite, he asks pointed questions without stammering. When the interviewee says something unexpected, Lamb is right there with follow-up. It might take the discussion off on a totally new and fascinating tangent.

Brian Lamb listens and not only asks the questions I would like to ask, but also those I never would have thought of. He can be gentle or tough. The man's interviews are riveting.

A classic Brian Lamb interview
In surfing the TV channels, I stumbled across Brian Lamb in a 1996 interview with Denis Brian, author of *Einstein: A Life*. Denis Brian, an older guy with a neat gray beard and horn-rimmed glasses, was wearing a blue button-down shirt and red tie.

I have no head for physics or science, but Brian Lamb and Denis Brian engaged in a staccato conversation about Einstein's private life and career aimed at viewers like me. For example, Denis Brian was asked to define the Theory of Relativity and he did so with an old joke.

"If a fat, ugly girl is sitting your lap for a minute it seems like an hour," Denis Brian said. "If a beautiful girl sits on your lap for an hour it seems like a minute. That's relativity."

When Einstein was told this definition, he loved it!

The craft of interviewing
The interview veered off course when Brian Lamb brought up Denis Brian's 1973 title, *Murderers and Other Friendly People: The Public and Private Worlds of Interviewers.*

To create the book, Denis Brian interviewed world-renowned interviewers about how they got their subjects to talk candidly and honestly. Denis Brian's advice:

- Know your subject thoroughly. Do as much research as you can on the person. Research and interview others who are familiar with the subject.

- Know so much about your interview subject you can give him information about himself he never knew.

- Know more about him than his wife knows.

- Create rapport. When Truman Capote interviewed Marlon Brando — a very unlikely pair — Brando mentioned his alcoholic mother. Capote also had an alcoholic mother and they traded stories and bonded. Capote got much more information than he had hoped for.

From Denis Brian's wonderful *Murderers and Other Friendly People: The Public and Private Worlds of Interviewers:*

> HARRISON SALISBURY: Try to get into the personal because it is a very good way of getting an insight. But I don't force it, because in some cases it's very embarrassing, as is true with some of those Communists who regard their personal life as a sort of closed book. But if they give me a little bit of an inkling, as they sometimes do, or if I am able to introduce the subject or something about my own situation, my own family, then this opens up a little avenue I can move down. I'll dart down it as fast as I can.
>
> TRUMAN CAPOTE: If you're having a difficult time with a subject, then you, in effect, change roles. And you, the interviewer, begin by making little confidences of your own that are rather similar to things that you think you will draw out of them. And suddenly they'll be saying: "Ah, yes, my mother ran away with five repairmen, too." See what I mean? Or: "Ah, yes, my father robbed a bank and was sent to prison for ten years, too. Isn't it extraordinary we should have those same things happen in our lives?" And then you find you're off to the races.
>
> REX REED: Catching people at off-moments is the dream of any interviewer. Ava Gardner, for example, was quite loaded when I interviewed her. It was the most honest interview she ever did. And later, she told a very close friend, Terence Young, as a smatter of fact, when he was directing her in *Mayerling* ... you know she was quite angry about the piece, I think at the time, and later they were talking about it on the set of *Mayerling* and she said, "That son-of-a-bitch knows me better than I know myself." And I would never have gotten that interview that way, unless she had been in an off-moment.
>
> HARRISON SALISBURY: In the early days ... I had a series of very sharply defined questions and I was in a great hurry to put them across, bing, bing, bing. And as the years went on I've taken to a much more relaxed technique which I think is more effective, of letting the interview develop its own pace and establish a sort of mood of interchange before bringing in the sharper questions.
>
> GAY TALESE: I go as a portrait painter goes, not as a photographer. I'm interpretive. I try to get inside the character I'm writing about very deeply. And I believe some of the truths of these individuals are things that are going to be revelations to themselves, when they read about them, as much as they are to me when I discover them.
>
> HUGH SIDEY: I have no theory other than I have short, rather blunt, open, simple questions, and I encourage, in a very low-key way, the source to talk. Another kind of secondary theory is not to be afraid to ask about inconsequential things. I have discovered that I have wasted more hours by asking people about the great, sweeping question of policy ... I certainly tried some of these questions, but immediately sensing that the guy wasn't going to talk about them, it's never been below me to ask when he got up, how he felt,

how he treated his kids, what books did he read, what movies had he seen. And I must say in my years in journalism, these insights into personality prove invaluable.

What to ask presidential candidates

In 1947, my father Alden Hatch was commissioned by Liberty magazine to write a series of monthly interviews of the major candidates for president in the upcoming election. Among them:

- President Harry Truman (D-MO)
- Gov. Thomas E. Dewey (R-NY)
- Sen. Arthur H. Vandenberg (R-MI)
- Former Gov. Harold E. Stassen (R-MN)
- Sen. Robert A. Taft (R-OH)

My father concluded each interview with the following question: "At poker, do you draw to an inside straight?"

Every Republican challenger said, "Never."

President Truman replied with obvious relish, "Always!"

Against all odds, Truman's balls-to-the-wall campaign was successful. He beat out the heavily favored Thomas Dewey, who came off as uptight and conservative. Short, with a pencil-thin mustache, Dewey could not shake off the withering description by Teddy Roosevelt's daughter, Alice Longworth. She said Dewey looked like "the little man on the wedding cake."

How I interview

For me, touch-typing has been a godsend. My fingers are an extension of my thought process.

For example, when I interview someone for a story, I use my laptop and can take down what is being said while maintaining eye contact with my subject.

I never use a tape recorder; I would rather concentrate on the questions and answers in my head and in the computer.

This intensity beats sitting through a casual interview twice — once during the recording and a second time transcribing the tape with all the "ums," "ers," "ahs" and pauses. In 50 years of using this system, not one of my subjects has ever accused me of being misquoted.

"[Studs Terkel] uses a tape recorder and I feel that's a great mistake," Truman Capote told Denis Brian. "Because the moment you introduce a mechanical device into the interview technique, you are creating an atmosphere in which the person isn't going to feel really relaxed, because they're watching themselves."

EXCEPTION: It is imperative to flesh out the notes as soon as possible. If you know you can't get to them within 48 hours, my suggestion would be to use a tape recorder.

Off-the-record

Here's a warning to anyone being interviewed. Many in the media are far more interested in making news and spreading the fact they made news rather than reporting it. File this traditional warning away in your brain and never forget it:

There is no such thing as off-the-record

The prime example was Republican candidate Mitt Romney's speech to high-roller campaign contributors who paid $50,000 a plate to attend a fund-raising dinner in Florida. Thinking his talk was "off-the-record," Romney proclaimed 47 percent of Americans were freeloaders who took no responsibility for their own lives. The speech was taped by bartender Scott Prouty and went viral around the world. This very likely cost Romney the 2012 presidential election.

Can you trust an interviewer?

Many years ago — when Peggy and I were running *WHO'S MAILING WHAT!* out of our basement in Stamford, Connecticut — a reporter from (I think) *National Review* phoned me. He was assigned to do a story on political direct mail and asked to come see my archive.

I said okay and would not charge him anything if my newsletter and archive service got a mention in *National Review*. He agreed.

He came to Stamford and I spent a lot of time with him. then sent him back to New York with samples to use as illustrations.

The story was published with no mention of the newsletter, the archive or me. I called him on it. "I had it in there, but my editor took it out."

I sent the guy a bill for $1,000 consulting services — very likely twice the amount he was paid for writing the story.

I got my mention in the next issue of *National Review.*

How I am different

I am not part of the traditional media. Being in the trade press, my goal is to provide useful information to my readers.

When an interview subject tells me something is "off-the-record," my hands immediately leave the computer keyboard. They remain conspicuously off the keyboard until it is mutually agreed we are back on the record.

When I have the first draft of a story done, I often send it to the interviewee with the following request:

- Kindly read it over.
- If you feel I have misquoted you, tell me and I will correct it.
- Did I get any facts wrong?
- Would you like anything removed?
- Anything we did not cover you would like to add?

Interview basics from Jim Hall, Virginia Commonwealth University

• Phrase your questions in a neutral way. Not: Don't you agree that this speaker should be banned from campus? Mix open-ended questions, such as, "Tell me about your love for antique cars," with closed-ended ones, such as, "How old are you?" The closed-ended ones elicit basic information; the open-ended allow the interviewee to reveal information or feelings that you did not anticipate.

• Decide how you will dress. You would dress differently for a hockey player than for the mayor. Ask yourself, how will my subject be dressed? Avoid anything in your dress or grooming that could be considered impertinent, flashy, sloppy or rebellious.

• Think of your meeting with the subject as a structured but friendly conversation, not an interview. As writer Studs Terkel said, "I realized quite early in this adventure that interviews conventionally conducted were meaningless. The question-and-answer technique may be of value in determining favored detergent, but not in the discovery of men and women. It was simply a case of making conversation and listening."

• Try to establish a rapport with the person early on. You may want to wait a bit before pulling your notebook out. This meeting stage may determine how the rest of the interview will go. Do you share a common interest or friend? If so, mention that.

• Look the subject in the eye and listen carefully to his/her answers. Be sure to smile. A smile, they say, is lubrication for the words and collaborator of the eyes in contact. A smile helps both you and your subject relax.

• When the source is speaking, nod or make some verbal remark to show you are listening and understand. Sit on the edge of your chair and lean forward. This is a posture that projects an eager, positive attitude.

• Observe and record the person's body language, mannerisms, dress, physical features, distinctive characteristics and interactions with others. These allow you to paint a word picture for your reader and may reveal something that is not being said. Observe and record the sights and sounds of the surroundings. Take good notes during the interview in a handwriting you will be able to read later. Take too many notes rather than too few.

Takeaways to Consider

• Know your subject thoroughly. Do as much research as you can on the person. Research and interview others who are familiar with the subject.

• Know so much about your interview subject you can give him information about himself he never knew.

• Know more about him than his wife knows.

• Create rapport. When Truman Capote interviewed Marlon Brando — a very unlikely pair — Brando mentioned his alcoholic mother. Capote also had an alcoholic mother and they traded stories and bonded. Capote got much more information than he had hoped for.

• Finally, my 55-word review of a horrendous interview experience:
***Ava Gardner: The Secret Conversations** by Peter Evans and Ava Gardner. The fascinating and unbearable angst of a ghostwriter and his neurotic subject — once the most beautiful woman in the world (and one of the most highly-sexed). After two strokes in her sixties — and strapped for cash — she agreed to the interviews. The day Evans finished the book, he dropped dead from a massive heart attack. Simon & Schuster, 304 pp, ISBN-13: 978-1451627695, $26 hardcover, Kindle $11.04. —DH, July 7, 2013

—

CHAPTER 37

Are Footnotes (or Endnotes) Necessary? Nah.

Research and footnotes
Are footnotes necessary?

My answer is no.

Footnotes are a nuisance to authors, readers and publishers.

Once upon a time it was de rigueur to drive readers nuts with footnotes — especially in prose out of academia.

The problem is these devices intentionally interrupt the thread of comprehension. Asterisks, little numbers in superscript (e.g., [1]), daggers, double daggers, diacritical marks (to show phonetic pronunciation) and footnotes — all take the readers eye off the ball.

A biography where footnotes were longer than the text
I once bought a short biography of Winston Churchill. Not only were footnotes on every page, but also in many cases the footnotes were longer than the actual text. I got past four pages, discovered the entire book was formatted half-text and half-footnotes and chucked it out.

Where you never see footnotes
Open any newspaper or popular magazine, and you'll never see footnotes in the stories, features or opinion pieces. Either you believe in the publication — and its journalists — or you don't.

The importance of footnotes
For a reporter, it is imperative to keep a record of where your research was obtained. If questioned about veracity, you can cite the source and be done with it.

"Never use an asterisk in direct mail," wrote Herschell Gordon Lewis. The reason is obvious. When a writer is deep into a sales argument, an asterisk is the equivalent of a bright red octagonal STOP sign. It could send the reader on a hunting expedition to find the reference. Whereupon the thread of concentration is broken and very likely the order is lost.

> **Traditional footnote choices**
> • Use tiny superscript number[1] in the text and put the references at the bottom of the page.
>
> • Put all references to the superscript numbers as endnotes in a special section at the end under "Notes and Bibliography."
>
> • No superscript numbers in the text. Instead create a "Notes and Bibliography" section at the back is arranged by chapter and page with the identifying

word or phrase, followed by the endnote. This is the least interruptive of the reading experience but the most difficult for the reader to research.

The beauty of footnotes on Kindle and e-books
With Kindle, you can click on a footnote reference — a tiny superscript number — and you'll be taken directly to the footnote. Press the "Back" bar and you are in the text where you left off. No searching for footnotes at the bottom of the page or in the back of the book.

Some e-authors use a tiny superscript number[1] to indicate a source and a tiny superscript lettera to indicate an informative anecdote or bit of history not essential to the text, but of possible interest.

Let's assume every reader of yours and mine is computer-literate and is comfortable using the Internet. (Those who are not can seek help from friends.)

If a reader of this book wants the precise source of a quote, story or statistic, chances are it can be data-entered into Google — surrounded by quotation marks — and the answer will be onscreen in less than a second.

My opinion: footnotes are vestigial
I think you can tell by now I researched the hell out of this book. It's based on 60 years in business and dealing with the English language.

Before Google, footnotes were essential.

Fast-forward to the 21st century: If a reader of this book wants the precise source of a quote, story or statistic, chances are it will turn up on Google in less than a second.

Takeaways to Consider

• Footnotes are vestigial.

• Keep your own records of where your research took you, but don't break the reader's thread of concentration.

• Newspapers and magazines don't use footnotes, so why should you?

• Google is civilization's greatest source for footnotes. It is the magnificent database to keep all writers honest.

CHAPTER 38

Good Design: Why It Died and How to Resuscitate It

The dot-com boom of the mid-1990s was huge. Many thousands of young, inexperienced designers with no training and no experience were hired by a legion of young, inexperienced entrepreneurs.

In terms of reading, my sense is very few of these hotshots ever got beyond *Peter Rabbit* and *Johnny Crow's Garden*. They were not readers. In their skewed minds they were hired to make websites look pretty. Website design is about them, not about the reader.

"The Internet is a new medium, a new paradigm," we geezers were told. "This is a world of new rules. We make the rules now. We don't need your old rules and we don't need you, chum."

After the crash of 2000 — where trillions of dollars evaporated — many of these smug, full-of-themselves amateur designers lost their jobs.

Unfortunately, their deeply flawed ideas became the norm and are all over the Internet.

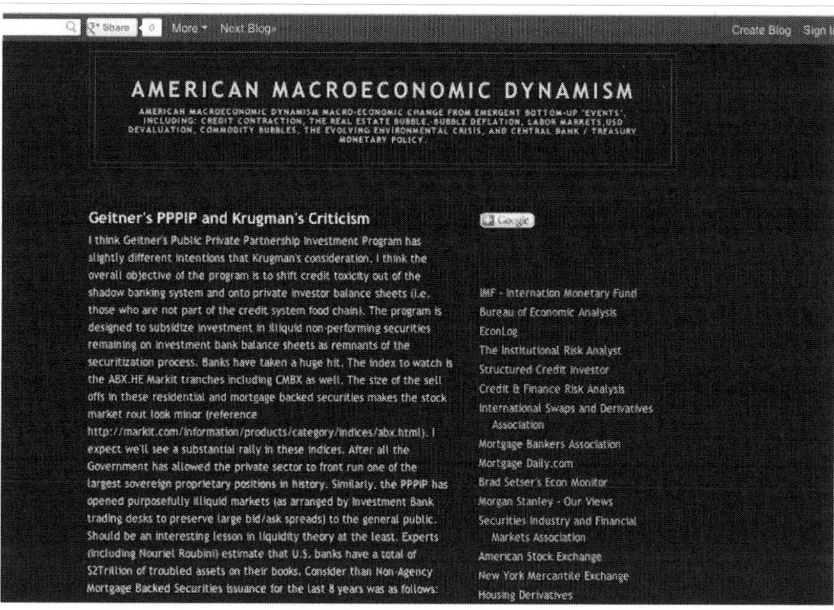

Most of the rules of print on paper apply to the digital world. *(See Chapter 14.)* In this case, white type dropped out of a black background is impossible to read.

Ask a Web designer why a site looks the way it does, the answer will be: "This is how it's done."

Ask a Web designer why type is in unreadable pastel hues or faint gray and the response is the same: "That's the fashion today."

Online readability: the optimal line length
I had an exchange with Christian Holst of the Baymard Institute in Copenhagen. Here are the nuts-'n'-bolts of making it comfortable for the online reader:

> Having the right amount of characters on each line is key to the readability of your text. It shouldn't merely be your design that dictates the width of your text, it should also be a matter of legibility.
>
> The optimal line length for your body text is considered to be 50-60 characters per line, including spaces (*Typographie*, E. Ruder). Other sources suggest that up to 75 characters is acceptable. So what's the downside of violating this range?
>
> **Too long** — if a line of text is too long the visitor's eye will have a hard time focusing on the text. This is because the length makes it difficult to get an idea of where the line starts and ends. Furthermore it can be difficult to continue from the correct line in large blocks of text.
>
> **Too short** — if a line is too short the eye will have to travel back too often, breaking the reader's rhythm. Too short lines also tend to stress people, making them begin on the next line before finishing the current one (hence skipping potentially important words).
>
> It turns out that the subconscious mind is energized when jumping to the next line (as long as it doesn't happen too frequently). At the beginning of every new line the reader is focused, but this focus gradually **wears off** over the duration of the line (*Typographie,* E. Ruder).
>
> In order to avoid the drawbacks of too long and too short lines, but still energize your readers and keep them engaged, we suggest keeping it within the range of **50-75 characters per line.** *—Christian Holtz, Baymard Institute*

Vertical vs. horizontal
The problem: A sheet of stationary, a book or a magazine is a vertical format. As readers, we are used to vertical documents. Our eyes are comfortable with text up to 75 characters wide.

With the exception of smart phones and tablets, the computer screen is horizontal. Sadly, many of these know-nothing Web designers abhor white space. So they fill this horizontal space with type. Often it runs double the optimal maximum width of 75 characters.

Ergo, a nasty reading experience has been created.

The solution
Use wide margins. Set the copy at the preferred width — no more than 75 characters (including spaces) — for ease of reading.

Don't worry about a lot of white space. After all, we're not talking about the cost of paper. This is the digital world. White space is free.

The reader needs care and feeding — not the white space.

Cunard's website

Peggy and I have always dreamed of crossing the Atlantic old style — in the slow paced world of a great Cunard ocean liner. As book critic Dwight Garner wrote in *The New York Times:*

A crossing on the *Queen Mary 2* is the sort of thing people put on their bucket lists. More than a few passengers on our crossing seemed perilously close to kicking that bucket ... the average age on our crossing, I'd guess, was well over 60. There was an abundance of wheelchairs, walkers and canes, so many that if everyone had tossed theirs overboard at once they would have created an artificial reef.

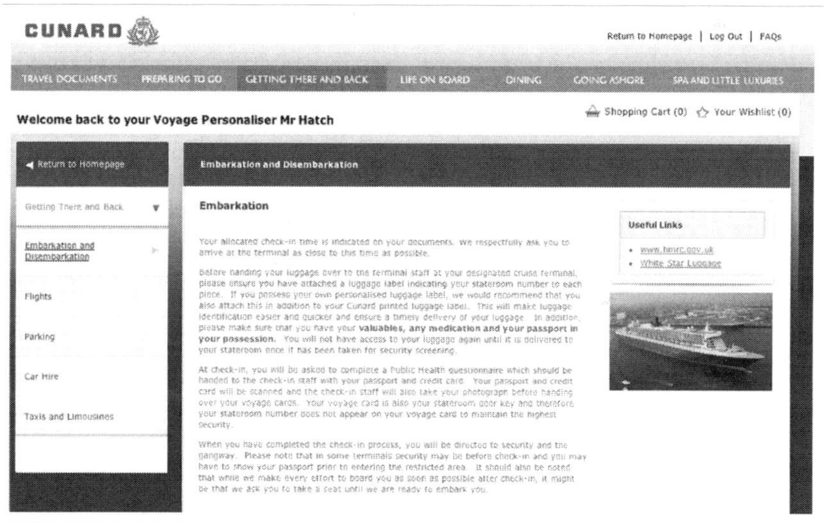

The Web designers at Cunard are totally insensitive to its customers. Senior citizens (*VERY* senior citizens) should not be forced to read mouse-type messages in a light gray font.

The only time to use gray type is when you absolutely do not want people to read the text. *(See Chapter 21 "Masters of Obfuscation.")*

As John Prince, management and branding consultant, wrote to me:

> As for gray mouse-type, I believe it's an age thing. The 20-something designers with 20/20 eyesight enlarge that section on their 32" retinal display monitors and it looks great to them. Really cool. It'll probably win a design prize. The problem is, of course, they're not the audience.
>
> Goes back to the sign on my studio wall: "Looks great! But will it sell anything?"

Most Web designers have never served an apprenticeship and have never been mentored in design and readability. One reason: potential mentors — the people who hire the designers — have never designed anything and never been mentored themselves. These ignorant vice presidents hire ignorant managers who allow ignorant website designers to amuse themselves creating the unreadable.

The result is a total communications disconnect between websites and readers. Tom Friedman of *The New York Times* wrote a fascinating column on current hiring problems:

> "The market is broken on both sides," explained [HireArt founder Eleonora] Sharef. "Many applicants don't have the skills that employers are seeking, and don't know how to get them. But employers also ... have unrealistic expectations." They're all "looking for purple unicorns: the perfect match. They don't want to train you, and they expect you to be overqualified … " Too many of the "skills you need in the workplace today are not being taught by colleges."

How design affects comprehension
My French client told me the story of a designer he was working with.

"I am designing a beautiful website for you," the guy said. "I need some content to fill in the spaces."

"I fired him," my client said.

The great copywriter Malcolm Decker wrote about the place of design in direct mail advertising:

> Finally, it's important to remember that in direct mail, the word is king. Copy is the architect of the sale. Design and art are strongly supportive interior designers that often set up the sale.
>
> Because lookers are shoppers while readers are buyers, if you can firmly engage your prospect — and keep him engaged — through reading, you're on your way to a sale.

The word is also king in magazine and newspaper articles, annual reports, résumés, business letters and business cards — just about any business, personal or literary communication.

The reader should never be conscious of design or typeface or literary style. All of it should disappear in the mist, so nothing remains but the author's mesmerizing prose going directly into the reader's brain.

Designing covers for books, reports, magazines, etc.
The main purpose of cover design is to enable the reader to immediately discern what the product is. Quite simply, a cover design should pop. The two tests of correct cover design:

- Can you read it from across the room?
- Can it be read and understood when reduced to a one-half-inch square on a computer screen or a catalog?

An example of cover design perfection

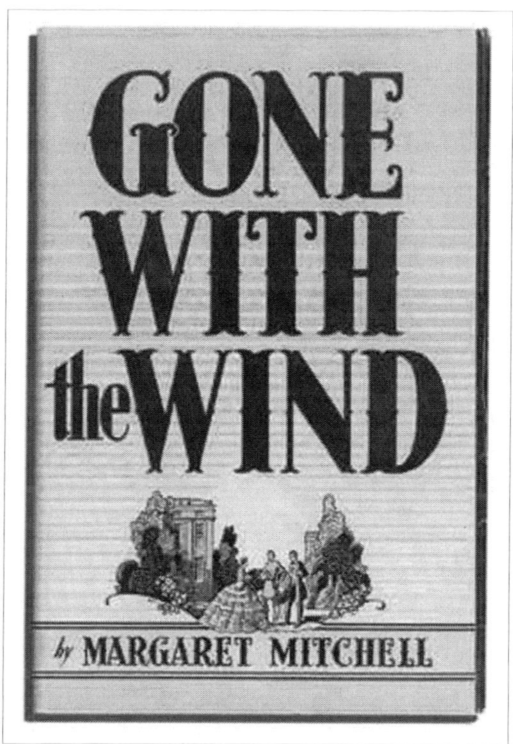

Gone with the Wind was the greatest success by the unknown author of a first novel in American history. Margaret Mitchell was a housewife in Atlanta who produced several thousand pages of manuscript. Harold Latham, a traveling book editor from New York, stumbled upon it on a trip to Atlanta in 1935.

Even in its raw, unedited form, the narrative blew Latham away and he persuaded his management at Macmillan to publish it.

The book won the 1937 Pulitzer Prize and was made into a blockbuster movie starring Clark Gable, Vivian Leigh, Hattie McDaniel and Leslie Howard. Released in 1939, the film went on to win 10 Oscars.

The book jacket for the original hardcover edition is a masterpiece. In a bookstore window, it was readable from across the street.

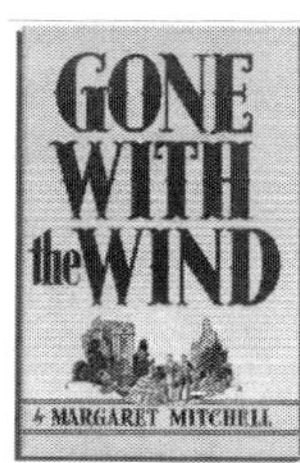

In a book catalog, newspaper ad or Internet listing the title is always readable in any size.

The worst book cover designer in America today

My vote for winner of this dubious distinction goes to Chipp Kidd (b. 1964), who has achieved rock star status in the publishing world. Many of his covers cannot be read or understood from either across the room or in a small online listing. His work is the epitome of self-indulgent design. A sampling:

Takeaways to Consider

• Before hiring a designer for a project, first determine the purpose of the design. Is it to be a logo, billboard, magazine illustration, sales brochure, annual report, newspaper ad or book cover?

• Communicate to the designer precisely what you want the design to accomplish.

• I have found designers can be very patronizing to executives, saying in effect, "You don't know anything about creative; leave that to me."

• If you feel uncomfortable with the design, then the design is wrong. Period.

• Be prepared to sit on the designer — especially Web designers — and have the job done over and over again. It must satisfy you and the original intent. Not the designer.

• Web designers are especially in need of adult supervision.

• If the designer whines you're stifling creativity, get another designer immediately.

• Make a black-and-white photocopy of the design — ad or page or cover. If it's difficult to read the type, send it back to the designer for surgery.

• For example, red type sprinted on a black background will show up as dark, unreadable mush. This becomes immediately obvious when subjected to a black-and-white photocopy.

• The only time to use gray type is when you absolutely do not want people to read the text.

CHAPTER 39

Danger! Safeguard Your Work!

Lost manuscripts
A number of horror stories exist where authors have lost their manuscripts and were forced to start again from scratch:

• T.E. Lawrence *(Lawrence of Arabia)* left the original manuscript of his *Seven Pillars of Wisdom* in the café of the Reading railroad station in England and never found it.

• Welsh poet Dylan Thomas, an alcoholic, lost the manuscript to his play, *Under Milk Wood*, three times.

• Thomas Carlyle's novel about the French Revolution was mistaken for waste paper by a maid who burned it. He had to start all over again.

• In 1922, Ernest Hemingway's wife, Hadley Richardson, bundled up both the original manuscripts and carbon copies of his early short stories and lost them on a train in the Gare de Lyon in Paris. They were never found.

• Best-selling novelist Robert Ludlum lost the manuscript of his first work during a night of drinking as a U.S. Marine on leave in San Francisco.

My father's technique
As a kid, I vividly remember how my father worked. He scrawled all 40 of his books in unreadable penciled script on lined paper. Every couple of days we would drive over to the house of his secretary, who typed two copies — an original and a carbon. The first copy was for editing. The second copy was immediately stored in the trunk of the car, so if the house burned down, his work would not be lost.

How I guarantee the safety of my work
Whenever I finish working on a file, I copy it into a flash drive always in my computer. Once a week, I update the archive and transfer the contents of my computer to the external drive to make a second copy.

I then transfer the week's work to my laptop for a third copy and store the external drive in our fireproof safe.

If I am working on the road, I'll e-mail the latest work to myself at Yahoo, which means it's retrievable from the cloud.

The last resort: Carbonite
I also subscribe to the Carbonite service. These folks have perpetual access to my computer. If a gas explosion takes out my house (and not me), I can retrieve my files from Carbonite.

If I have been for away for week or more, I will receive an e-mail from Carbonite with a warning that no new material has been generated. Carbonite also contacts me if our connection is down. The cost: $59 per year per computer — a worthwhile insurance policy.

Takeaways to Consider

- Don't take a chance on losing your work.
- Copy the day's output onto a flash drive.
- Back up your computer to a separate hard drive at least once every week.
- You can e-mail current work to yourself at your in-box, where it will be held by your service provider.
- Look into Carbonite or another backup system.

CHAPTER 40

Three of the Greatest Letters Ever Written

The Wall Street Journal's **billion-dollar bonanza**

What follows is the fabled "Two Young Men..." letter written by freelancer Martin Conroy and first sent out in 1974 and mailed continuously for over 25 years. It may still be in the mail today.

I don't know when it first dawned on me that this was a very special letter. I kept seeing it over and over and over again — month after month, year after year. I decided to research it.

Late in 1991, I called *Wall Street Journal* circulation manager Paul Bell and ran some numbers by him:

> **HATCH:** Would you say that the average mail order circulation of the Journal over the past 18 years was about one million?
>
> **BELL:** [Pause.] Yes, that's about right.
>
> **HATCH:** Am I right in assuming that the average subscription rate of The Wall Street Journal over the past 18 years has been about $100 a year?
>
> **BELL:** [Pause.] Yes, that's about right.
>
> **HATCH:** Is it safe to assume that 55 percent of all your mail order subscribers over the past 18 years have come in as a result of Martin Conroy's "Two Young Men..." letter?
>
> **BELL:** We have a lot of other sources — telemarketing, subscriptions as a result of newsstand sales, supermarket take-ones, inserts. But, yes, I think 55 percent is a fair estimate.
>
> **HATCH:** Paul, 1 million subscribers per year time $100 equals $100 million times 18 years is $1.8 billion times 55 percent equals $1 billion. If these numbers are correct, the Martin Conroy letter is directly responsible for bringing in $1 billion in revenue to *The Wall Street Journal*, and is, therefore *THE MOST SUCCESSFUL SINGLE PIECE OF ADVERTISING IN THE HISTORY OF THE WORLD!*
>
> **BELL:** [Long silence. Then in a small voice.] Uh, please don't tell Marty Conroy. He'll raise his prices.

THE WALL STREET JOURNAL.

World Financial Center, 200 Liberty Street, New York, NY 10281

Dear Reader:

On a beautiful late spring afternoon, twenty-five years ago, two young men graduated from the same college. They were very much alike, these two young men. Both had been better than average students, both were personable and both—as young college graduates are—were filled with ambitious dreams for the future.

Recently, these men returned to their college for their 25th reunion.

They were still very much alike. Both were happily married. Both had three children. And both, it turned out, had gone to work for the same Midwestern manufacturing company after graduation, and were still there.

But there was a difference. One of the men was manager of a small department of that company. The other was its president.

What Made The Difference

Have you ever wondered, as I have, what makes this kind of difference in people's lives? It isn't a native intelligence or talent or dedication. It isn't that one person wants success and the other doesn't.

The difference lies in what each person knows and how he or she makes use of that knowledge.

And that is why I am writing to you and to people like you about The Wall Street Journal. For that is the whole purpose of The Journal: to give its readers knowledge—knowledge that they can use in business.

A Publication Unlike Any Other

You see, The Wall Street Journal is a unique publication. It's the country's only national business daily. Each business day, it is put together by the world's largest staff of business-news experts.

Each business day, The Journal's pages include a broad range of information of interest and significance to business-minded people, no matter where it comes from. Not just stocks and finance, but anything and everything in the whole, fast-moving world of business. . .The Wall Street Journal gives you all the business news you need—when you need it.

Knowledge Is Power

Right now, I am looking at page one of The Journal, the best-read front page in America. It combines all the important news of the day with in-depth feature reporting. Every phase of business news is covered. I see articles on new inflation, wholesale prices, car prices, tax incentives for industries to major developments in Washington, and elsewhere.

(over, please)

And there is page after page inside The Journal, filled with fascinating and significant information that's useful to you. The Marketplace section gives you insights into how consumers are thinking and spending. How companies compete for market share. There is daily coverage of law, technology, media and marketing. Plus daily features on the challenges of managing smaller companies.

The Journal is also the single best source for news and statistics about your money. In the Money & Investing section there are helpful charts, easy-to-scan market quotations, plus "Abreast of the Market," "Heard on the Street" and "Your Money Matters," three of America's most influential and carefully read investment columns.

If you have never read The Wall Street Journal, you cannot imagine how useful it can be to you.

A Money-Saving Subscription

Put our statements to the proof by subscribing for the next 13 weeks for just $44. This is among the shortest subscription terms we offer—and a perfect way to get acquainted with The Journal.

Or you may prefer to take advantage of our better buy —one year for $149. You save over $40 off the cover price of The Journal.

Simply fill out the enclosed order card and mail it in the postage-paid envelope provided. And here's The Journal's guarantee: should The Journal not measure up to your expectations, you may cancel this arrangement at any point and receive a refund for the undelivered portion of your subscription.

If you feel as we do that this is a fair and reasonable proposition, then you will want to find out without delay if The Wall Street Journal can do for you what it is doing for millions of readers. So please mail the enclosed order card now, and we will start serving you immediately.

About those two college classmates I mention at the beginning of this letter: they were graduated from college together and together got started in the business world. So what made their lives in business different?

Knowledge. Useful knowledge. And its application.

An Investment In Success

I cannot promise you that success will be instantly yours if you start reading The Wall Street Journal. But I can guarantee that you will find The Journal always interesting, always reliable, and always useful.

Sincerely,

Peter R. Kann
Publisher

PRK: id
Encs.

P.S. It's important to note that The Journal's subscription price may be tax deductible. Ask your tax advisor.

David Ogilvy's letter to New York commuters
Mark Phillips, founder of the Bluefrog Agency, recounted the story of this 1968 masterpiece — the year David Ogilvy agreed to become chairman of the United Negro College Fund.

How Ogilvy broke the rules
A direct mail campaign always goes direct to a person at an address — either at home or in a place of business. Some mailings go to an address alone. Even today we get mailings addressed to:

> Resident
> Address
> City State ZIP

Generally this is dangerous marketing. When you rent a magazine subscription list or a list of catalog buyers, you know the name of the person. In addition, you know something about your prospect's behavior.

Rent a cheap compiled list — the equivalent of the telephone book arranged by Zip code — and you have no idea whether the person reads mail or buys anything by mail or even has a credit card or a bank account.

For this United Negro College Fund effort, Ogilvy did not even have an address. The letter — along with a reply envelope — was placed on the seat of every afternoon commuter train leaving New York's Grand Central Terminal. The bulk of the passengers lived in the upmarket towns of Westchester County, New York, and suburban Connecticut.

Ogilvy deduced most of these folks were college educated and had good jobs in the city. Otherwise they could not afford the commute.

This fundraising letter brought in $26,000 after just three hours of exposure.

United Negro College Fund, Inc.

June 24, 1968

FROM: David Ogilvy

TO : Commuters

When this train emerges from the tunnel at 108th Street this evening, look out of the window.

You may see some of the 1,125 boys and girls from New York ghettos who are now on vacation from our Negro colleges.

At least you will see some of the homes(?) from which they come. They are "high risk" students--with high potential. Your own college won't take them, because they cannot qualify for admission.

In the New England colleges there are now 300,000 students. How many of them, do you guess, are black? About 2,000--two thirds of one percent. Words fail me.

If you are like most of the commuters on this train, you are a college graduate--and you have supported your college faithfully over the years.

After dinner tonight, will you do something imaginative? Will you write a check for a group of colleges whose alumni, through no fault of their own, are simply unable to carry the whole load of supporting their alma mater?

I refer, of course, to Morehouse and Fisk and Tuskegee and the 33 other predominantly Negro colleges which belong to the United Negro College Fund.

About 40,000 students--most of them Negro--are now enrolled in these colleges. Their graduates include 85 percent of all Negro doctors, and most of the leaders of the Negro community. The vast majority of them have very small incomes--compared with yours.

Last year 50 predominantly white colleges received $416,000,000 in gifts. For our 36 Negro colleges, we

59 East 54th Street
New York, N.Y. 10022
PLaza 1-1436

are trying to raise $6,500,000 this year. Will you help?

Without equality of education, there can never be equality of opportunity. This is the heart of the country's most urgent problem. Will you help?

I dare to suggest that you send our Fund a percentage of the amount you are giving to your own college. Ten percent? Fifty percent? You be the judge. (Don't reduce your gift to your own college; simply give our Fund something on top.) Here are the guts of the situation:

1. The doors to our UNCF colleges are open to all--regardless of race, creed or national origin. They are not segregated, nor are they educating their students for a segregated world. Their faculties and their Boards are integrated, and the number of their white students is growing every year.

2. Our average cost of tuition, books, room and board is $1,375. This compares with $2,400 at predominantly white colleges. Three out of four of our students are working their way through our colleges.

3. On top of that, our colleges give financial assistance to more than half of their students. A great many more need it.

4. UNCF is the largest fund drive devoted to any Negro cause. Many people feel it is also the most constructive.

Says John W. Gardner, "These colleges have an immensely important part to play in the education of Negro Americans. And the education of Negro Americans is one of the crucial tasks of our time...I can tell you with some authority that the predominantly Negro colleges need help."

Please decide now what percentage of your gift to your own college you wish to send to UNCF, and mail it in the envelope I have enclosed. Perhaps you will then sleep a little better during the long hot summer.

Yours sincerely,

David Ogilvy

Chairman

P.S. A gift of stock would be equally valuable.

Hank Burnett's Admiral Byrd Society letter

In 1966, a Harvard University dean approached the legendary Dick Benson to help raise money for an unusual 23-day adventure. Under the auspices of the Admiral Byrd Society, it was to be a round-the-world adventure unlike anything ever conceived before.

What made the excursion unique was the circumnavigation would be north-south — going over both poles.

The offer was reminiscent of Ernest Shackleton's *Times of London* ad, Dec. 29, 1913. It reportedly drew hundreds of responses.

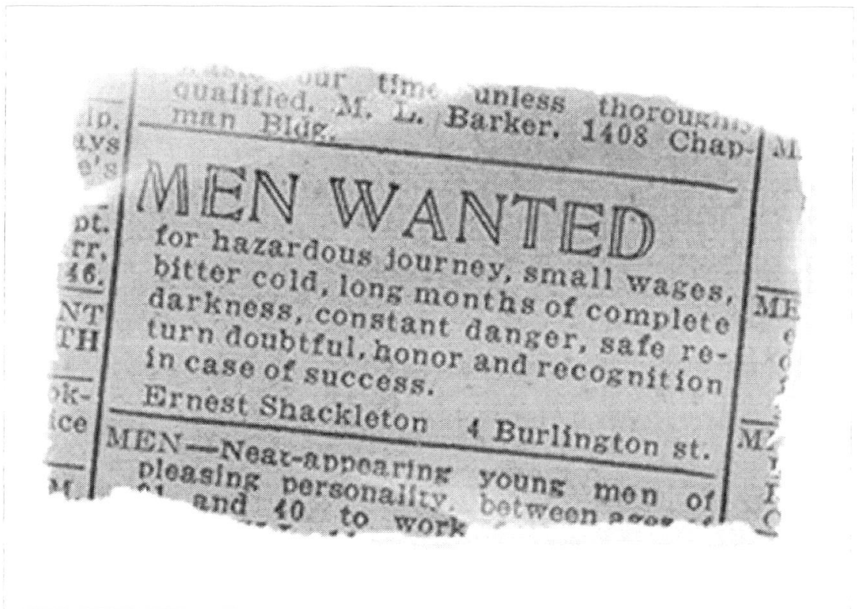

MEN WANTED

for hazardous journey, small wages, bitter cold, long months of complete darkness, constant danger, safe return doubtful, honor and recognition in case of success.

Ernest Shackleton 4 Burlington st.

Hank Burnett's lede:

> As Chairman of the Admiral Richard E. Byrd Polar Center, it is my privilege to invite you to become a member of an expedition which is destined to make both news and history.
>
> It will cost you $10,000 and about 26 days of your time. Frankly, you will endure some discomfort, and may even face some danger.
>
> On the other hand, you will have the rare privilege of taking part in a mission of great significance for the United States and the entire world. A mission, incidentally, which has never before been attempted by man.

This was a big deal. For starters, the $10,000 price tag was the equivalent of $61,000 in 2012 dollars.

The allowable budget for marketing was a paltry $5,000. But the list wizardry of consultant Dick Benson coupled with the copy brilliance of Hank Burnett paid off. The first seven-page direct mail letter in history generated 72 paid responses — $720,000 gross — and the trip went off without a hitch.

EDWARD C. BURSK
SOLDIERS FIELD
BOSTON, MASSACHUSETTS, 02163

EDITOR
HARVARD BUSINESS REVIEW

Please reply to me in care of:
Transpolar Expedition
Admiral Richard E. Byrd Polar Center
18 Tremont Street
Boston, Massachusetts 02108

September 3, 1968

Mr. Richard N. Archer
121 Corlies Ave.
Pelham, N.Y. 10803

Dear Mr. Archer:

As Chairman of the Admiral Richard E. Byrd Polar Center, it is my privilege to invite you to become a member of an expedition which is destined to make both news and history.

It will cost you $10,000 and about 26 days of your time, Frankly, you will endure some discomfort, and may even face some danger.

On the other hand, you will have the rare privilege of taking part in a mission of great significance for the United States and the entire world. A mission, incidentally, which has never before been attempted by man.

You will personally harp the chance to help enrich mankind's fund of knowledge about two of the last earthly frontiers, the polar regions.

I am inviting you to join a distinguished group of 50 people who will fly around the world longitudinally, over both poles, on an expedition which will commemorate Admiral Richard E. Byrd's first Antarctic flight in 1929.

Among the highlights of this transpolar flight - the first commercial flight ever to cross both poles and touch down on all continents - will be stopovers at the American military/scientific bases at Thule, Greenland, and McMurdo Sound, Antarctica.

Because this expedition has the interest and support of much of the Free World, you and your fellow members will be honored guests (in many cases, even celebrities) at state and diplomatic receptions throughout the itinerary. You will have the opportunity to meet and talk with some of the world's important national leaders and public figures, such as Pope Paul VI, the Emperor of Japan, General Carlos Romulo, and many others who are already a part of history.

By agreeing to join this expedition, you will, in a sense, establish yourself in history too. For you will become a Founding Trustee of the new Admiral Richard E. Byrd Polar Center, sponsor of the expedition.

Your biography will be recorded in the Center's archives, available to future historians. The log, photographs and memorabilia of the expedition will be permanently displayed in the Center. And your name will be inscribed, with those of the other expedition members, on a bronze memorial tablet.

Before I continue with the details of the expedition, let me tell you more about the Byrd Polar Center and the reasoning which led to its establishment this summer.

Located in Boston, home of the late Admiral and point of origin for each of his seven expeditions, this nonprofit institution will house, catalog and preserve the papers and records of both Admiral Byrd and other Arctic and Antarctic explorers.

But the Center will have a more dynamic function than merely to enshrine the past. It will be a vital, viable organization devoted to furthering peaceful development of the polar regions, particularly Antarctica.

It will become, in effect, this country's headquarters for investigation and research into the scientific and commercial development of the poles. The Center will sponsor, support, initiate and conduct studies and expeditions. It will furnish comprehensive data or technical assistance to the United States, or to any university, institution, foundation, business organization or private individual legitimately interested in polar development.

In other words, the Center has set for itself a course which the Admiral before his death endorsed wholeheartedly. He foresaw that mankind would one day benefit enormously from development of Antarctica's vast potential. And he perceived that Antarctica's unique and diverse advantages and resources might best be developed by private capital in a free enterprise context.

The Byrd Polar Center is dedicated to these objectives. And the essential purpose of this commemorative expedition is to dramatize the role that private enterprise - and private citizens - can play in the opening of these last frontiers.

At the same time, the expedition should help prove a few other important points. It should demonstrate the feasibility of shrinking the world through longitudinal navigation. It should also help blaze a trail for commercial air travel over the South Pole. Presently, to fly from Chile to Australia, you must go by way of Los Angeles, even though a straight line trans-Antarctic route would be far shorter.

There is another factor I should mention, one which I think lends a certain urgency to the work of the Center. Development of the polar regions enjoys a high official priority in the Soviet Union - higher, some believe, than in the United States.

The Center's activities can provide a tangible, effective complement to those of our own government, and over the long term, contribute meaningfully to preservation of the Arctic and Antarctic regions for peaceful purposes.

These objectives, I think you will agree, are entirely valid. And important, for the future of humanity. It is for this reason that the inaugural activity of the Byrd Polar Center will be an expedition of such scope and magnitude.

The expedition will be led by Commander Fred G. Dustin, veteran of six polar expeditions, advisor to Admiral Byrd and one of the intrepid group which spent the winter of 1934 in Little America on Byrd's Antarctic Expedition II. Commander Dustin is a member of the U.S. Antarctica Committee and President of the Byrd Polar Center.

Considered the ranking American authority on the polar regions, Fred Dustin is probably better qualified to lead this expedition - and brief members on virtually every aspect of the polar regions - than any man on earth. The Center and the expedition are fortunate to have Commander Dustin, as you will discover should you decide to participate.

The flight will be made in a specially outfitted, four-engine commercial jet with lounge-chair-and-table cabin configuration. A full flight crew of six will be headed by Captain Hal Neff, former pilot of Air Force One, the Presidential plane. Special clothing and equipment, such as Arctic survival gear, will be provided by the expedition and carried aboard the plane.

The expedition members will meet in Boston on the evening of November 7, 1968, for briefing and a reception and send-off party with the Governor of Massachusetts, Mayor of Boston, local officials and directors of the Byrd Polar Center. Next day, we will take off, head due north from Boston's Logan International Airport and follow this itinerary (as I have not yet visited all these places myself, I have drawn on the descriptions submitted to me by Commander Dustin and the other experienced people who have planned the expedition):

<u>Thule, Greenland</u>

Far above the Arctic Circle, past the chill reaches of Baffin Bay, lies desolate Thule, the northernmost U.S. air base. Almost 400 miles further north than the northern tip of Alaska, Thule was originally surveyed as a possible military site by Admiral Byrd and Commander Dustin. Here, in the deepening Arctic winter, you will get your first taste of the rigors of polar existence. You will have the chance to inspect the installation and meet the men for whom Arctic survival is a way of life.

<u>North Pole</u>

According to those who have crossed the North Pole, you will completely lose your day-night orientation. Sunrise and sunset can occur within minutes of each other, a strange and unforgettable phenomenon. After Thule, you will cross the geographic North Pole, just as Admiral Byrd did in his pioneering trans-Arctic flight with Floyd Bennett in 1926. A memorial flag will be dropped.

<u>Anchorage, Alaska</u>

After crossing the pole, the plane will bank into a 90□ left turn and head south, over the Arctic Ocean and Beaufort Sea, past Mt. McKinley, North America's highest peak, and on to Anchorage. There, you will meet the Governor and key officials.

<u>Tokyo, Japan</u>

The highlight of your stopover in Japan will be an opportunity to meet the Emperor and Premier. (Fishing; excursion to Hakone and Atami by bullet train; tea ceremony at private homes.)

Manila, Philippines

General Carlos Romulo, the legendary patriot and statesman, an old friend of Admiral Byrd, will give the expedition a warm welcome in Manila. (Folklore performance; hunting for duck, deer, wild boar and a special species of water buffalo; fishing for tuna and marlin.)

You will note that here and elsewhere we have prearranged a considerable amount of hunting, fishing, and so on. These activities are optional. (Members of the expedition will be asked to indicate their preferences 30 days before the flight.) For those who do not want to participate in any of these events, there will be sight-seeing, golf and many other things to do.

Darwin, Australia

Hard by the Timor Sea, tropical Darwin offers some of the world's most superb beaches. You will have time not only to sample the sand and water sports, but to see Australia's great outback. With its spectacular chasms, canyons and gorges, the rarely visited outback is a scenic match for our own West.

Sydney, Australia

You can look forward to an enthusiastic reception in Sydney by the Prime Minister and government officials. For one thing, Australia is on particularly good terms with the United States. For another, Australia has traditionally been in the vanguard of nations involved in Antarctic exploration and development. (Hunting for kangaroo, crocodile, buffalo, wild boar, duck, and geese; or off-shore fishing for rifle fish, salmon, and giant grouper.)

Christchurch, New Zealand

This is our staging point for the flight to Antarctica, and it couldn't be more appropriate. Most of the early expeditions departed from New Zealand, and Admiral Byrd is still considered a national hero there. New Zealand is Antarctic-conscious and its people take almost a proprietary interest in the frozen continent. You will be something of a celebrity in New Zealand, and can expect a thoroughly enjoyable visit while the expedition awaits favorable weather reports from McMurdo Sound. (Deer hunting - where deer are so plentiful that they pay a bounty; fishing for all of the great species of - in an area known for the greatest marlin fishing in the world - also Mako shark.)

McMurdo Sound, Antarctica

I am told that only a total eclipse of the sun is comparable, in emotional impact, to the first sight of Antarctica. Once experienced, neither can be forgotten. If you prove to be like most who have seen Antarctica, you will need somehow, someday, to return. And when you do, the emotional impact will be just as profound. That is what the Antarctic veterans say.

For Antarctica exists well beyond the boundaries of the world you know. You will see there a sun you have never before seen, breathe air you have never before breathed. You will see menacing white mountains towering for thousands of feet over a black ocean in which, with luck, you might survive for 45 seconds. You will see the awesome Ross Ice Shelf, as large as France, with its 50 to 200 foot ice cliffs cleaving the sea for 400 miles. You will see the active volcano, Mt. Erebus, 13,000 feet of fire and ice.

And you will see the huts, so well preserved they seem to have been inhabited only yesterday, which Shackleton used in 1908 and the ill-fated Scott in 1911. Antarctica, apparently, is not subject to the passage of time as we know it.

At McMurdo Base, you will meet the military men and scientists who inhabit this strange, alien territory. And you will inhabit it for a while too - long enough to feel its bone-chilling cold, to hear its timeless silence, to perceive, at the very edge of your composure, the terror of its mindless hostility to human beings.

While you are there, you will learn, as few men have ever had the opportunity to learn, about Antarctica. You will learn about survival, but more important, about what men must accomplish to truly open this formidable frontier.

<u>South Pole</u>

Admiral Byrd was the first man to fly over the South Pole. In all of history, probably fewer than 200 men have crossed the pole, by air or otherwise. As a member of this expedition, you will join that select group.

<u>Punta Arenas, Chile</u>

From the South Pole, you will fly to Punta Arenas, on the tortuous Strait of Magellan which separates continental South America from bleak Tierra del Fuego. The visit here will be brief, but you should get some idea of the flavor of this nearly forgotten outpost.

<u>Rio de Janeiro, Brazil</u>

This memorable stopover will include a diplomatic reception. You will also have a chance to relax and sample the sights and sounds of fabulous Rio. (Special plane to Belo Horizonte for hunting boar, duck, jaguar, panther, water buffalo, crocodile and deer.)

<u>Dakar, Senegal</u>

You may never have expected to see Dakar, but you will on this expedition. (Tribal dancing; safari.)

<u>Rome, Italy</u>

No trip would be complete without a stop in Rome, where we will be received enthusiastically. During our stay there we will have a private audience with the Pope.

trip will exceed costs, the activities of the Polar Center will be accelerated.

To reserve your place in the expedition, just drop me a note on your letterhead or personal stationery, with your deposit check for $2,500, made out to the United States Trust Company. Incidentally, if anything prevents your leaving as planned, you can send another in your place; otherwise, cancellations cannot be accepted later than 30 days before departure.

If you have further questions, please write to me in care of the Trans-polar Expedition, Admiral Richard E. Byrd Polar Center, 18 Tremont Street, Boston, Massachusetts 02108.

I hope we may hear from you soon - and that we will welcome you to the expedition.

Sincerely yours,

Edward C. Bursk

KCB:EHK

P.S.: We have just made arrangements for a professional camera crew to accompany the flight, and as a result we will be able to provide you with a short film clip and sound tape of your experiences.

Bibliography

Bly, Robert W. (Bob)
• *The Copywriter's Handbook, Third Edition: A Step-By-Step Guide to Writing Copy That Sells*
• *Start Your Own Home Business After 50: How to Survive, Thrive, and Earn the Income You Deserve*

Bird, Drayton
• *Commonsense Direct & Digital Marketing*
• *How to Write Sales Letters That Sell*

Brian, Denis
• *Murderers and Other Friendly People: The Private Worlds of Interviewers*

Caples, John
• *Tested Advertising Methods*
• *Making Ads Pay: Timeless Tips for Successful Copywriting*
• *How to Make Your Advertising Make Money*

Cruikshank, Jeffrey L. and Arthur W. Schultz
• *The Man Who Sold America: The Amazing (but True!) Story of Albert D. Lasker and the Creation of the Advertising Century*

Collier, Robert
• *The Robert Collier Letter Book*

Friesen, Pat
• *Cross-Channel Copywriting Handbook*

Hatch, Denny
• *Million Dollar Mailings*
• *Method Marketing: How to Make a Fortune by Getting Inside the Heads of Your Customers*
• *The Secrets of Emotional Hot-Button Copywriting: How to Employ the 7 Key Copy Drivers that Make People Act*
• *Career-Changing Takeaways: Quotations, Rules, Aphorisms, Pithy Tips, Quips, Sage Advice, Secrets, Dictums and Truisms in 99 Categories of Marketing, Business and Life*

Hemingway, Ernest
• *A Movable Feast*

Hopkins, Claude
• *My Life in Advertising*
• *Scientific Advertising*

Jayme, Bill
• *Bill Jayme Collection: Master of Direct Mail Marketing*

Levine, Michael
• *Guerrilla P.R. 2.0: Wage an Effective Publicity Campaign without Going Broke*

Lewis, Herschell Gordon
- *On the Art of Writing Copy*
- *Direct Mail Copy That Sells*
- *Effective E-Mail Marketing: The Complete Guide to Creating Successful Campaigns*
- *On the Art of Writing Copy: The Best of * Print * Broadcast * Internet * Direct Mail*
- *Power Copywriting: Dynamic New Communications Techniques to Help You Sell More Products and Services*
- *How to Handle Your Own Public Relations*
- *Selling on the Net: The Complete Guide*

Nicholas, Ted
- *The Golden Mailbox: How to Get Rich Marketing Your Products*
- *Magic Words That Bring Your Riches*
- *How to Publish a Book & Sell a Million Copies*

Ogilvy, David
- *Ogilvy on Advertising*
- *Confessions of an Advertising Man*

Rapp, Stan & Tom Collins
- *Maxi-Marketing: The New Direction in Advertising, Promotion and Marketing Strategy*
- *The Great Marketing Turnaround: The Age of the Individual—and how to Profit from It*

Roman, Kenneth
- *The King of Madison Avenue: David Ogilvy and the Making of Modern Advertising*

Sackheim, Maxwell
- *My First 65 Years in Advertising*

Schwab, Victor O.
- *How to Write a Good Advertisement*

Schwartz, Eugene M.
- *Breakthrough Advertising*

Updegraff, Robert R.
- *Obvious Adams: The Story of a Successful Businessman*

Watkins, Julian
- *The 100 Greatest Advertisements*

Wheeler, Elmer ("Sizzle")
- *Tested Sentences That Sell: How To Use "Word Magic" To Sell More And Work Less!*
- *Sizzlemanship: New Tested Selling Sentences*

Wunderman, Lester
- *Being Direct: Making Advertising Pay*

About Denny Hatch

Since 1976, Denny Hatch has been a consultant, copywriter and designer in the field of direct marketing.

In past lives Denny has been a page at the NBC television studios, book publicist (Prentice Hall), book salesman (Franklin Watts) and advertising salesman (*Library Journal*); run book clubs (Macmillan, Meredith, Grolier); and been a copywriter for a direct mail agency (The Weintz Co.).

In 1984, with his wife Peggy, he launched the newsletter, *WHO'S MAILING WHAT!*, out of their home in Stamford, Conn. It was based on his massive library of direct mail samples.

To create the newsletter, Denny scanned 1,000 to 2,000 direct mail packages a month in more than 200 categories — business, consumer, non-profit and catalogs — and presided over a library of more than 200,000 direct mail samples; for a fee, subscribers could get copies of any of these mailing packages.

The *WHO'S MAILING WHAT!* archive not only exists, but is thriving, with thousands of direct mail (and e-mail) samples available online.

In 1992, his company was acquired by North American Publishing Co. in Philadelphia. He continued to publish the newsletter, as well as edit *Target Marketing* magazine, which was on life support. After five years with *Target Marketing*, the publication was once again highly profitable.

He went back on his own in 1997.

Currently Denny is a regular columnist of the Target Marketing Group.

On Sept. 25, 1989, Denny was the subject of a front-page article in *The Wall Street Journal*; has been quoted in *Time*, *Newsweek* and *Forbes*; and has appeared on NBC's *Today* program.

Denny has been a frequent speaker at direct marketing seminars and conferences in the U.S., the U.K, Canada and the Far East.

He is the son of biographer Alden Hatch, author of more than 40 biographies. Among them: the first life story of Dwight D. Eisenhower as well as Franklin D. Roosevelt, Clare Boothe Luce, three popes, the Mountbattens and many others.

Denny is the nephew of 1930s screwball comedy writer Eric (*My Man Godfrey*) Hatch.

Index

A

Abraham, Jay (b. 1949), Marketing consultant and teacher, sometimes called "The Wizard," 117,
Ace, Goodman (1899-1982), American humorist, radio and TV writer, 125, 132
Admiral Byrd Society, 275-281
Advice on the Art of Writing Short Stories, 215
Aeschines (389-314 BCE), Athenian statesman and orator, 32, 36
Albany Medical College, 173
allthingsd.com, 220, 223, 224
Amazon, 41, 83, 84, 208, 228, 229, 230, 231
Ambrose, Stephen (1936-2002), American historian, author, 44
Americans, The, 212
American, The, 214
American Heritage, 176
American Pastoral, 214
American Psycho, 214
American Theater Wing, 117
American Tragedy, An, 214
Andersson, Axel, Founder, Axel Andersson Akademy, Hamburg, renowned direct mail expert, 64, 78, 200, 201
Arden, Eve (1908-1990), Film and radio actress, 195
Armstrong, Richard, Freelancer, author of *God Doesn't Shoot Craps: A Divine Comedy,* 222, 224
Ascender Corporation, 107
Avis, 53

B

Baier, Bret (b. 1970), Fox News anchor, 240
Bain Capital, 66
Baldwin, Sandy, President, United States Olympic Committee, 173
barnesandnoble.com, 41, 208
Barnicle, Mike (1943-), American print and TV journalist, 44
Baskind, Tom, P.R. master practitioner, 158
Bastian, Jill, verticalresponse.com/blog, 192
Baymard Institute, 193, 260
BBDO, Batten Barton Durstine & Osborn, Ad agency, 1, 53
Bedell, Clyde (1898-1985), Advertising copywriter, author of *How to Write Advertising That Sells*, 5
Bell, Paul, Circulation director, *The Wall Street Journal*, 269
Bennett, Joan (1910-1990), Film actress, 195
Benson, Richard V. (Dick) (1921-1996), Legendary direct marketing consultant and guru, 125, 132, 179, 183, 198, 275

C

D

De Beers, Diamond mining company founded by Cecil Rhodes, 53
Decker, Malcolm, Consultant, freelance copywriter, 22, 24, 148, 156, 179, 224, 225, 262
DeGeneres, Ellen (b. 1958), Comedienne, television host, 208
Demosthenes (384-322 BCE), Greek orator and statesman, 32
Derr, Richard, (1919-1982), Stage and screen actor, 195
Devil May Care: The New James Bond Novel, 216
Dewan Shaila, Correspondent, *The New York Times*, 110-111
Dewey, Thomas E. (1902-1971), Governor of New York, losing Republican candidate for president 1944, 1948, 253
De Wyngaert, Richard, Proprietor of Headhouse Books, Philadelphia, 211
Digg, 199
Direct Mail Copy That Sells, 125
Direct Marketing Association, 77, 233
Direct Marketing Days New York, 77, 233
Dolman, Bob, Freelance direct mail copywriter, 109
Dolnick, Edward, Author of *The Forger's Spell*, 217
Double Down: Game Change 2012, 66
Doyle, Dane Bernbach, Ad agency, 53
Drawbaugh, Kevin, Reuters, 43
Dream Girl, Play by Elmer Rice, 195, 196
Drucker, Peter (1909-2005), Legendary management consultant and writer, 124
Duenwald, Mary, American journalist with *Bloomberg View*, formerly with *The New York Times*, 66, 78
Duncan, George, Book marketing copywriter and consultant, 75
Dusenberry, Philip (1936-2007), Chairman, BBDO North America, 1
Durrenberger, Carl, Chemical engineer, Hewlett-Packard Company, 43

E
Edelston, Martin (1929-1013), Founder of Boardroom Publications, 160
Edsel, 29, 30, 31
Effective Mail Marketing, 125
Eisenhower, Dwight D. (1890-1969), WWII commander of U.S. forces in Europe, 34th President of the United States, 97, 207, 221, 222, 241, 248
Elements of Typographic Style, 101
Eliot, T.S. (1888-1965) American Nobel Laureate Poet, 44
Ellehuus, Christoffer, Managing Director, Corporate Executive Board, 147
Ellis, Joseph (1943-), Pulitzer Prize winning professor of History at Mount Holyoke College, author of *Founding Brothers*, 173
Elliott, Ed, Designer, Response Creative, Plano, Texas, formerly with Phillips Publish ing International, 94, 140
Engel, Louis (1909-1982), Former managing editor of *Business Week* and partner and vice president of Merrill Lynch, 92, 93, 94
Ezell, Will, "That results guy," 170, 171, 172

F
Facebook, 74, 199
Factiva Study, 245
Fanning, Shawn (b. 1980), Founder of Napster, 39
Faulkner, William (1897-1962), American author, 132

G

H

Hansen, Evan, Editor-in-chief, wired.com, 35
Hardball, 244
hardtofindseminars.com. 51
Hardwicke, Sir Cedric (1893-1964), British stage and screen actor, 195
Harris, Jacob, Data journalist, *The New York Times*, 234
Harris, Julie (1925-2013), Six-time Tony award-winning American stage, film and tel evision actress, 121
Hatch, Alden (1898-19760), Biographer and historian, 40, 41, 253,
Hauptman, Don, Freelance copywriter, 68, 179, 180
Hayes, Chris (b. 1979), MSNBC anchor, 240
Heilemann, John (b. 1966), American author and political commentator, 66
Hemingway, Ernest (1899-1961), American author, Nobel laureate, 23, 24, 48, 49, 82, 132, 135, 267, 283
Hernandez, Raymond (b. 1966), Investigative reporter, *The New York Times*, 173
Hewitt, Don (1922-2009), CBS News television producer, director, founder of *60 Minutes*, 238
Hirsch, Steven (b. 1961), Co-chairman Vivid Entertainment, 9
Hitler, Adolf (1899-1945), 34
Hoax, The, 215
Hodgson, Dick (d. 2006), Direct marketing consultant, founder Sargent House, 187
Holliday, Judy (1921-1965), Academy Award-winning stage and screen actress, 195
Holst, Christian, Baymard Institute, 260, 193
Hopkins, Claude (1866-1932), Advertising pioneer, copywriter, author of *Scientific Advertising*, 7, 10, 63, 21, 71, 77, 95, 118, 180, 283
Hotchner, A.E. (b. 1920), Author of *Papa Hemingway*, 132
hotjobs.com, 163
Howell, Elsworth (1916-1971), Founder, Grolier Enterprises and Howell Book House, xi, 131, 219
Huch, Scott E., President, The Delta Group, 99, 111, 130
Huey, Craig, Newsletter publisher and consultant, 105
Humphrey, Hubert H. (1911-1978), U.S. senator (D-MN), U.S.Vice President and presidential candidate, 237, 238

I

Ingraham, Laura (b. 1964), Conservative commentator, author, 205
In FED We Trust: Ben Bernanke's War on the Great Panic, 215
Internet Archive, 215
Isherwood, Charles, Theater critic, *The New York Times*, 117
Italie, Hillel, Reporter, Associated Press, 43
Ivory Soap, 53
Ivoryton Playhouse, 195, 199

J

Jackson, Brooks, Journalist, proprietor of factcheck.org, 34
Jackson, Don, Direct marketing insurance consultant, 45
Jaglom, Henry (b. 1938), British-born actor, film director and writer, 213
Jakes, Bishop T.D. ("Thomas Dexter") (b. 1957), pastor of The Potter's House, a Dallas megachurch with 30,000 members, 239
James, P.D. (Phyllis Dorothy) (b. 1920), English crime writer, 214
Jargon, Julie, Reporter, *The Wall Street Journal*, 60

M

Mayer, Ed, Direct marketing guru and teacher, 200
Mayer, Marissa, CEO of Yahoo, 219, 220, 222, 224
Mayerling, 252
MBA Magazine, 52
McCabe, Ed, Former CEO RCA Record Club, 29, 36
McCafferty, Megan (b. 1973), American novelist, 43
McCaffrey, Shannon, Journalist, Associated Press, 35
McCall-Crabbs: Standard Test Lessons in Reading, 134
McCann-Erickson, Ad Agency, 53
McConnell, Mitch (b. 1942), R-KY, Senate Minority Leader, 239
McGraw, Harold Jr. (1918-2010), CEO, McGraw-Hill, 159
McLuhan, Marshall (1911-1980), Pioneering media guru and author, 5, 237
McPhee, John (b. 1931), American writer, 47
mediabistro.com, 245
Metcalf, Ben, Former literary editor, Harper's magazine, 4
Meyer, Joyce (b. 1943), Christian author and TV lecturer, 239
MGM Mirage, 173
Mikkelsen, Randall, Editor, *Global Regulatory Briefing*, Reuters, 35
Miklaszewski, Jim (b. 1949), NBC Pentagon correspondent, 240
Miller, Claire Cain, Journalist, *The New York Times*, 220
Miller, Drew Allen, Marketing strategist, publisher, Board Report Publishing Company, 75
Miller Lite, Beer, 53
Milton, John (1608-1674), English poet, 135
Mincer, Jilian, Reporter, *The Wall Street Journal,* 60
Mitchell, Margaret (1900-1949), Author of *Gone With the Wind*, 135, 263
monster.com, 163
Montgomery, Ward, 144
Moon River and Me: A Memoir, 216
Morton salt, 53
Mossberg, Walter, Technology guru, *The Wall Street Journal*, 230
Motel 6, 53
Mouçon, Renaud de (1183-1217), Bishop of Chartres, 143
Mount Holyoke, 173
Murderers and Other Friendly People: The Public and Private Worlds of Interviewers, 251, 252
Murdoch, Rupert (b. 1931), Australian media mogul, owner of News Corp. and Fox, 60, 61
Murdock, Mike (b. 1946), Televangelist, 239
Musgrove, Mike, Technology reporter, *The Washington Post,* 190
Myers, Steve, Managing editor, the Poynter Organization, 190

N

Nagourney, Adam (b. 1954), Political reporter, *The New York Times,* 117
Napster, 39
National Observer, 44
Needleman, Sarah E., Reporter, *The Wall Street Journal,* 132
Neil, Dan, Pulitzer prize-winning automotive critic, *The Los Angeles Times,* 26
Nelson, Lord Horatio (1758-1805), Heroic British admiral, 221
Newman, Barry, Reporter, *The Wall Street Journal,* 60

Q

R

T

U

V

W

8037440R20169

Made in the USA
San Bernardino, CA
28 January 2014